The Ronald Reagan
Presidential Library and Museum

Library Edition

Suppression, Deception, Snobbery, and Bias

Suppression, Deception, Snobbery, and Bias

Why the Press Gets So Much Wrong—And Just Doesn't Care

ARI FLEISCHER

BROADSIDE BOOKS

SUPPRESSION, DECEPTION, SNOBBERY, AND BIAS. Copyright
© 2022 by Ari Fleischer. All rights reserved. Printed in the
United States of America. No part of this book may be used
or reproduced in any manner whatsoever without written
permission except in the case of brief quotations embodied
in critical articles and reviews. For information, address
HarperCollins Publishers, 195 Broadway, New York, NY 10007.

HarperCollins books may be purchased for educational, business,
or sales promotional use. For information, please email the
Special Markets Department at SPsales@harpercollins.com.

Broadside Books™ and the Broadside logo are
trademarks of HarperCollins Publishers.

FIRST EDITION

Library of Congress Cataloging-in-Publication Data

Names: Fleischer, Ari, 1960- author.
Title: Suppression, deception, snobbery, and bias : why today's
    media doesn't care they get so much wrong / Ari Fleischer.
Description: First edition. | New York : Broadside Books, 2022.
    | Includes index. | Identifiers: LCCN 2021058506 (print)
    | LCCN 2021058507 (ebook) | ISBN 9780063112759 (hardcover)
    | ISBN 9780063112773 (ebook)
Subjects: LCSH: Journalism--Objectivity--United States. | Press--
    United States. | Journalistic ethics--United States. | Reporters
    and reporting--United States. | Broadcast journalism--United
    States.
Classification: LCC PN4888.O25 .F54 2022 (print) | LCC
    PN4888.O25 (ebook) | DDC 302.230973--dc23/eng/20220301
LC record available at https://lccn.loc.gov/2021058506
LC ebook record available at https://lccn.loc.gov/2021058507

22 23 24 25 26 LSC 10 9 8 7 6 5 4 3 2 1

Contents

Suppression,
Deception,
Snobbery,
and Bias

Chapter One

ORIGINAL SIN

On January 25, 2020, CNN's Don Lemon hosted a panel discussion with anti-Trump political commentators Rick Wilson and Wajahat Ali to talk about the latest news, meaning it was a discussion of how rotten President Donald Trump was. But this time, they went beyond the usual castigation of Trump. Instead, they went after the tens of millions of people who supported him.

"This is an administration defined by ignorance of the world," said Wilson. "That's partly him playing to their base and playing to their audience, the credulous, boomer rube demo that backs Donald Trump."

Then Wilson broke into a phony southern accent and condescendingly played the role of a Trump backer, saying, "Donald Trump's the smart one—and y'all elitists are dumb!"

Ali chimed in, pretending to be a Trump supporter: "You elitists with your geography and your maps and your spelling!"

Lemon burst out laughing. His guests continued their mockery of Trump supporters.

"Your math and your reading," Wilson said.

"Your geography, knowing other countries, sipping your latte," Ali continued, as all three laughed out loud. "Only them elitists know where Ukraine is."

After he collected his breath, Lemon summed things up, saying, "That was a good one. I needed that."[1]

For liberals and much of the media, the moment made perfect sense. It was hard for them to see how *anyone* could support Trump. Mocking half the country made good sense to them and they didn't think anyone in their newsrooms would criticize them for their narrow-minded stereotyping of tens of millions of Americans. For conservatives, the moment went viral not only because the mockery was just the latest rude and condescending bit of "reporting" from the mainstream media, but also because it made no sense. Trump was from New York City and didn't have a southern accent, as if that should matter. Trump won the 2016 election thanks to swing voters in the Midwest, from Michigan to Wisconsin. The reliably Republican southern states didn't elect him. Swing voters in Pennsylvania and in the Midwest did. Plus, among white college graduates, Trump beat Hillary Clinton, 48 to 45 percent.[2] I guess those white college graduates include the dumb rubes Wilson was referring to.

Lemon and his guests were able to laugh at this ridiculous stereotype because they spend too much of their time with people in newsrooms who are badly out of touch with much of America. It's an America they don't respect, which is why they could so happily go on the air and mock conservatives and Trump voters, with the laughing support of a CNN anchor. It's a mindset that's killing journalism and the pursuit of truth. It's a reflection of how too many newsrooms have abandoned objectivity for subjectivity. It's an approved-at-the-top, close-minded way of thinking that has led journalists to engage in suppression and deception instead of old-fashioned reporting.

It's a window into how predominantly urban, college-educated Democrats run newsrooms where they publish information designed to appeal to other urban, college-educated Democrats. Day after day, night after night, the reporters and editors who make up the mainstream media have convinced themselves that their audiences—and their opinions—are superior to other people's thinking. The others are akin to deplorables. They're racists ready to riot. They're rubes who can't read a map or they're rednecks who don't know how to spell.

Half the country is keenly aware that they are routinely mocked and looked down upon by much of the media. How the media think this is good for America is beyond me. The disdain shown by too many reporters for too many Americans is a major reason our nation is polarized and divided. It's not just politicians who are at fault. The mainstream media's small-minded approach to its job and routine dismissal of conservative or populist thought is an important contributor to our nation's divisions. This snobbery and lack of respect and understanding of conservatives and populists breeds resentment and increased polarization. The media play a significant role in driving the American people apart.

This is a book about how and why the American people have lost faith in the media. It's about a once-trusted institution that is now at the bottom of the barrel in terms of trust. Most Americans no longer think the media tell the news fully, fairly, and accurately. It's what happens when a group of mostly college-educated Democrats, out of touch with much of the country, determine what is and isn't news, suppressing news they don't like, repeating deceptions that they do, in a way that resonates with fellow college-educated Democratic readers and viewers, alienating pretty much everyone else.

If you are a conservative or independent in America, you know the media is not fair. However, conservatives often get this conflict wrong. We misread what the media is trying to do, and we misinterpret why they are doing it. There is no secret meeting where liberals decide how to pervert the news. There is no central source of propaganda. It's worse than that. It comes naturally to the media because they're too much alike. They have a diversity problem.

Interestingly, liberals, too, suffer because of media bias. America's liberal base is increasingly untethered from reality. Thanks to a press corps that couldn't possibly conceive of a Donald Trump victory, Democrats have had a hard time understanding why and how Hillary Clinton did not win the 2016 election in a much-anticipated landslide. There had to be a deeper, more sinister reason. Voila, collusion. Based on media reporting, Democrats *knew* Special Counsel Robert Mueller would deliver and indict Trump and his top aides. Democrats and much of the media are still having a tough time accepting that Trump and his campaign never did the things they were accused of doing concerning Russia.

In the pages that follow, I'm going to argue that, for all our debates about lies, misinformation, and polarization, we are ignoring a fundamental cause of a crisis driving our country apart: the media itself. So long as the mainstream media continues to engage in suppression, deception, snobbery, and bias, our nation will be harmed. When you hear about Russian collusion, narrow-minded intolerant Republicans, Nicholas Sandmann (the Covington Catholic High School kid on the steps of the Lincoln Memorial), mostly peaceful protesters, and college football celebrations instantly labeled as "super-spreader events" while Democratic celebrations of Joe Biden's 2020 election victory are not so labeled, but you don't hear about President Biden's ethical problems, the Democratic Party chairman in a Texas county who called Senator Tim Scott (R-SC) an "Oreo," and the Democratic National Committee staffer who opposed hiring straight, white men, and when you read and see descriptions of GOP policies that make Republicans look bad, you will see what's really been happening. You'll see an activist press corps that has its thumb on the scale. A press corps that increasingly, aggressively takes sides in our national debates. A press corps that is out of touch, gets things wrong—and just doesn't care.

To understand why the media is an institution held in such low regard, let's go back to the beginning. To the original sin of who becomes a reporter in the first place.

ON MARCH 31, 1998, IN room 1129 of the Longworth House Office Building in Washington, DC, a dozen students from the prestigious Columbia Journalism School were in town for a working field trip, learning about their chosen profession.

I was the communications director for the House Committee on Ways & Means and was asked to meet with them, which I was happy to do. I talked to them about how news is made and how spokespeople and reporters work together. When I was done, I had a question for these future reporters.

"In the 1996 election, how many of you voted for Bob Dole and how many for Bill Clinton?" I asked. I suspected most had voted for the Democrat, Bill Clinton, but I wanted to see how lopsided it was. Eight to four? Nine to three?

"Clinton first," I said, looking to see how many voted Democratic. Eleven hands shot up. "So only one of you voted for Dole?" I asked in disbelief.

"No," said the owner of the twelfth hand, "I voted for Ralph Nader." Nader was the Green Party candidate who ran to the left of Clinton. A 12:0 ratio. That's just great, I thought.

Flash forward twenty-two years.

In March 2020, I was again invited by the Columbia Journalism School to meet with future reporters, this time on Columbia's campus in New York City. (It would be my last trip prior to the coronavirus shutdown.)

At this meeting, they asked me to participate in a mock press briefing. The roughly one dozen students played White House reporters, and I took to the podium to pretend I was President Trump's press secretary. I was happy to do it to help these young journalists get some real-life training.

When we were done, I decided to repeat my question from 1998 to this new generation of reporters. "In the 2016 election," I asked, "how many of you voted for Donald Trump and how many for Hillary Clinton? Hillary first."

Every hand in the room went up.

Journalism has a great weakness, an original sin. The people who go into journalism do not represent the breadth and depth of the United States of America. They don't look like America, nor do they sound or think like America. They are overwhelmingly cut from the same cloth, a fabric that is largely liberal, like-minded, and way too unfamiliar with the circumstances and needs of many Americans, especially those without college degrees, those who come from rural areas, and those who are conservative or Republican. It's no wonder the media has a hard time understanding 74 million Americans who voted for Donald Trump's 2020 reelection.[3]

JOURNALISM IS SUFFERING. BIAS IS rampant. Reporters take sides. News gets suppressed; deceptive stories run wild, in the hands of an increasingly activistic press corps. Our free and independent press, an essential part of American democracy, is dying.

In an October 2020 survey conducted by the Pew Research Center, eight in ten American adults said that they get different facts depending on where they turn to for news.[4] A significant number of Americans think journalists cannot be trusted and that they have agendas.[5] Journalists are seen as people who can't understand what many Americans are experiencing. They're out of touch, and the stories they cover, especially the palace intrigues in Washington, aren't important to their readers' lives. They're largely seen as very well-educated liberal Democrats who understand fellow Democrats but tend to be intellectually dismissive of many Republicans, especially conservatives and working people.

A recent survey shows just how out of touch the press has become. According to a 2018 study by the Pew Research Center, the only group of Americans who say the press understands them are college-educated Democrats. The majority of Americans with a high school education or less feel misunderstood by the news media. Nearly three-quarters of Republicans say the news media "don't understand people like them."[6] These numbers are devastating. It's gone beyond the old issue of liberal bias—it's deeper. People used to count on the press to tell them the facts and the truth. But now, many Americans conclude the press do not even understand them, let alone tell them the truth.

Except for one notable group. College-educated Democrats. They're the one group, according to Pew, that thinks the press can relate to them.[7] That's a rotten position for the press to be in. It's a narrow position, out of touch with most of the country.

How could the press have distanced themselves so much from their readers and viewers? Ask any reporter, and they will tell you that journalism is about serving the public and providing them with the information they need to make decisions about things that are important in their lives. But today, too much of journalism is written by college-educated Democratic voters for college-educated Democratic voters. It's a slice of America that talks to a slice of

America, without acknowledging how out of touch with America they truly are.

Which takes me back to the Columbia Journalism School, where young, college-educated, mostly Democratic voters are trained how to become journalists by older, college-educated, mostly Democrat-voting professors.

For the rest of society—especially for those without college degrees, gun owners, religious people, most independent voters, people in rural areas, conservatives, and Republicans—the media are not credible, in touch, or trustworthy. We don't trust the media because the media doesn't trust us. Much of the media looks at conservatives and concludes: If only "these people" would read the *New York Times* or watch CNN, they would understand the facts and not support Donald Trump, Senator Ted Cruz, Senator Tom Cotton, Governor Ron DeSantis, Governor Kristi Noem, or numerous other Republicans. It's why many reporters condescend to these Republican voters, thinking the only people in America who support extremes and think narrow-minded thoughts are conservative Republicans. It's why Don Lemon laughingly declared, "That was a good one. I needed that."

For much of society, journalism is broken.

Jim VandeHei is the cofounder and CEO of *Axios*, an influential, highly read online group of newsletters that provide in-depth coverage of all things Washington. He cofounded *Politico* and was a White House reporter for the *Wall Street Journal* and the *New York Times*.[8]

Two weeks after the 2020 election, he wrote a stunningly critical analysis of the state of journalism:

> The media remains fairly clueless about the America that
> exists outside of the big cities, where most political writers

and editors live. The coverage missed badly the surge in Trump voters in places obvious (rural America) and less obvious (Hispanic-heavy border towns in Texas).

Let's be honest: Many of us under-appreciated the appeal of Trump's anti-socialism message and the backlash against the defund-the-police rhetoric on the left.

The media (and many Democrats) are fairly clueless about the needs, wants and trends of Hispanic voters. Top Latinos warned about overlooking and misreading the fastest-growing population in America—but most didn't listen. Hispanics will shape huge chunks of America's political future, so a course correction is in order. . . .

The media filter bubble is getting worse, not better. Look at what's unfolding in real-time: Trump supporters feel like Fox isn't pro-Trump enough, while reporters and columnists bolted *The New York Times*, Vox Media, and others because they were not "woke" enough.

- This is an urgent sign that we are collectively losing the battle for truth and open debate. . . .

Twitter is a mass-reality-distortion field for liberals and reporters. The group-think and liberal high-fiving was as bad as ever and continues to be a massive trap and distraction for journalists.[9]

VandeHei is right. Journalism is in deep trouble.

If America wants good journalism—fair and neutral—then six hands should go up for Hillary and six for Trump when asked whom they voted for. Six for Bill Clinton and six for Bob Dole. But when it's 24–0, journalism has a problem, and all Americans suffer the consequences.

Imagine if twenty-four hands went up for Trump and none for Biden. Or twenty-four for Dole and none for Clinton. If you don't think journalism would be different with those results, then you don't understand the reality of newsrooms today. This imbalance is the core of journalism's problem. Journalism will never fix itself until it fixes who becomes a reporter in the first place. Liberal self-selection of journalism as a career is killing fairness in journalism. I don't care how neutral a journalist is taught to be—if the field of journalism consists mostly of liberals and Democratic voters, it will never be fixed.

It will only get worse.

In 2013, three professors, two from the University of Indiana and one from Syracuse University, conducted an in-depth research project titled "The American Journalist in the Digital Age: Another Look at U.S. News People."[10] The study, later published in 2018, found that journalists were four times more likely to be Democrats than Republicans, way out of proportion to the roughly even split among the American people. The survey also showed only 7 percent of reporters consider themselves to be Republicans. Additionally, the survey found most reporters consider themselves independents, an assertion I find to be window dressing. It's an assertion reporters use so they can tell themselves they're not biased toward either party. I don't buy it, and I'll show why throughout this book.

During the 2016 presidential campaigns of Hillary Clinton and Trump, all you had to do was follow the donor trail to uncover journalists' overwhelming support for Clinton. In 2016, according to the *Columbia Journalism Review*, "People identified in federal campaign finance filings as journalists, reporters, news editors or television anchors—as well as other donors known to be working in journalism—have combined to give more than $396,000 to the presidential campaigns of Clinton and Trump, according to a Center for Public Integrity analysis."[11]

The story's headline was "Journalists Shower Hillary Clinton with Campaign Cash."

CJR reported that more than 96 percent of that cash went to Clinton: About 430 people who work in journalism had, through August 2016, combined to give about $382,000 to the Democratic nominee. About 50 identifiable journalists had combined to give about $14,000 to Trump. (Talk-radio ideologues and paid TV pundits are not included in the tally.)

Jane Coaston is the host and editor of the New York Times' opinion podcast The Argument. She was previously senior politics reporter at Vox. In May 2021, Coaston appeared on Hugh Hewitt's radio show, where she was asked a series of questions about the makeup of her fellow mainstream journalists. Her answers blew the cover off the press as she revealed how lopsided her colleagues are.

Hewitt stipulated there are some 5,000 elite people who make up the mainstream media, consisting of reporters and producers at the New York Times, the Washington Post, the Wall Street Journal, Associated Press, Reuters, Bloomberg, networks ABC, NBC, CBS, PBS, CNN, and MSNBC, the Atlantic, the New Republic, and Time magazine, along with the Sunday shows and most columnists.[12]

How many of these 5,000, Hewitt asked Coaston, voted for Trump in 2020?

Her reply was 2 percent.

How many for Trump in 2016? he asked.

About 4 percent, she said.

What about Romney in 2012?

Maybe 7 or 8 percent, she replied.

McCain in 2008?

Coaston estimated 4 percent for McCain.

Bush in 2004, she said, came in at about 7–9 percent.

Hewitt continued: "I love that you're doing this with me. Thank you. A lot of media refuse to play this exercise, but it's very useful for the audience. What percentage of that legacy elite media are pro-choice, do you guess?"

Her answer was, "Access to pro, yes. Writ large? I would say seventy-eight percent."

"How about own a gun?" Hewitt asked.

"Ooh, I would say, interestingly, I would say probably about ten percent would own a gun."

"What percentage of elite media favored confirmation of Amy Coney Barrett [to the Supreme Court]?"

"Five percent."

"What percentage of elite media favored confirmation of Brett Kavanaugh?"

"Oh, three percent."

Hewitt kept asking, and Coaston kept answering, blowing the whistle on how liberal reporters are compared to the American people.

"Okay, what percentage are solidly pro-Israel, I mean, solidly pro-Israel like Hugh Hewitt pro-Israel in the current war?"

"Hmm, twelve percent."

"Okay, what percentage think climate change is an 'existential threat'?"

"Seventy to seventy-five percent."

"What percentage of elite media, legacy media as previously de-fined, these five thousand people who make the news, favor building the border wall to its proposed length of 850–900 miles?"

"Ooh, that would be pretty low. I would say eight percent."

You get the picture.

While most reporters would refuse to play along with Hewitt or would claim to be independents, Coaston told the truth. I suspect her sentiment about how far left most reporters are is right on target.

In August 2017, *Politico* and *Morning Consult* took a poll of registered voters, and they asked a simple question regarding the political leanings of various entities.[13] "Generally, would you consider each of the following liberal, conservative or centrist/nonpartisan?" Among the groups *Politico* and *Morning Consult* asked respondents to think about was the "national news." If you think the American people perceive the media as centrist or nonpartisan, you guessed wrong. If you think the American people perceive that the press is liberal, you guessed right. Very liberal or somewhat liberal clocked in at 54 percent. Very conservative or somewhat conservative barely registered at only 16 percent.

Sometimes you don't have to scratch very hard to find the bias that lurks below the surface of the national news.

Listen to Ken Stern, the former CEO of liberal National Public Radio. Stern undertook a yearlong trip to better get to know Republicans, especially those who live in rural areas. He wrote about it for the *New York Post* in 2017.[14]

"Most reporters and editors are liberal—a now-dated Pew Research Center poll found that liberals outnumber conservatives in the media by some 5 to 1, and that comports with my own anecdotal experience at National Public Radio," Stern wrote. "When you are liberal, and everyone else around you is as well, it is easy to fall into groupthink on what stories are important, what sources are legitimate and what the narrative of the day will be."

In Stern's travels, he went hunting and handled a gun for the first time in his life.

He observed, "Gun control and gun rights is one of our most divisive issues, and there are legitimate points on both sides. But media is obsessed with the gun-control side and gives only scant, mostly negative, recognition to the gun-rights sides."

He came to know devoutly religious conservatives and National Rifle Association members. By getting to know them, he saw them in a different, less political, more personal light.

He bemoaned his industry's loss of trust as he reflected on what he learned.

"Some of this loss of reputation stems from effective demagoguery from the right and the left, as well as from our demagogue-in-chief [President Trump], but the attacks wouldn't be so successful if our media institutions hadn't failed us as well."

Good for Stern. He's on to something important. He recognized that his industry is out of touch with much of the country, and he also knows that the media has failed.

When I say the press is mostly a group of college-educated Democratic voters, it's a fact. Reporters who care to think deeply and reflect upon their industry realize that. Even if they don't want to be biased, there are few people around in newsrooms to tell them when they are engaging in bias. Some may continue to deny it or say it doesn't matter because they're professional reporters who know how to shed their bias. They're wrong.

Start with the White House press corps, the elite of the elite. They as a group are tremendously influential in setting the national agenda as they and their editors decide what is and is not news, and how, or if, the information will be shared.

The White House briefing room has forty-nine seats. On June 7, 2021, every seat was filled for the first time in over a year as the social distancing rules resulting from the COVID pandemic were relaxed.

By a ratio of 12:1, the seats were occupied by Democrats!

Only one reporter—just one—was an identifiable Republican, John Gizzi of the conservative publication *Newsmax*.

While twenty-two reporters, a plurality, registered as independent voters, twelve reporters were registered Democrats.

Yamiche Alcindor of PBS was a registered Democrat.

Katie Rogers of the *New York Times* was a registered Democrat.

Molly O'Toole of the *Los Angeles Times* was a registered Democrat.

Justin Sink of Bloomberg News was a registered Democrat.

Asma Khalid of NPR was a registered Democrat.

An additional nine reporters live in states without party registration information, but based on which party's primary they voted in, six were likely Democrats, two were likely Republicans, and one was likely an independent. (Five reporters are foreigners who can't vote in U.S. elections.)

Throw these nine into the mix, and the ratio is still lopsided for the Democrats. No matter how you cut it, the White House briefing room does not look, sound, or register to vote like America.

To find this information, all of which is publicly available, I did what reporters do. I dug into the facts.

I hired a Washington, DC–based research firm, Delve, and they looked through public registration information of the forty-nine reporters sitting in those seats. Most of these reporters are registered to vote in Washington, DC, or Maryland, where people register by party if they choose.

Delve prepared a chart showing who sits where and how they're registered.

From entry-level reporters leaving journalism schools to the peak

Mike Memoli NBC	Peter Doocy Fox News	Nancy Cordes CBS	Josh Gerstein Politico	Cecilia Vega ABC	Steve Holland Reuters	Phil Mattingly CNN
Ken Thomas Wall Street Journal	Steven Portnoy CBS Radio	Justin Sink Bloomberg	Asma Khalid NPR	Tyler Pager Washington Post	Katie Rogers New York Times	Maureen Groppe USA Today
Sebastian Smith Agence France Presse	Andrew Feinberg The Independent	Francesca Chambers McClatchy DC	April Ryan TheGrio, CNN	Natasha Korecki Politico	Molly O'Toole Los Angeles Times	Karen Travers ABC
Shannon Pettypiece NBC News Digital	Takaaki Abe Nippon Television	David Sherfinski Thomson Reuters Foundation	Brett Samuels The Hill	Jared Halpern Fox News Radio	Steve Herman VOA	George E. Condon Jr. National Journal
Courtney Rozen Bloomberg Industry	Brian Bennett TIME	Blake Burman Fox Business	Jonathan Tamari Philadelphia Inquirer	Steven Nelson New York Post	Philip Wegman Real Clear Politics	Yamiche Alcindor PBS
Christian Datoc Washington Examiner	Chris Johnson Washington Blade	Juliane Schäuble Tagesspiegel	*John Gizzi* *Newsmax*	Emily Goodin Daily Mail	Fabian Reinbold T-Online	Bob Costantini Self-Employed
Douglas Christian Reel Political News	Todd J. Gillman Dallas Morning News	Liz Goodwin Boston Globe	Eric Philips CBN News	Tara McKelvey BBC	Raquel Kräbenbühl GloboNews	Hiba Nasr Asharq News

Democratic	*Republican*	Other

of the profession at the White House, reporters' political habits are out of line with the American people. Most reporters, at least publicly, will furiously claim none of this matters. They report the news fairly and honestly, they will claim, regardless of any individual points of view they hold. This book will show that's not true.

I guess the good news is that the ratio wasn't 24:0, like it was during my encounters with students at Columbia Journalism School. It was *only* 12:1.

But why isn't the ratio 12:1 *Republican* to Democrat? If fewer Democrats became reporters and the field was dominated by Republicans (and independents), don't you think the news would come out differently? Of course, it would.

IN 2020, THE PRESS WAS hit by a stinging indictment in the form of a study conducted by the Gallup organization and the Knight Foundation.

The study showed that a plurality of Americans thinks the press is failing in its most important job—providing objective news reports to the American people. Almost a majority, 44 percent of those surveyed, said the media is doing "poorly" or "very poorly" providing objective news reports, while only 28 percent said the media was doing "well" or "very well."[15]

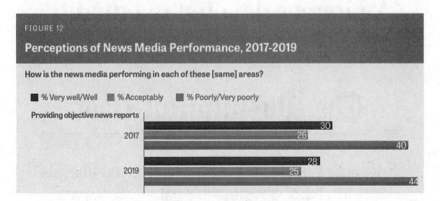

FIGURE 12

Perceptions of News Media Performance, 2017-2019

How is the news media performing in each of these [same] areas?

■ % Very well/Well   ■ % Acceptably   ■ % Poorly/Very poorly

Providing objective news reports

2017 — 30, 26, 40

2019 — 28, 25, 44

Source: Gallup/Knight Foundation Survey. American Views 2020:
Trust, Media, and Democracy. November 9, 2020.

When asked the simple question "What is your overall opinion of the news media in the United States today?" 46 percent said it was "very" or "somewhat" unfavorable. Just 31 percent said it was "very" or "somewhat" favorable.[16]

Democrats, however, do like the press. Fifty-three percent of Democrats have a "somewhat" favorable or "very" favorable opinion of the news media, while only 46 percent of Democrats have a "very" or "somewhat" unfavorable opinion.[17] Of course, Democrats like the press. The press tells them the news they want to hear.

When Supreme Court justice Antonin Scalia died in 2016, it was a front-page banner headline in the *Washington Post*.

Four years later, when Justice Ruth Ginsburg died, she, too, received a banner, front-page headline from the *Post*, but the headline for the liberal icon read differently than the one for the conservative champion. Ginsburg's headline read "A pioneer devoted to equality." Scalia's headline read "Supreme Court conservative dismayed liberals."

Source: *Washington Post*, September 19, 2020.

Source: *Washington Post*, February 14, 2016.

One justice was devoted to equality—and she received a glowing headline upon her passing. The other justice was, for *Washington Post* editors, devoted to dismaying liberals—and he got a nasty, political headline upon his passing.

No wonder, according to Gallup, 73 percent of Republicans hold an unfavorable view of the media, with only 13 percent holding a favorable view.[18] A majority of independents have a low opinion of the media as well.[19] If the press wonders why conservatives don't trust them, it's because of headlines like these.

Everyone knows Republicans don't hold the media in high regard. But when voters of all parties see how the press lionized Ginsburg and taunted Scalia, everyone should blow a whistle. Republicans aren't the enemy. They shouldn't, especially in death, be slapped. No one in America is served well when the press loses objectivity and takes on the role of activists.

The press is in trouble, but they sure do not act like it. The only change they are willing to make is, amazingly, to become even *more* opinionated and out of touch. They can read the polls, too, but they stopped trying to do anything about them a long time ago.

Chuck Todd is the host of *Meet the Press* on NBC. He is a longtime Washington reporter, who wrote for *Politico* just prior to Joe Biden's inauguration:

> One of the laziest tropes in conservative circles is the issue of media bias. It's such a reflexive response these days.
>
> It's about all many conservative infotainment hosts on TV and radio have left to fire up an audience, since Trump presents no seriously identifiable ideology to promote or defend. Media bashing works with much of the GOP grassroots; that's translated into various Senate GOP press shops wanting to avoid poking the rabid right-wing bears by appearing on legitimate news shows.

It's obviously hard to watch the media get abused this way so a few grifters can sell more newsletters or scam a few bucks. But such is the state of how the current Trump-centric conservative ecosystem works.[20]

Grifters? Scam a few bucks?

Chuck Todd and any reporter who thinks like him remain in denial. For decades, independent pollsters like Pew and Gallup have reported a longtime decline in people trusting the press. But Todd has his head in the sand if he thinks this is a Trump-driven, conservative trope. Any other business that has lost as many customers as the media would react by asking, "What's wrong with us? What can we do differently or better?" Instead, the press concludes there is something wrong with its customers, especially those customers who don't have high school degrees, come from rural areas, are religious, pro-life, conservative, and those who voted for Donald Trump.

There is almost no one left in America who *doesn't* think the press is biased. Except perhaps those who work in the press.

Right on cue, four days after Chuck Todd's dismissal of media bias as a conservative trope, *Axios* headlined a story, "Media Trust Hits New Low."[21]

The story read:

> For the first time ever, fewer than half of all Americans have trust in traditional media, according to data from Edelman's annual trust barometer shared exclusively with Axios. Trust in social media has hit an all-time low of 27%.
>
> • 56% of Americans agree with the statement that "Journalists and reporters are purposely trying to

mislead people by saying things they know are false or
gross exaggerations."

- 58% think that "most news organizations are more
  concerned with supporting an ideology or political
  position than with informing the public."[22]

Most Americans think the press misleads people and that the
media is politically biased. Don't tell that to Chuck Todd. He knows
better than his readers and viewers.

Michael Steel was the press secretary for Republican Speaker of
the House John Boehner, and he also served as Congressman Paul
Ryan's press secretary when Ryan ran for vice president on Mitt
Romney's 2012 ticket. He graduated from Columbia Journalism
School in 2003, in a class of about two hundred students.

He told me he was one of three Republicans in his class.[23]

Steel recalled a visit by a guest lecturer in the famed Pulitzer Hall
on Columbia's campus who asked the assembled class whom they
voted for in the 2000 election: Al Gore, George Bush, or Ralph Nader.

"It was an even split between Gore and Nader," Steel told me
with a chuckle. "Two people raised their hands for Bush. I was a third
Republican in the room but didn't raise my hand because I was a re-
porter in 2000 and didn't vote."

Recalling his discussions with classmates about political issues,
he said he used to tell them, "I can only argue with two of you at
once."[24]

So long as journalism schools fail to confront their diversity prob-
lem and continue to crank out mostly liberal, Democratic-voting fu-
ture journalists, journalism's problems will only get worse.

Chapter Two

DECEPTIONS AND DOUBLE STANDARDS

In 2019, Speaker Nancy Pelosi and other congressional leaders had a meeting at the White House with President Trump. It was a typical meeting between Pelosi and President Trump, meaning it did not go well. The various sides disagreed about pretty much everything, prompting Pelosi at one point to rise from her seat, point her finger at the president, and make her case.

The president later took to Twitter to show Pelosi's finger point, writing, "Nervous Nancy's unhinged meltdown!"[1]

Pelosi liked Trump's tweet so much she made it a pinned tweet on her Twitter account.[2]

The press loved it and praised Pelosi for it.

"Iconic photo," said Mika Brzezinski on MSNBC's *Morning Joe.*[3]

CNN's Dana Bash gushed: "One woman standing up and you know giving it to the President of the United States at a table with all men there. I mean, of course she's going to own that."[4]

Source: Donald Trump. Twitter. @realDonaldTrump. October 16, 2019.

The *New York Times* ran a story on the incident with the headline "Viral Photo Captures Power Dynamic Between Trump and Nancy Pelosi." The subheading read: "President Trump tweeted a photograph meant to mock Ms. Pelosi, but it soon went viral as the opposite: an iconic image capturing Washington's most powerful woman standing up to him."[5]

Flash back, however, to an encounter between then-governor of Arizona Jan Brewer and President Barack Obama in 2012. Brewer, with her finger, did unto Obama as Pelosi did unto Trump. The press skewered Brewer for it, as Brewer pointed out in a tweet of her own.

According to the *Arizona Daily Independent*, "Brewer was photographed shaking her finger at Obama on the tarmac at Phoenix-Mesa Gateway Airport in January. According to Brewer, Obama was 'a little disturbed about her book,' 'Scorpions for Breakfast,' in which she describes him as 'patronizing' during an earlier meeting."[6]

For MSNBC, CNN, and the *New York Times*, Brewer was anything but iconic. "The photo captured last night of Republican Arizona governor Jan Brewer pointing her finger in President Obama's face.

The news media hails @SpeakerPelosi as a hero for pointing her finger at @POTUS @realDonaldTrump but when I stood up to @BarackObama I was vilified as rude and racist. Such Hypocrites!

2:17 PM · Oct 17, 2019 · Twitter for iPhone

Source: Jan Brewer. Twitter. @GovBrewer. October 17, 2019.

It's an image that doesn't connote respect for the highest office in the land, does it?" intoned Chris Matthews on MSNBC's *Hardball with Chris Matthews*.[7]

On CNN, John King opened his interview with Governor Brewer by saying, "A lot of people are saying he's the president of the United States. Whether you disagree or not, perhaps you should have shown him a bit more respect."[8]

On CNN's *Early Start*, Ashleigh Banfield wasn't gushing: "Jan Brewer and Barack Obama getting testy on the tarmac and Brewer even pointed her finger, shaking it, wagging it at the president."[9]

CBS echoed the reprimanding tone. The *CBS Evening News* with Scott Pelley led its newscast with the story about "that picture that has caused quite a stir." CBS's Norah O'Donnell followed up saying, "It's this picture with the Republican governor's finger in the president's face that has Jan Brewer on the defensive today."[10]

"Who have you ever seen talking to the president like this?" asked Brian Williams on *NBC Nightly News* in his lead-up to a report critical of Brewer.[11]

For the *New York Times*, the exchange between Brewer and

Obama wasn't a power dynamic, but a run-in that could potentially boost Obama's popularity among Hispanic voters. The *Times* headline read: "In Airport Run-in, Democrats See Help for Obama Among Hispanics."[12]

Don't ask me to explain that one. I really can't.

Writing in an opinion piece for the *New York Times* nearly three years later, journalist Timothy Egan blasted Brewer for treating President Obama "as if he were some errand boy and not the commander in chief."[13]

Point your finger at Trump. The press loves it. Do it to Obama. There's something wrong with you. When the media tell us that Pelosi was brave and stood for what she believes in, while Brewer was rude and violated the norms, they're really saying that Republicans are a bunch of unworthy rubes who act badly, can't be trusted, and probably are missing a few teeth. That's today's hypocritical, defend-Democrats, attack-Republicans mainstream media for you.

In October 2021, Gallup asked Americans, "How much trust and confidence do you have in the mass media—such as newspapers, TV and radio—when it comes to reporting the news fully, accurately and fairly—a great deal, a fair amount, not very much or none at all?"[14]

The results were terrible for the press.

Only 36 percent of the American people reported having a great deal or fair amount of confidence that the media would report the news fully, accurately, and fairly.

Telling the news fully, accurately, and fairly is the press's *job*. It's the heart of what they're supposed to do for a living. It's what makes them the so-called fourth pillar of our democracy. It's a vital role we need them to play. Yet, more than half of Americans don't feel confident that the press is upholding its responsibilities. It wasn't always like this. Forty years ago, the press was a highly trusted institution. If the mainstream media, typically the *New York Times*, the *Washington*

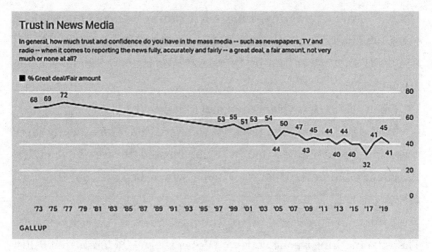

Source: Gallup Survey. Media Use and Evaluation, "Trust in News Media."
https://news.gallup.com/poll/1663/media-use-evaluation.aspx.

Post, or the network news shows, reported something, people took it as true. In 1977, according to Gallup, 72 percent of the American people had a great deal or fair amount of trust and confidence in the press.[15] The press's decline should be worrisome to all Americans, but make no mistake: The press has done this to themselves. They did it by being biased, and in too many cases, by being just plain wrong.

Red-hot, breaking news stories, particularly those with major consequences, often lead to incorrect information making it onto the air and into print. These critical mistakes happen in part because reporters are under intense pressure to break news. In complex situations, like a bombing or mass shooting, information often changes as investigations unfold.

Back on April 15, 2013, two terrorists detonated two bombs near the finish line of the Boston Marathon. They killed three people and injured hundreds.

It was instant, massive, live coverage everywhere. It also was full of mistakes. Mistakes that could have had dire consequences for the FBI's investigation—a point that the FBI made clear in a statement it issued on April 17: "Over the past day and a half, there have been a number of press reports based on information from unofficial sources that has been inaccurate. Since these stories often have unintended consequences, we ask the media, particularly at this early stage of the investigation, to exercise caution and attempt to verify information through appropriate official channels before reporting."[16]

Good luck with that.

According to a *New York Times* article that followed up on the FBI's admonishment to the media, "Numerous organizations, including *The Associated Press*, *The Boston Globe*, and several local Boston television stations, erroneously reported Wednesday afternoon that an arrest had been made, or that a suspect was in custody, citing unnamed law enforcement sources. . . . CNN and Fox News spent about an hour discussing the news of an arrest with various correspondents and experts before backing off when they received further information."[17]

The media debacle surrounding the Boston Marathon bombings came just four months after the media made several major errors in its initial reporting of the Sandy Hook Elementary School shootings in Newtown, Connecticut.

In its *Morning Edition* piece, "Coverage Rapid, and Often Wrong, in Tragedy's Early Hours," NPR noted that the "bedlam" involved major news outlets—including CNN, CBS, FOX News, the Associated Press, the *New York Times*, and NPR among others—erroneously reporting on the who, what, where, when, why, and how of the shooting. NPR noted that "many of the reports relied on unnamed law enforcement officials, typically federal, or even the vaguer 'the authorities' in at least one instance."[18]

Wise reporters should sit tight and wait to broadcast or print information until it is verified. But today's reporters are so caught up in the race to break news that they roll the dice and then do their best to catch up with evolving stories. Critical reporting mistakes are also symptomatic of a modern-day journalism curse: anonymous sources. The media today has gotten drunk from anonymous sources. These sources might be right. They might be wrong. But so long as what the source says is treated as news, sources can get away with telling reporters almost anything. In these situations, readers and viewers have no clue whom to believe. Whenever I see a story quoting only anonymous sources, I note the "news," wonder if it might be true or not, then slide right past it. It's not worth my time to ponder if it's true until a source goes public or until the information can be fully evaluated.

During the Trump presidency, anonymous sources were weaponized against President Trump, his family, and the White House. Sometimes the reports turned out to be true. Often they were false. Typically, however, these anonymous sources were only giving us the piece of the story they wanted us to know about, which was fine with most of the press.

Journalism's credibility crisis reached a crescendo on Friday, December 8, 2017. It began when CNN's Manu Raju broke a self-described "exclusive" story, based on what he claimed were "multiple sources," all anonymous, alleging that Donald Trump Jr. had received an email "offering a decryption key and website for hacked WikiLeaks e-mails."[19] In other words, team Trump was given advance access to Hillary Clinton's hacked documents and emails *prior* to WikiLeaks releasing them in an effort to harm Clinton's presidential campaign.

It was huge news, reported far and wide as a CNN scoop. Social media exploded as Trump's critics believed CNN had found a smoking gun.

If it were true, the president's son would have been caught in a lie, since he, along with spokespeople for the White House and the Trump 2016 campaign, stated they had no advance notice of the leaked emails. It might also have been a crime for Trump Jr. to be in possession of stolen material, many commentators said live on the air.

Shortly after CNN's bombshell, CBS News "confirmed" it.

MSNBC jumped into the act, with NBC News national security and intelligence correspondent Ken Dilanian claiming he had independently "confirmed" the damaging news from "two sources with direct knowledge of this."[20]

The bombshells were going off everywhere now.

After several hours of "breaking news" about the "latest developments," with commentators, Democratic congressmen, and news anchors hyperventilating about how serious a story this was and how it might lead to criminal charges against Trump Jr. and others on the campaign, the story fell apart.

The story was never accurate. Not even close.

Instead, a source had dangled something juicy to make Trump look bad, and CNN bit. They accepted their sources' word about the email, even though CNN reporters never saw the email with their own eyes.[21] They took the word of their anti-Trump source as gospel and filled the airwaves with false information.

CNN's "multiple" sources who described the email said it was dated September 4, 2017, more than a week in advance of the WikiLeaks release of Hillary's emails. But later that day, the *Washington Post* did obtain a copy of the email, and the date on it was not September 4. It was September 14, *after* the hacked information was already in the public domain.[22]

Think about this. CNN said it had "multiple" sources. How could they all misread the date on the email and tell CNN's reporter that the email was dated September 4, not September 14? I can see how one person could make a simple mistake like that. But multiple sources?

How could CBS and MSNBC confirm this story? They claimed to have sources, plural, who also, amazingly, made the same mistake.

All these smart sources somehow misread the same date on the same email? I've often wondered, when a news outlet is quick to "confirm" a major scoop, if they really have any source at all who confirmed the scoop, or if a reporter under pressure told an editor he or she had confirmed the story in order to keep up with the competition. As for the first story, I suspect two anti-Trump congressional aides, or members of Congress, agreed to peddle the story. Who knows if they even read the date on the email. It doesn't matter. They peddled the story and got CNN to bite. When other media outlets called to "confirm" it, reporters likely called the same two clowns, who of course confirmed it, since it was their story to begin with. A cesspool of wrong reporting was swirling around these two sources, and I'm sure they loved it.

Since all these sources are anonymous, no reader or viewer can know for sure. We're supposed to simply accept the media's word that it's true.

In the case of Donald Trump Jr., the allegations were not true. Far from it.

Neither CNN, CBS, nor MSNBC ever explained how they got the story wrong. They corrected the date on the email, but they did not tell their readers and viewers how this happened in the first place. Notably, CNN changed the number of sources from the "multiple" it originally claimed to just "two sources" when CNN corrected its mistake.[23, 24] Next time you hear CNN, or any media outlet, claim to have "multiple" sources, bear in mind that it might only be two people, hardly the definition of multiple.

The damage, however, was already done.

As independent journalist Glenn Greenwald wrote during his tenure at the *Intercept*: "It's hard to quantify exactly how many people were deceived—filled with false news and propaganda—by the CNN story. But thanks to Democratic-loyal journalists and operatives who decree every Trump-Russia claim to be true without seeing any evidence, it's certainly safe to say that many hundreds of thousands of people, almost certainly millions, were exposed to these false claims."[25]

Greenwald's story was headlined, "The U.S. Media Suffered Its Most Humiliating Debacle in Ages and Now Refuses All Transparency Over What Happened."[26]

I can't help but wonder if this story would have made it on the air if CNN's newsroom, and other newsrooms, weren't so anti-Trump to begin with. If CNN's newsroom was half for Trump and half for Biden, they likely would have been more guarded and more accurate.

When reporters and editors are almost universally against someone, as they are with former president Trump, they let down their guard. If the news is anti-Trump, they *want* it to be true. It doesn't take much time, or scrutiny, before the news is aired. If it's pro-Trump, it's harder to get on the air. Let's be more careful. Where's the hard evidence? Let's check it out, they're told.

In this instance, why didn't editors at CNN tell Raju that unless he saw the email himself, CNN couldn't put the accusation on the air? If he had seen it, I presume he would have noticed the date was not what his sources told him.

But when a journalism school, and a newsroom, consist of people who overwhelmingly think one way, it's easier to air information that supports their points of view, especially if it comes from an anti-Trump anonymous source.

The same thing happened in January 2021 to the *Washington Post*.

An anonymous source told the *Post* that President Trump made a phone call to an election inspector in Georgia as part of the former president's claim that he won the state.

The *Post* headlined its January 9, 2021, story, "'Find the fraud': Trump pressured a Georgia elections investigator in a separate call legal experts say could amount to obstruction."[27]

The story was based on an anonymous source who told the *Post* that Trump told Frances Watson, Georgia secretary of state's chief election investigator, to "find the fraud" and that Watson would be a "national hero" for doing so.

Other media outlets chased the story.

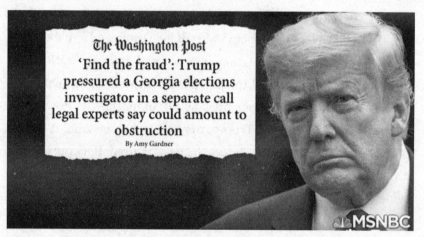

Source: Screenshot. MSNBC's *Weekends with Alex Witt*. January 9, 2021.

Except that's not what Trump said.

Once again, the press trusted an anti-Trump anonymous source. Once again, the press failed the public.

Two months after the *Post* ran its accusatory story against Trump, an audiotape of the call was found and released by Georgia election officials. The *Post* quickly changed its tune as it quietly corrected its story.

The *Post* misquoted Trump's comments on the call, based on in-formation provided by a source. Trump did not tell the investiga-tor to "find the fraud" or say she would be "a national hero" if she did so. Instead, Trump urged the investigator to scrutinize bal-lots in Fulton County, Ga., asserting she would find "dishonesty" there. He also told her that she had "the most important job in the country right now."[28]

Once again, the media too easily fell for the word of an anonymous source. In this case, the source turned out to be Georgia's deputy secretary of state, Jordan Fuchs. Trump publicly fought with Fuchs's boss, Secretary of State Brad Raffensperger, about the accuracy of Georgia's election results.

The *Washington Post* wasn't the only media outlet that fell for the lines they were given about Trump's call to Watson. In a repeat of when other media outlets "independently confirmed" CNN's phony story about Donald Trump Jr. and WikiLeaks, the *Federalist* reported that "[s]everal other major media outlets—including NBC, ABC, USA Today, PBS, and CNN—'confirmed' the fabricated quotes from the *Post*'s anonymous source by, get this, citing *their own anonymous sources.*"[29]

The media just don't learn, do they?

Today, it seems, scoops and clicks in support of a cause are too often more important than truth, accuracy, and fairness. It's no wonder the fourth pillar is collapsing.

Former journalist Ron Fournier served as White House correspondent and bureau chief for the Associated Press. In early January 2018, Fournier tweeted, "Most journalists get into the business to make things better, to force change, to move the needle. That can't happen in DC right now."[30]

What a refreshing tweet. Fournier didn't say people go into journalism to cover the news. He didn't say people become reporters to inform the public about events by providing facts.

He admitted that most people become journalists to carry out an agenda by forcing change or moving a needle.

Whose needle? What kind of change? How do you define better?

I assure you it's not movement of the needle in a conservative, small government, pro-life, free enterprise direction. Make no mistake— for the four years of the Trump presidency the media's point of view was decidedly anti-Trump. They were determined to move the needle against a president they intensely disliked. Many reporters decided Trump was a threat to America and they needed to save the republic. Good and fair reporting be damned.

The CNN-WikiLeaks imbroglio hit at a particularly bad time for the press.

Just a few days earlier, ABC News was forced to retract a story by its longtime chief investigative correspondent Brian Ross alleging that then-candidate Trump directed retired general Michael Flynn, at the time a campaign adviser, to contact Russia *during* the 2016 campaign.[31]

In a tweet that was later deleted, ABC News reported, "Michael Flynn promised 'full cooperation to the Mueller team' and is prepared to testify that as a candidate, Donald Trump 'directed him to make contact with the Russians.'"[32]

Once again, the media got its timing wrong. Another anti-Trump bombshell turned into a dud.

Shortly after Ross broke the news, he unbroke it.

In another tweet, which for some odd reason was deleted by ABC, the network reported, "Clarification of ABC News Special Report: Flynn prepared to testify that President-elect Donald Trump directed him to make contact with the Russians *during the transition*— initially as a way to work together to fight ISIS in Syria, confidant now says."[33]

During the transition. Not during the campaign.

So ABC News told its viewers that Trump initially directed a top aide to work with Russia during the campaign, implying that Trump colluded with Russia on who knows what. But the truth was that

Trump did what every president-elect does: He directed his foreign policy experts to work with foreign countries as part of his transition to office.

ABC suspended Brian Ross for four weeks without pay over this mistake and ultimately parted ways with him a few months later—presumably fed up with the numerous other mistakes Ross had made over his career. (When I was press secretary, Ross reported that Saddam Hussein was behind the 2001 anthrax attacks in the United States, despite my warning ABC News not to go with that story because it was false. Ross went with the story and later had to reverse his claims.)[34]

Throughout the Trump years, immigration was a red-hot topic. Trump came into office vowing to build a wall along the Mexican border and stop illegal immigration into the United States.

His critics, along with much of the media, viewed his actions as xenophobic and bordering on racist.

In November 2019, the media ran with a report claiming that the United States had detained more than 100,000 immigrant children at detention facilities throughout the United States. It was the perfect story. It showed how cruel Trump was, detaining children in massive numbers, giving credence to the argument that he was racist, and his actions were inhuman.

According to the *Washington Examiner*:

Various news outlets, including Agence France-Presse, the Associated Press, National Public Radio, and Reuters, reported this week that a United Nations study showed that there are "more than 100,000 children in migration-related U.S. detention."

That sounds pretty bad. It means America has "the world's highest rate of children in detention," in violation of international law.[35]

But guess what? The author of the United Nations study clarified that the figure of more than 100,000 detained children was drawn from 2015 data, the latest data point available at that time.[36]

Barack Obama was the president in 2015. Not Donald Trump. Media interest instantly dried up. News organizations that heralded the anti-Trump news now rushed to withdraw it.

Again according to the *Examiner*:

"AFP is withdrawing this story," the French newsgroup announced Tuesday. "The author of the report has clarified that his figures do not represent the number of children currently in migration-related U.S. detention, but the total number of children in migration-related U.S. detention in 2015. We will delete the story."

Reuters has also withdrawn its equally shoddy and false article. In its place is now an editor's note that reads, "A Nov. 18 story headlined 'U.S. has world's highest rate of children in detention—U.N. study' is withdrawn. The United Nations issued a statement on Nov. 19, saying the number was not current but was for the year 2015. No replacement story will be issued."

NPR likewise issued a note stating that it has "temporarily withdrawn [its] story because the study's author has acknowledged a significant error in the data."[37]

But why didn't these news organizations rerun their stories to say that new information had come to light from the UN showing that under President *Obama*, a cumulative total of 100,000 children were held in American detention facilities throughout the year 2015?

If it was immoral of the United States to detain so many children over the course of a year, what difference did it make if the year was 2015?

If the detention of children is the news, the stories still should have run, but this time blaming President Obama, not President Trump. Don't Democrats deserve to know the truth about President Obama? Don't all Americans? But the media did not want to blame Obama, especially during the Trump years. Running a story like that would have put President Trump's actions into context. It would have shown that President Trump's course of action wasn't an outlier; it was consistent with what his predecessor did. But when the media is broken, and reporters are driven to tell only one side of a story, news that might cast a Democratic president in a negative light goes away. It vanishes. When it vanishes like that, it distorts the truth that Democrats and independents deserve to know and it angers Republicans. It also hinders our nation's ability to solve complex problems because one side looks at the other as immoral—because that's largely how the press covers one side of the debate. Instead of the media reporting the news fully, accurately, and fairly, the news about Obama's detention of 100,000 children simply vanished. It was suppressed.

One of the best ways to measure what the press wants to come true is how they cover polls, especially during the Trump presidency. If they're bad for the GOP, they're hyped. If they're bad for the Democrats, they're downplayed. The result is that many Democrats think the majority of Americans agree with their favorite policies and politicians.

In the sixth year of his presidency, George W. Bush was not very popular.[38] As a result of the war in Iraq, his job approval had plunged, and Republican control of the Senate and House was in jeopardy.

According to the Media Research Center, the network news shows (ABC, CBS, and NBC) ran 124 stories between January 1, 2006, and August 31, 2006, on how low Bush's poll numbers were.[39]

Fast-forward eight years.

In the sixth year of his presidency, Barack Obama was not very popular.[40] As a result of his policies, his approval rating had declined sharply, and Democratic control of the Senate in 2014 was in jeopardy. A Gallup poll in September of that year reported Obama's job approval was only 39 percent.[41]

Guess what? The same three networks that ran 124 stories about Bush's low numbers ran just *nine* on Obama's low numbers, the Media Research Center found.[42]

The networks minimized Obama's polling woes. They didn't focus on them like they did during the Bush years. Reporters' protect-Obama reflex kicked in. Given how easy their coverage was on Obama, is it really a surprise? Voters who don't support Obama must be misinformed, was the message sent by suppressing the anti-Obama poll results. But everyone knows Bush is bad for the country, so those anti-Bush polls were worth sharing with viewers. That's not how a fair and neutral media should cover the news. Either both Bush and Obama should have received heavy coverage of their low polling numbers, or neither should. But once again, the media's double standard, which somehow doesn't get trained out of them in journalism school, triumphed.

In 2020, the polls told a different story: a very favorable story for Joe Biden and the Democrats. The media covered the polls extensively. And they turned out to be very wrong.

In June 2020, Chris Cillizza of CNN wrote a story headlined, "Donald Trump is facing the prospect of a landslide loss."[43] His story cited two polls by the *New York Times* and Siena College that showed "Trump trailing former Vice President Joe Biden by double digits in Michigan (Biden +11), Wisconsin (Biden +11) and Pennsylvania (Biden +10) and by mid-single digits in North Carolina (Biden +9), Arizona (Biden +7) and Florida (Biden +6)."[44]

None of those polls turned out to be close to accurate. None.

In late September, six weeks before Election Day, the *Washington*

Post's Jennifer Rubin wrote an opinion piece headlined, "The chances of a blowout are high." She continued, "The most recent Washington Post–ABC News poll shows former vice president Joe Biden leading by 10 points—a huge margin—with voting already underway. The New York Times–Siena College poll shows Biden with an eight-point lead. By historic standards, a presidential election with such a lead in the popular vote would be somewhere between 'commanding' and a 'blowout.'"[45]

Virtually everywhere you looked, the media tone was set. Trump was going to lose in a landslide, Republicans would get blown out in the Senate, and Democrats under Nancy Pelosi would gain seats in the House.

A year's worth of stories like that have an impact. When the media puts its finger on the scale, it moves the needle. It hurts fundraising, depresses the "losing" side's morale, and creates inaccurate impressions that inform reporters' stories. This leads to a cynical cycle of stories that report the polls are bad and, therefore, the GOP is in trouble. And the more the GOP was seen to be in trouble, the more the polls worsened.

Make no mistake—it *is* putting a finger on the scale. It's exactly why the culture and mentality of college-educated, largely Democratic-leaning newsrooms accepted and covered bad Bush polls, but the networks for nine months in 2014 *didn't* cover most of the doomsday Obama polls. They wanted one set of stories (anti-Bush) to be true while they hoped the other story (anti-Obama) would not turn out to be true. This isn't a new phenomenon, nor was it unique to the 2020 election cycle.

In 2014, Republican senator Mitch McConnell from Kentucky easily defeated his opponent, Alison Lundergan Grimes, by 16 points.[46] You would never have expected a McConnell landslide if you followed the news.

One week before Election Day in 2014, the *New York Times* told its readers that McConnell was "locked in a tight re-election race."[47]

Also in late October 2014, the *Washington Post* headlined a story, "People don't like Mitch McConnell. That's why Alison Lundergan Grimes still has a shot."[48]

The *Post* told its readers, "A Western Kentucky University poll released Tuesday is the latest to show Alison Lundergan Grimes (D) remaining competitive with McConnell, the Republican Senate minority leader. McConnell leads 45–42, within the poll's margin of error. It's the latest poll to show the race is still tight, despite national Democrats having pulled ads from the state."[49]

CNN's John King told viewers on October 21 that Kentucky was "a close race. This is close to the end."[50]

These reporters were banging a drum that had been sounded all year. In April, MSNBC's Steve Kornacki, relying on a *New York Times/Kaiser* poll that showed Kentucky was a 1-point race, told his viewers that Kentucky was "a true toss-up" and "we knew that Kentucky was going to be a close race."[51] Except it wasn't.

I remember watching the election results in 2014, looking at McConnell's 16-point victory, thinking to myself, who in the world thought this would be close? Anyone who relied on the mainstream media, that's who.

If reporters in 2020 wrote stories that were more reflective of the truth about the presidential race, the American people would have read headlines showing, "Race Looks Dead-Even," "Trump vs. Biden Likely to Go Down to the Wire," "Battleground States Could Go Either Way." Headlines like those were rare in 2020. Headlines predicting landslides and gains for Democrats were commonplace.

If the polling headlines matched reality, the 2020 landscape would have been different. The GOP would have raised more money. Republican morale would have been higher, and journalists' stories would have been more nuanced, putting less pressure on Trump and Republicans. Republicans very well may have won even more seats, possibly including the presidential race, and they might have taken control of the House of Representatives.

"What they were trying to do was discourage Election Day turnout of Trump voters with really bad polls," Trump pollster John McLaughlin told reporter John Solomon.[52]

Reporters couldn't get enough of these anti-Republican polls. In late September 2019, the *Los Angeles Times* reported, "Trump is on track for a level of defeat in California not seen since the Civil War."[53] The Civil War!

The story cited a University of California, Berkeley, Institute of Governmental Studies poll showing Trump was winning just 29 percent of the vote, while 67 percent said they would not vote for Trump, a 38-point gap. The story pointed out that Trump lost to Hillary in 2016 by 30 points in California.

"On the statewide level, Trump has acted as a drag on his party's candidates for other offices, and that could worsen in 2020, said Mark DiCamillo, director of the Berkeley poll."

"'Trump's declining electoral fortunes in California could dispirit Republican voters here, reducing GOP turnout in next year's primary and general elections,'" DiCamillo was quoted as saying. "'This could spell trouble for Republican candidates running in competitive elections for Congress, Assembly and state Senate,' DiCamillo said." Like so many polling stories, this one was wrong. Wildly wrong.

In reality, Trump lost California by 29 points in 2020, one point *better* than he did against Hillary. So much for the doomsday Civil War scenario. As for those congressional races, the GOP *picked up* four congressional seats in the state.[54] Pretty much everything about the story's hype and hysteria was wrong.

Not to be outdone, the media's October 2020 polling was even worse in many key battleground states.

The ABC News/*Washington Post*'s final poll in Wisconsin showed Trump losing the state by a massive, unbelievable 17 points.[55] The final *New York Times*/Siena poll showed Trump losing Wisconsin by 11 points.[56] He lost by 0.7 points.[57]

CNN's final poll in battleground North Carolina showed Biden winning by 6 points.[58] The final NBC News/Marist poll also showed Biden up by 6 points.[59] Trump *won* North Carolina by 1.3 points.[60]

It was the same story in swing state Florida. The final Quinnipiac poll showed Biden winning Florida by 5 points.[61] It also showed Biden winning Ohio by 4 points. Trump *won* Florida by 3.3 points, and he *won* Ohio by 8 points.[62]

A similar anti-Republican tilt showed up in numerous U.S. Senate races.

A September Quinnipiac poll in Maine showed Democratic challenger Sara Gideon up 12 points over incumbent Senator Susan Collins.[63] Collins won by 8.6 points.[64]

The final NBC News/Marist poll in North Carolina showed Democratic challenger Cal Cunningham winning by 10 points.[65] Incumbent Republican Thom Tillis won by 1.8 points.[66]

Writing about the Iowa U.S. Senate race between Republican incumbent Joni Ernst and Democratic challenger Theresa Greenfield in October 2020, the *New York Times* headlined its story, "Ernst Struggles in Iowa as Republicans Battle to Hold Senate Amid Trump's Woes."[67]

The story said, "Ms. Ernst, who has tightly embraced the president even as his standing has fallen, has trailed Ms. Greenfield in every poll for the past month, and in a recent New York Times–Siena poll, as many Iowans had a negative view of her as those who had a positive one. The survey underscored a bitter reality for the first woman to represent Iowa in Congress: Mr. Trump's troubles, particularly with female voters, are doing real damage to Republicans down the ballot."[68]

Ernst comfortably won reelection by 6.5 points, and the GOP down-ballot *gained* seats in the House of Representatives.[69]

In the House of Representatives, the experts and the press were overwhelmingly wrong.

Just one week before Election Day 2020, the *New York Times* continued to pound Republicans, telling its mostly Democratic readers what they wanted to hear.

"Pushing Deep Into G.O.P. Turf, Democrats Are Poised to Expand House Majority," read the headline in one story.[70]

"That has left Republicans, who started the cycle hoping to retake the House by clawing back a number of the competitive districts they lost to Democrats in 2018, straining to meet a bleaker goal: limiting the reach of another Democratic sweep," the *Times* reported.[71]

The story highlighted an open-seat race in Indiana as one in which "Democrats view the district as one of their best opportunities to flip a seat" from Republican to Democrat. One week later, the Democratic candidate there lost by 4.1 points.[72] It wasn't even very close.

It was the same story at the *Washington Post*.

"Democrats target districts in Trump territory as party grows optimistic about expanding House majority," ran a headline one week prior to Election Day.[73]

Despite the *Post* being warned by a spokesman for the National Republican Congressional Committee that the story was "laughable," much of the story read as an advertisement for Democratic talking points.

House Democrats are increasingly bullish that they will flip multiple seats in districts where President Trump will win on election night, outrunning the top of the Democratic ticket and giving House Speaker Nancy Pelosi (D-Calif.) a chance to expand her majority.

In a sign of how serious Democrats are about gains in Trump territory, the Democratic Congressional Campaign Committee is airing TV ads in 11 GOP districts Trump won by double digits in 2016. In nine, the Democrats—candidates, the campaign committee and their outside allies—are outspending GOP incumbents and their backers.

At the same time, nonpartisan analysts continue to move races that once seemed unfathomable for Democrats to win in their direction. Among them are Alaska and Montana, as well as GOP strongholds in rural Minnesota to conservative parts of Virginia, including one district that hasn't backed a Democratic candidate for president since Harry S. Truman.

"I don't think too many people would have thought [this] at the beginning of this cycle, but we're playing deep into Trump country," said DCCC Chairwoman Cheri Bustos (D-Ill.). "I'm confident in saying this: We're going to hold on to the majority; we're going to grow our majority. . . . We're well positioned to have a good night."

House Democrats won't put a number on their projections, but outside analysts say they could gain from three to 15 seats as Trump sees his advantage shrink over Joe Biden.[74]

What a joke.

Nationwide, Republicans *gained* twelve seats,[75] almost taking back control of the House. The Democrats lost every one of the races mentioned in the *Washington Post* story as possible Democratic pickups. Every. Single. One.

The same media that thought Donald Trump had no chance of

winning in 2016 learned nothing and made many of the same mistakes again in 2020. Is it any wonder so few Republicans and independents believe they can get accurate reporting from the mainstream media?

Is it any wonder that Democrats are susceptible to the argument that their voters are being "suppressed"? When the media spend a year telling you you're likely to win and you don't, it's only natural to wonder what else could be going on. Bad and biased reporting doesn't only harm Republicans, it harms Democrats who also deserve to know the honest state of play—especially when it's bad for them.

Nationwide, the average of all polls assembled by Real Clear Politics predicted that Biden would win nationwide by 7.2 points. He won by 4.5 points.[76] The final CNBC/Change Research poll predicted a 10-point win for Biden.[77] The final NBC/*Wall Street Journal* poll also showed a 10-point Biden victory,[78] as did the Quinnipiac poll.[79]

But in a race in which a record-breaking 158 million votes were cast,[80] if a total of fewer than 50,000 had switched from Biden to Trump in Arizona, Nevada, Wisconsin, and Georgia, Trump would have won.

That's how close the race was. Despite Biden's 4.5-point margin and 306 electoral votes, the 2020 presidential race went down to the wire.[81] It was so close, the final result wasn't even announced until four days after Election Day. A handful of vote changes in four states would have reelected Donald Trump.

But no one would have known that by reading a year's worth of coverage. Instead, for a year, the media wrongly informed the country about the shape of our politics. Stories that made Trump and Republicans look bad were played up. Stories that raised doubts about Biden and Democrats were played down or outright suppressed by the media and giant tech companies like Twitter and Facebook.

The press was not neutral. They were biased and wrong. Stories like this don't only hurt Republicans; they hurt Democrats and they hurt our nation. Based on media accounts, the Democrats thought they would win the White House decisively and gain seats in the House. Their media-based expectations were not realized. Instead of forming judgments based on a neutral, fair-minded portrayal in the media, Democrats were led astray. While it's nice to have the press on your side, it would be even better if both sides concluded that the press played it down the middle and that their stories were often accurate.

Many reporters' worst errors spring from the fact that too many reporters, especially political ones, think alike, act alike, and view events alike, and they can't stand Donald Trump. They are unable or unwilling to open their minds to the possibility that half the country is proudly, happily, and intelligently different. Reporters let their anti-Trump animus cloud their judgment and consequently misinform their readers and viewers. Their dislike of Trump is understandable. He picked fights with them, and they picked fights back. They picked fights with him, and he picked fights back. The hostility was palpable. Trump pushed limits and engaged in behavior, particularly after the election, that many view as going too far.

But a dislike for a president—whether justified or not—doesn't give reporters license to put their fingers on the scale and misinform the country in so many ways.

Liberal, anti-Trump groupthink is why Hillary Clinton was endorsed by 229 daily newspapers and 131 weeklies, while Trump received the endorsement of 9 dailies and 4 weeklies, according to a study done by the Nieman Lab. That's a 27-to-1 difference.[82]

It was a similar story in 2020. According to the American Presidency Project at the University of California, Santa Barbara, of the nation's largest newspapers, 47 endorsed Biden in 2020, and only 7 endorsed Trump.[83]

But the press was so blinded by their disdain of President Trump that they missed many of the stories that were in front of them every day, especially the close race for the White House in 2020.

The press is not the enemy of the people. But they sure can be their own worst enemy.

The damage they are doing to themselves and the nation is severe. The American people *want* to get their news straight. They want someone who can give them honest reporting based on facts. But most Americans have concluded they can no longer get truth and facts from the mainstream media. Remember that Gallup poll that showed almost 60 percent of the country lacks faith that the media reports the news fully, fairly, and accurately? Judging from how wrong the coverage was throughout 2020, it's easy to see why.

This is what happens when journalism schools throughout the country, for decades, graduate similar-minded, liberal-oriented, college-educated, mostly Democratic voters into the ranks of the news media, where the stories they tell are tailored to mostly liberal-oriented, college-educated, mostly Democratic readers and viewers.

FOX News is an exception, especially their evening opinion shows. So is talk radio, although few of the most listened-to talk-radio hosts are journalism school graduates. Recognizing the hostility of mainstream newsrooms to conservative thought, a number of new, internet-based conservative publications have arisen in recent years, such as the *Federalist*, the *Washington Examiner*, and the *Daily Wire*.

At ABC, CBS, NBC, CNN, the *New York Times*, the *Washington Post*, the Associated Press, and most of the mainstream media, newsrooms lack ideological diversity; the dominance of groupthink is destroying the integrity of journalism within these newsrooms. For many in mainstream media, the definition of diversity is racial, or gender, or sexual orientation. They pride themselves on being "diverse" so long as this diversity doesn't involve ideas.

They pride themselves on looking like America, but in reality, they only look like half of America.

It's why the press is broken. Unless and until journalists are able to see the world and the country through a fair and neutral lens, the institution of journalism will continue to collapse under the weight of its own activism, and America's trust in the media will continue to erode. Until newsrooms are full of people who understand voters from across America, journalism will continue to suppress the news and deceive the people.

Chapter Three

REPORTERS HAVE
LOST THEIR MINDS

There was a time not long ago when reporters prided them-
selves on being fair and neutral. Donald Trump's campaign for
the presidency in 2016 and his four years as president blew that to
smithereens.

From then–CNBC correspondent John Harwood's (now CNN's
White House correspondent) question to candidate Trump at a 2016
debate, "Is this a comic book version of a presidential campaign?"[1] to
the *New York Times*' 2016 Hillary Clinton campaign reporter, Amy
Chozick, who acknowledged in her campaign memoir that she broke
down and cried the day after Hillary lost,[2] to the fawning coverage of
Joe Biden and Kamala Harris's campaign for the White House, too
many members of the press have abandoned neutrality and fairness in
reporting the news. Fair and neutral are no longer considered valuable
qualities in being a good reporter.

It has become more fun and interesting for too many reporters to become a party to one side of the story—and it's seldom the Republican side, and virtually never the Trump side.

As the former president of CBS News and FOX News, Van Gordon Sauter, wrote in a May 2020 op-ed in the *Wall Street Journal*, "To many journalists, objectivity, balance, and fairness—once the gold standard of reporting—are not mandatory in a divided political era and in a country they believe to be severely flawed. That assumption folds neatly into their assessment of the president. To the journalists, including more than a few Republicans, he [Trump] is a blatant vulgarian, an incessant prevaricator, and a dangerous leader who should be ousted next January, if not sooner. Much of journalism has become the clarion voice of the 'resistance,' dedicated to ousting the president even though he was legally elected and, according to the polls, enjoys the support of about 44% of likely 2020 voters."[3]

I have lost track of the number of wacky conspiracy theories launched against Trump and the GOP in service to the resistance.

Collusion with Russia was the mother of all unfair accusations seized on by the media. The amount of ink spilled to further false collusion allegations is astounding. Many of the stories that launched the Russian collusion narrative were based on a leak about the 2016 Steele Dossier, the memos written by former British intelligence officer Christopher Steele alleging links between Trump and Russia. The dossier's allegations turned out to be false,[4] but it seems like much of the press *wanted* the dossier to be true.

The dislike for Trump personally among college-educated Democrats was so severe that it blinded most media outlets to the instincts reporters once prided themselves on: namely, cynicism to anonymous accusations that sound so far over the top that they likely cannot be true. But when someone loses their mind, it is hard to expect them to think straight. And make no mistake, Donald Trump made the press lose their minds.

It's hard to say who is more hostile to whom. Candidate Trump in 2016 was brutal to the press (and to anyone who crossed his path) and the press returned the favor. I don't know who was the chicken and who was the egg, but regardless of who attacked first, Trump and the press have been at each other's throats ever since.

The press is paid to cover the president, and their job is to rise above whatever inequities they perceive. Their *job* is to be fair. They stopped doing their job. Trump, for better or worse, is an outsider who was elected to do the job his way. Plus, if it is right for the media to give bad coverage to someone who treats them with disdain, is it right for the media to give good coverage to someone who treats them nicely? The answer in both cases should be a resounding no. The press's job is to report the news. Their job is to inform the American people about the news fully, fairly, and accurately, without bias, regardless of whom they cover, independent from how much they like or dislike the president.

They failed.

In early 2017, shortly after Trump took office, a wave of bomb threats was called into more than one hundred Jewish community centers across the United States.[5] It did not take long for the media to link the threats to President Trump.

The *New York Times* on February 28, 2017, ran the following headline: "Threats and Vandalism Leave American Jews on Edge in Trump Era."[6] Without establishing any connection between the new president and the threats, the *Times* wrote, "the calls have stoked fears that a virulent anti-Semitism has increasingly taken hold in the early days of the Trump administration." According to the *Daily Beast*, "President Trump reportedly suggested that the threats may have been done to 'make others look bad.'"[7] Numerous columnists and talking heads blamed the anti-Semitic phone threats on the new president. The Democratic National Committee condemned Trump's suggestion that the attacks might not have come from anti-Semites.[8]

Congressman Jerry Nadler (D-NY) appeared on CNN and was asked about the bomb threats and the president's handling of them. He said, "Maybe [Trump] doesn't want to denounce his own supporters because some of his own supporters are responsible for this."[9]

CNN's anchor didn't press Nadler for what evidence he had that Trump's supporters were responsible. Nadler's claim was, as they say, without evidence.

It turned out that the source of the threats was a mentally unstable Israeli teenager and a liberal American journalist.[10] Neither was inspired by Trump.[11] The truth did not matter, because the truth got fewer clicks. The narrative of Trump-is-at-fault was more important. That false narrative dominated coverage of virtually everything in the Trump era. It has dominated coverage over important, substantive issues and it has even worked its way into frivolous coverage. That's what happens when reporters and editors lose their minds and become determined to cover the news in a biased way, designed to appeal to readers and viewers who can't stand Trump.

In November 2017, Trump traveled to Japan for a summit meeting with Prime Minister Shinzo Abe. On the way to lunch, the two leaders walked to a balcony overlooking a koi pond on the Akasaka Palace grounds for a ceremonial feeding of the koi fish below. Abe demonstrated the koi fish feeding technique to Trump by putting a spoon in his box of fish food, and then he dropped a small scoop of it into the water. Trump did the same. Abe dropped a few more scoops. So did Trump. Then Abe poured the full contents of his box into the water, which Trump also did.[12]

But that's not what CNN's viewers saw. They saw Abe feed the fish with a spoon while Trump, the boor, dumped his entire box into the water. CNN edited the video to zoom in on Trump, neglecting to show or report that Abe had poured the contents of his fish food box into the pond before Trump followed suit.[13]

Veronica Rocha of CNN reported, "Trump feeds fish, winds up pouring entire box of food into koi pond."[14]

The media saw an opportunity to embarrass Trump and pounced.

According to a report in the *Washington Examiner*, "CNN was given an assist in getting this bogus story rolling by Bloomberg White House correspondent Justin Sink, who tweeted that Trump and Abe were 'spooning fish food into the pond' when the U.S. president, 'decided to just dump the whole box in for the fish.'"[15]

On Twitter, ABC News posted a cropped video of the feeding. The video showed both world leaders spooning the fish food and then zoomed in to show only Trump dumping his full box of fish food into the koi pond.[16]

The *Guardian* ran with the Twitter headline "trump dump."

Source: *Guardian*. Twitter. @guardian. November 6, 2017.

Monica Alba of NBC News couldn't resist jumping into the fray.

"President Trump empties his fish food container while feeding koi with Prime Minister Abe at Akasaka Palace," she tweeted.

"Big Stupid Baby Dumps a Load of Fish Food on Japanese Koi Pond," read the Twitter headline of the news website Jezebel.[17]

The misleading headlines dominated the news. Yet, as *Time* White House reporter Alana Abramson pointed out: "[the White House] pool report explicitly notes that both Trump and Abe—not just the president—initially took portions of the fish food from the box before tossing out the remnants: 'The two leaders then leaned out and began throwing spoonfuls of the food into the water, before eventually turning over the bowls and dumping the rest out,' the pool report reads."[18] Full video of the ceremonial feeding also documented Trump following Prime Minister Abe's lead.

I'm sorry, but who cares? Why was Trump's manner of feeding the fish a story, even if what the media were alleging *was* true? Of course, the media's reporting was false. Totally false. But why would the press make this an issue in any case?

As media critic Joe Concha wrote in *The Hill*, "So the obvious question is this: Why pick a fight with Trump . . . over something so ridiculous as fish-feeding? By doing so, it only perfectly makes the argument for Trump that the media is not only overwhelmingly negative in covering him, as study after study shows, but it's at times also hostile, adversarial and—most importantly in this case—fake."[19]

As the White House pushed back against the bogus coverage and as video surfaced showing Trump's fish feeding technique was the same as Abe's, reporters rushed to erase their tweets and update their coverage.

I went to see former president Trump in April 2021 to interview him about the mainstream media and its coverage of him.[20] I played for him the media's clip of him dumping his koi fish food, and I showed him the negative coverage he received.

"I couldn't believe it," Trump told me. "I just did what he [Abe] did."

He told me his reaction upon learning of the fish feeding frenzy was "That can't be a story. That was a very elegant, beautiful evening.

We're standing on this beautiful pagoda on the patio, and I said I believe he did it, and I just followed him. They [the media] just want to show crudeness."

When it came to the mainstream media's coverage of Donald Trump, too often it was marked by deceptive reporting, constantly aimed at undermining Trump's legitimacy and his presidency.

In August 2020, First Lady Melania Trump welcomed reporters to a newly renovated Rose Garden. The famous Rose Garden outside the West Wing had not undergone a comprehensive renovation since it was established in the early 1960s by President Kennedy. Melania focused on restoring the Rose Garden to its original design while adding better audio equipment along with a redesign of the plantings and the placement of new limestone walkways.[21] Drainage was improved, along with fixes to underground cables used by the media to broadcast live from the Rose Garden.

Because the first lady's last name was Trump, her mild and necessary Rose Garden renovations were attacked.

"First Lady Melania Trump's renovation of the White House's famous Rose Garden stripped it of historic colorful, bold and diverse appearance," wrote the Obama administration's Wendy Sherman in *USA Today*.[22] The same Wendy Sherman who negotiated the Iran deal.[23]

Architectural Digest reported, "Since the Rose Garden [renovation] was revealed, social media has crackled with fury, condemnation, personal attacks, and, as always, misinformation. . . . 'This is just a sad quadrangle,' former NPR executive producer Kitty Eisele said in a dispirited Tweet. NBC chief foreign affairs correspondent Andrea Mitchell retweeted a photograph of the garden posted by the presidential historian Michael Beschloss and the plaint 'What happened to the trees?'"[24]

But no one went as far as journalist Howard Fineman, who once served as chief political correspondent and deputy Washington bureau chief for the former heavyweight *Newsweek* magazine. Fineman is now a contributing correspondent to MSNBC and NBC News.[25]

Source: Howard Fineman. Twitter. @howardfineman. August 22, 2020.

A neofascist parade ground.

Reporters love to complain about Donald Trump going too far and violating norms, only to do it themselves. But when the media go too far against conservatives and populists, it's because, in the eyes of many reporters, *those* people deserve it. Democrats from time to time do or say crazy things—but the press would prefer to keep their attention on Republicans. Especially if they can call Republicans fascists, or Nazis.

When Trump was elected in 2016, there was no honeymoon. None.

He was instantly greeted by large protests outside his home on Fifth Avenue in New York City. Quickly, a social media movement was launched called "#NotMyPresident." A powerful opposition formed, even before he took office, known as "the Resistance."[26] The Resistance was also the name used by French citizens who fought the Nazi occupation of France during World War II. When the press labeled those who opposed Trump "the Resistance," I recall thinking how offensive that was, likening an American president-elect to the Nazis, with little admonishment for those using such offensive terms.

Boy, was I naïve.

It didn't take long for Trump's critics to flat out call him a Nazi. It began during the campaign, led by some celebrities and *Saturday Night Live*.

According to the *Washington Post* in March 2016:

> If there's one comparison you never make, it's comparing some-one to Adolph Hitler. It just isn't done, because almost no one in history was as bad as Hitler was.
>
> But in an election season that has broken a lot of the bound-aries that used to dictate what could and couldn't be said in pres-idential politics, that particular trope just won't go away.
>
> Louis C.K. and "Saturday Night Live" both went there this weekend when it comes to Donald Trump and Hitler. But they were hardly the first. In fact, it's party [*sic*] of a growing chorus, mostly coming from celebrities.
>
> Bill Maher called Trump's rallies "Hitler-y" during an epi-sode of his HBO show, as a montage of rough treatment of pro-testers at Trump rallies played onscreen.[27]

"Hitler-y." So, it's not just Trump who is Hitler-like. It's also the people who support him.

Four months later, *New York* magazine headlined a column: "How Hitler's Rise to Power Explains Why Republicans Accept Donald Trump."[28]

I'm sure these reporters thought they were calling it as they see it. Trump offended them and they called him Hitler. I'm also sure that what they never understood is the more they called Trump and his followers "Hitler-y," the more they emboldened potential Trump sup-porters to be for Trump. If there's one thing populist outsiders can't stand, it's to be dictated to by the intelligentsia. Even those who had doubts about Trump resented being told that support for Trump was support for Hitler. These voters knew this was just another way the mainstream media looked down on them. It was another way highly educated reporters dismissed much of the country, thinking no sane person could support Trump unless these voters were Hitler fans. This type of reporting is insulting. But many reporters failed to under-stand that.

Much of the press still doesn't understand how alienated a large segment of the country is from Washington and its "experts." If the Washington experts were so smart in 2016, why was the economy so bad? Why was Congress so unpopular and unresponsive? Why were so many American workers struggling? Why was the United States still involved in foreign entanglements in places most Americans wanted to leave? Why were the experts wrong so often? And why do reporters continue to talk down to and dismiss voters who don't sup-port the reporters' favorite candidates?

Trump as an outsider had tremendous appeal, yet many smart reporters dismissed him and his movement, using vitriolic language, including comparing him to Hitler. These insider experts derided his supporters. And the more the insiders told the outsiders that sup-port for Trump was support for Hitler, the more foolish the insid-ers sounded. The experts' extreme rhetoric, I believe, pushed many Republicans who were lukewarm for Trump *into* the Trump camp just to prove the experts wrong. These voters know they're not Hitler-like and they were determined to reject the condescending wisdom of the so-called experts.

When Trump announced his candidacy the year before, he re-ferred to some Mexican immigrants to the United States as "rapists."[29]

Politicians are not supposed to talk that way. Trump did it anyway. Trump's rise scared many Democrats and much of the media. They couldn't believe someone as rough, as blunt, and (at times) as rude as Trump might become the Republican nominee.

So, the media and the Democrats resorted to the worst criticism they could think of to explain it. They kept calling him Adolf Hitler.

According to the *Boston Globe* in March 2016, "Representative Seth Moulton [D-MA] compared the rise of Republican presidential front-runner Donald J. Trump to the election of Adolf Hitler and said Wednesday that constituents should warn 'that crazy uncle' against voting for the businessman if he wins the GOP nomination. . . . He said voters should read up on how the German people elected Hitler in the 1930s to gain a better understanding of how an educated society 'can elect a demagogue.'"[30]

The Boston Globe

Moulton compares Trump's rise to election of Hitler in 1930s

Source: Travis Andersen, "Moulton compares Trump's rise to election of Hitler in 1930s," *Boston Globe*, March 23, 2016.

Once they started, they never stopped.

November 9, 2020, was the eighty-second anniversary of Kristallnacht, or "Night of Broken Glass." On that day in 1938, the Nazi regime carried out horrific anti-Semitic violence across Nazi Germany—burning hundreds of synagogues, vandalizing Jewish homes and cemeteries, and shattering the storefront windows of Jewish-owned businesses. Nazis also rounded up 30,000 men who were taken to concentration camps.[31] On the anniversary of this immense tragedy, CNN's Christiane Amanpour compared Trump to Hitler on the air.[32] She later apologized.

That same month, two weeks after Election Day, Minnesota congresswoman Ilhan Omar (D-MN), in an interview with the *Washington Post*, referred to Trump's campaign rallies as "Klan rallies."[33]

Former MSNBC host Donny Deutsch repeatedly compared Trump to Hitler and equated Trump supporters with Nazis. In 2018, appearing on MSNBC's *Morning Joe*, he said, "If you vote for Trump, then you, the voter—you, not Donald Trump—are standing at the border like Nazis going, 'You here. You here,'"[34] a reference, according to the *National Review*, to what guards at Nazi extermination camps would say as they sent Jews to gas chambers or to work the barracks.[35]

Two years later, Deutsch turned it up a notch.

"There is no difference from what Donald Trump is preaching, from what Adolf Hitler preached in the early '30s. Let's just say it once and for all,"[36] he said from the safe harbor of *Morning Joe*, where once-sane people go to lose their minds without being challenged.

I understand anger against Donald Trump. America's political system has always been noisy and occasionally rude. Trump dished it out, and he should take it.

But the Democrats and the media's repeated denunciations of Trump as a Nazi are a big part of the problem with political coverage in America today. It goes too far. It crosses the bounds by which reasonable people are supposed to abide. Just because Trump himself could be pugilistic should not give license to the media to do the same.

Certainly, the biggest mistake made by Trump was his decision to host a rally on the Ellipse, a park by the White House, on January 6, 2021, the same day Congress was scheduled to vote to certify the results of the 2020 election. Tensions were high, and it was predictable that some of the protesters would head to Capitol Hill to make their voices known.

The violence, mayhem, rioting, and attacks on the police and on Congress that hundreds engaged in were crimes and one of the lowest moments in the history of our republic.

For Trump's critics, the January 6 riot convinced them that they had been right about this man all along—that Trump *was* Hitler. If they were wrong for four years, it didn't matter, they thought, because they were right on January 6.

For some, saying Trump is Hitler and Trump's supporters are Nazi-like may sound like objective reporting. For others, it's another example of how journalism is broken.

I was twenty-one years old when I worked on my first campaign. I got a job as the press secretary for a New York State assemblyman who was challenging the longtime Democratic congressman in Westchester County, New York.

It was my first job after college, and I loved it. I had a lot to learn.

One day, a coworker on the campaign mentioned to me that the incumbent congressman had a cocaine problem. "How do you know?" I asked him. He told me he didn't know, but that's what he had heard.

I recall thinking to myself that politics has a dark side. It didn't seem fair to me that someone would say that about a congressman if they didn't have proof. Our campaign never acted on that tidbit of what I always believed was false information, but one lesson I learned was the importance of not believing the worst in a political opponent. Some people in politics, however, want to believe the worst in their opponents. I try never to do that. I do my best not to question someone's motive or to accuse people of something that I can't prove. Being fair and reasonable is important in everything.

If only Trump's critics were more fair and reasonable. But their anger blinded them, and they regularly believed the worst.

In the summer of 2020, one of the wackiest theories about a political opponent that I had ever heard made the rounds. For a few weeks, it became a major story on all the networks and in the media: Donald Trump was removing blue mailboxes from street corners so that he could steal the presidential election.

In August 2020, a Florida Democratic activist, Thomas Kennedy, tweeted a photo that appeared to show Wisconsin USPS mailboxes at a dump. He alleged that "they" were trying to sabotage mail voting as part of a plan to steal the election. The photo went viral.

Source: Thomas Kennedy. Twitter. @tomaskenn. August 14, 2020.

Social media was ablaze. Photos of mailboxes being removed in several states fueled panic throughout the anti-Trump twittersphere—catching the attention of Joe Biden, Taylor Swift, and other twitterati.

"They're going around literally with tractor trailers picking up mailboxes. You oughta go online and check out what they're doing in Oregon. I mean, it's bizarre!" Biden said.[37]

Calling Trump a cheater, Taylor Swift joined the chorus and

tweeted, "Trump's calculated dismantling of USPS proves one thing clearly: He is WELL AWARE that we do not want him as our president. He's chosen to blatantly cheat and put millions of Americans' lives at risk in an effort to hold on to power."

Hundreds of thousands of people liked her tweet.[38]

Many Democrats, and many reporters, are so suspect of Trump and Republicans that they actually thought these stories might be true. Trump was going to remove mailboxes so he could steal the election. Trafficking in conspiracy theories is never good, but in this instance, much of the mainstream media and many Democrats flung their doors wide open to a fantasy, a far-fetched conspiracy theory from the paranoid and irrational left. Of course, when Republicans engage in conspiracy theories, the mainstream media is often the first group to slam the doors shut.

It didn't matter that the removal of postal boxes is a routine procedure carried out before and after elections, a practice going back to 1833 in New York City, where the very first street corner mailbox was placed.[39] (By the way, it's not there anymore. It was removed.) Those Wisconsin mailboxes that appeared to be at a dump in the photo that went viral? Those mailboxes were actually in a lot operated by a company that routinely refurbishes mailboxes for the U.S. Postal Service, and typically has stacks of mailboxes awaiting restoration.[40] Mailboxes need to be refurbished, and some locations change depending on how often they are used. Nothing lasts forever, including the location of mailboxes.

According to a 2016 notice issued by the USPS's inspector general, "Nationally, the number of collection boxes declined by more than 12,000 in the past 5 years."[41]

Note the year. It was *2016*. I don't recall President Obama being accused of stealing mailboxes.

In a year marked by a pandemic in which many people preferred to mail their ballots instead of voting in person on Election Day, people lost their minds. Trump thought mail-in voting was marked by fraud and regularly said so, discouraging GOP voters from voting by mail. Democrats, and much of the media, who believed the worst in Trump, pounced. Pretty soon, anytime a postal box was removed anywhere, it became a dark story with questions raised about its impact on the election.

"USPS Mailboxes Removed in Some New York Area Neighborhoods," reported NBC News in New York City.[42]

"Postal service removes Oakland collection boxes; leaders warn of election interference," reported the *San Francisco Chronicle*.[43]

The feeding frenzy was on. That's because when you're a Democrat accusing Trump of malfeasance, the mostly Democratic press corps is happy to oblige, even if the facts of the matter don't support the allegation. The point is Trump likely did it, so fire away. It amazes me to this day that sensible people could *actually* believe that Trump was stealing mailboxes. But after being fed years' worth of stories about how terrible Trump was, *any* conclusion was possible, no matter how wacky or conspiratorial. The press deserves much of the blame for how out of control the anti-Trump theories became. The Trump-is-stealing-mailboxes nonsense was deceptive, activist reporting at its worst.

Upon hearing that some mailboxes had been removed in the state of Montana, Senator Jon Tester (D-MT) said, "These actions set my hair on fire, and they have real-life implications for folks in rural America and their ability to access critical postal services like paying their bills and voting in upcoming elections."[44]

Tester lost not only his mind, but his hair.

Referring to the routine removal of postal boxes and other changes the USPS was making to be more efficient, Speaker of the House Nancy Pelosi accused Trump of launching a "campaign to sabotage the election by manipulating the Postal Service to disenfranchise voters."[45]

Sabotage. Disenfranchise. The anti-Trump attacks based on bad reporting kept growing worse, even though there was no truth—none—to the original allegations.

Turnout in the 2020 election hit a more-than-one-hundred-year high. Vote by mail surged to record heights. Some sabotage. Some disenfranchisement. Funny thing, when Nancy Pelosi accuses Trump of trying to steal an election, the press mostly goes along. When Donald Trump says his opponents are the ones stealing it, most of the press attack him. Time after time, the mainstream media just happen to see things from a Democratic point of view. Time after time, the media viewed Trump and many Republicans as sinister, unethical, and likely guilty, which is why stories about removing mailboxes to steal an election are published, while stories about Democratic misdeeds, including those involving Hunter Biden, are suppressed. More on that in chapter 5.

On February 24, 2019, President Trump sent out a save-the-date tweet, inviting the American people to a party on the National Mall to celebrate Independence Day. "HOLD THE DATE!" Trump tweeted. "We will be having one of the biggest gatherings in the history of Washington, D.C., on July 4th. It will be called 'A Salute To America' and will be held at the Lincoln Memorial. Major fireworks display, entertainment and an address by your favorite President, me!"

The president, inspired by a 2017 trip to France where he saw a French military parade, wanted to do something similar in the United States. Initially he wanted a major demonstration of military force to march down Pennsylvania Avenue.[46] Democrats and the media denounced Trump's idea.

Representative Jim McGovern (D-MA) tweeted, "Trump acts more like dictator than president. Americans deserve better."[47]

Representative Jackie Speier (D-CA), a member of the House Armed Services Committee, told CNN: "I was stunned by it, to be quite honest . . . we have a Napoleon in the making here."[48] This time Trump was not only Hitler-like, but he was also Napoleon in the making.

The online publication *Vox* panned the idea, running a headline that stated, "Trump wants a military parade 'just like France's.' It's likely to look more like China's."[49] After objections from the military, and due to the cost, Trump revised his grand plan and announced a much smaller "Salute to America" on the Mall. It didn't matter. His critics still lost their minds.

As military equipment started to show up in the streets of Washington, Laurence Tribe, an esteemed legal scholar at Harvard Law School, a man the media often cite as an expert, tweeted:

Source: Laurence Tribe. Twitter. @tribelaw. July 2, 2019.

His critics really should make up their minds. Is Trump a Nazi, a Russian, Napoleon, or Chinese? He can't be all four. Or maybe to his critics, he can be.

Without knowing what Trump would say, Democratic congressmen accused Trump of engaging in partisan politics on July Fourth. "Frankly, that's not what July 4th is about," House Majority Leader Steny Hoyer (D-MD) told NBC News. "It's sad that the president's turning it into—in my opinion and the opinion of many—a political rally."[50] "He can't resist injecting partisan politics into the most nonpartisan sacred American holiday there is: the Fourth of July," Representative Gerald E. Connolly (D-VA) said to the *New York Times*.[51]

The Fourth of July speech Trump gave contained not a word of partisanship. It was a stirring tribute to America's military and the men and women who serve. As Air Force One, Marine One, a B-2 stealth bomber, and other military aircraft flew overhead, the president's entire focus was to thank those who serve, on America's Independence Day. The event was a heartwarming patriotic tribute.

In his remarks, Trump told the story of America, from the signing of the Declaration of Independence to the Lewis and Clark expedition to the Civil War and beyond. "Devotion to our founding ideals led American patriots to abolish the evil of slavery, secure civil rights, and expand the blessings of liberty to all Americans," Trump said.[52]

The crowd repeatedly shouted, "USA, USA, USA!"

Trump paid tribute to Dr. Martin Luther King Jr., Frederick Douglass, and Harriet Tubman. He pointed to an elderly man on the stage with him, Clarence Henderson, one of the earliest civil rights advocates, who, when he was eighteen years old in 1960, participated in a sit-in at a Woolworth lunch counter in Greensboro, North Carolina. "Clarence, thank you for making this country a much better place for all Americans," Trump said as the crowd cheered.[53]

Trump then told war stories, highlighting the freedom-saving accomplishments of each branch of the military as the anthem for each was played to a wildly enthusiastic audience. After an hour of history spent on patriotism, pride, and exceptionalism, Navy Blue Angels fighters flew overhead as the band played "The Battle Hymn of the Republic," and the event came to a stirring end.[54]

People losing their minds did not.

CNN's counterterrorism expert, Philip Mudd, was asked for his reaction to Trump's speech. "I hated it," Mudd said, decrying Trump's focus on the military.[55] On the other hand, Stephen Collinson, a CNN political reporter, wrote, "President Donald Trump was as good as his word Thursday: He saluted America."[56]

"In one of the least polarizing speeches of his presidency, Trump paid tribute to America's armed forces at a July Fourth appearance before the Lincoln Memorial in Washington that unfolded amid stormy skies and criticism that he was politicizing the nation's Independence Day celebrations," Collinson wrote.[57]

But why did Trump's critics lose their minds in the first place? Why did the mention of a military parade set them loose on a misguided series of denunciations and accusations, which all too easily found safe harbor in the mainstream press corps?

When Trump lashes out at his political opponents, the press often inserts the words *without evidence* into their descriptions of Trump's actions. There was no "without evidence" inserted into the stories of the many Democrats who falsely accused Trump of turning July Fourth into a partisan campaign event. The press just ran with it.

It fits a pattern established during the Trump years. Trump antagonized the media. The media fired back. Democrats criticized the president. The press took the side of the Democrats. If you didn't watch Trump's actual speech, anyone watching or reading the media would have been led to believe the speech was one more authoritarian thing Trump did. Deceptions like this happened time after time.

One of the more amusing bits of "reporting" that combined lost minds, deceptive reporting, and pro-Biden bias occurred on November 7, 2020, the day Biden was projected the winner of the election. The reaction from American media outlets abroad, and particularly MSNBC at home, was hilarious. It was the perfect illustration of how newsrooms think most sensible people, including the people of London and Paris, are just like them in their fondness for Joe Biden and their disdain for Donald Trump.

The night Biden was declared the winner, fireworks went off across London. *ABC World News Tonight* assumed and tweeted that the fireworks were in celebration of Biden.

Source: *ABC World News Tonight*. Twitter. @ABCWorldNews. November 8, 2020.

CNN's Jeff Zeleny was carried away by the international celebrations for America's new president-elect. He told Wolf Blitzer, live on the air, "we heard church bells ringing in Paris. We saw fireworks in London. This is indeed a moment the world is watching. . . ."[58] Zeleny wasn't wrong. Church bells did ring in Paris. Fireworks did go off in London.

But as London correspondent to the *Washington Post* Karla Adam later pointed out, the church bells and fireworks had nothing to do with America's election results. Adam noted that bells rang that evening in Paris only because they were automatically programmed to announce the 6 p.m. mass. Similarly, in London, the fireworks were in celebration of Bonfire Night, a very British holiday commemorating the failed bombing of the British Parliament in 1605, which was intended to kill King James I.[59]

American media outlets, especially ABC News, were ridiculed. On *Good Morning Britain*, former host Piers Morgan said, "Americans are getting a little bit over-excited about the global reaction to Joe Biden's win. ABC News, that bastion of factual accuracy, tweeted . . . yesterday implying that all over this country we were celebrating Joe Biden's victory." Cohost Susanna Reid pointed out, "What's extraordinary is that we do this every year," which led Morgan to add: "Which means we've been celebrating Joe Biden's win for the last 500 years, ever since Guy Fawkes, Bonfire Night, started."[60]

Tim Graham of the Media Research Center reported a hilarious tweet mocking ABC News from Daniel Hannan, a conservative former member of the European Parliament. Hannan, responding to the ABC News tweet, wrote, "Shall we tell them? I wanna tell them!"[61] The version of the tweet he cited was deleted by ABC.

> **Daniel Hannan** ✔
> @DanielJHannan
>
> Shall we tell them? I wanna tell them!
> twitter.com/ABC/status/132...
>
> This Tweet is unavailable.
>
> 11:49 AM · Nov 8, 2020 · Twitter Web App
>
> **248** Retweets **41** Quote Tweets **1.9K** Likes

Source: Daniel Hannan. Twitter. @DanielJHannan. November 8, 2020.

The funniest moment of the night came from Ari Melber at MSNBC. As he showed video clips of bells ringing in Paris and fireworks exploding in London, Melber told his audience, "There were also celebrations abroad. Places like Paris, where the actual church bells were ringing. Listen to that. That doesn't happen for every election. That was the reaction there to mark Trump losing. Joe Biden becoming our president-elect. Or take London. Fireworks were set off, celebrating this historic win. Let's take this in."

At that moment, Melber stopped speaking. For almost eighteen seconds. Eighteen seconds! That's an eternity on live TV. Melber paused to take in the amazing scene of Londoners celebrating Biden's win. He was so moved he couldn't speak. He wanted to soak it in and enjoy every moment of British fireworks marking Biden's international triumph!

Melber then added, "Millions of people in dozens and dozens of countries stopping to reflect on what we did, what you did here in America yesterday."[62]

Who knew Melber was so devoted to King James I and the events of 1605?

Before the bells-for-Biden story was corrected, NBC's *Saturday Night Live* jumped into the act. Of course it did. The connection between the cultural/entertainment left and the media/political left is almost instant. "Do you know how bad you have to be for Paris to ring church bells when you lose?"[63] said *SNL* comedian Colin Jost.

This is what happens, however, when newsrooms are so ideologically and culturally lopsided. Of course people around the world celebrated Biden's win! Who wouldn't? The reporting that night was dismally inaccurate, biased, and deceptive. It was as wrong as wrong can be. Sadly, it *was* what the American people were told.

Sometimes, however, a firework is just a firework. And a church bell is just a church bell. But thanks to the media that aired these stories, I suspect many Americans still think the world celebrated Trump's defeat.

There's an old saying in local news—if it bleeds, it leads. There should be a new saying in national news—if it's anti-Trump, it gets a bump. The lose-your-mind lunacy extended well beyond the broadcasts and news pages of mainstream media.

In April 2017, the New England Patriots came to the White House to be honored for winning the Super Bowl two months earlier.[64] The *New York Times* sports section tweeted about it, comparing the number of players who showed up in 2015, when President Obama was in office and the Patriots won the Super Bowl, to 2017. The message the *Times* wanted to convey to its readers was that Obama was popular. Trump is not.

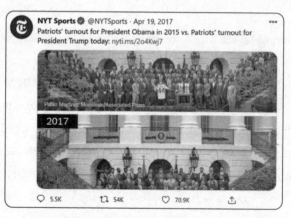

Source: NYT Sports. Twitter. @NYTSports. April 19, 2017.

Judging from the picture and the headline, you would think most players and people in the Patriots organization boycotted Trump. "Take that, Trump!" was the message sent by the *Times*. Except once again, the *New York Times* got its facts wrong.

A story in the *Times* was headlined:

Tom Brady Skips Patriots' White House Visit Along With Numerous Teammates

Source: *New York Times*, April 19, 2017.

The Patriots threw a penalty flag, saying the *Times* story was out of bounds. It lacked context.

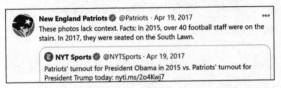

Source: NYT Sports. Twitter. @NYTSports. April 19, 2017.

The Patriots then tweeted again, reversing the *New York Times'* ruling on the field. "Comparable photos: The last time the #Patriots won two Super Bowls in three years, 36 players visited the White House. Today, we had 34."

To drive home its point that the *Times* had distorted facts and engaged in deceptive reporting in an effort to damage Trump's reputation, the Patriots supplemented their tweet with two photographs depicting the team's nearly equal White House attendance during the Bush and Trump presidencies.

As for Tom Brady, if a reader made it to the fourteenth paragraph of the story, they would have learned that Brady also hadn't attended the Patriots' Super Bowl honor when Barack Obama was president. In both instances, he stayed home to be with his family.[65]

This is minor-league, frivolous stuff. But it's indicative of the

Source: New England Patriots. Twitter. @Patriots. April 19, 2017.

routine way the media deceived the American people in an effort to make Trump look bad. The Patriots' White House visit wasn't the only frivolous occasion when reporters stepped in it.

There was the time Melania Trump wore Timberland boots.

In December 2018, the first lady accompanied her husband to Iraq for a surprise visit to the troops. She wore Timberland boots. Some in the media went nuts.

According to Yahoo Life:[66]

yahoo/life

Melania Trump gets mocked for wearing Timberland boots while visiting the troops

Source: Yahoo Life, December 26, 2018.

Whom did Yahoo Life cite for mocking the first lady? A bunch of random people on Twitter, whose tweets they elevated into their stories.

As of this writing, the tweet's author, @riverjordan19, has 834 followers, but somehow Yahoo Life found her tweet newsworthy.

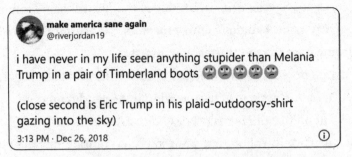

Source: Twitter. @riverjordan19. December 26, 2018.

It wasn't the first time the press criticized the first lady's shoe selection.

In October 2017, *Teen Vogue* blasted Melania Trump for wearing Timberland boots on a visit to hurricane victims in Puerto Rico. Like Yahoo Life, *Teen Vogue* found someone on Twitter and elevated a tweet into a story, subheadlined "Disaster Chic."[67]

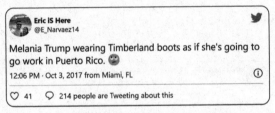

Source: Twitter. @E_Narvaez14. October 3, 2017.

Mr. @E_Narvaez14 has, as of this writing, 295 Twitter followers. I truly don't know how the press finds these critics. But I do know that the reason they elevate them into their stories is that when a newsroom is full of reporters and editors who don't like Donald Trump, anything anti-Trump is good enough to make it into print.

If only this foolishness about boots stopped here.

But guess what happened when Democratic vice presidential candidate Kamala Harris wore the same type of boots? As Tristan

Justice wrote for the *Federalist*, under the headlines, "Timberland Boots Only Look Fabulous On Democrats,"[68] "Trump Derangement Syndrome has infected the fashion industry."

Justice noted Yahoo Finance's editor at large Brian Sozzi, who said, "Kamala Harris may have made Timberland boots cool again." Sozzi went on to call Harris's shoe choice a "boss like move."

It wasn't only Yahoo that went loo-loo. Pointing out the blatant shoe hypocrisy, the *Federalist* reported:

> "Kamala Harris Wears Timberlands, Gets Sh*t Done," headlined *Marie Claire*, a health, beauty and fashion magazine.
>
> "Timbs and Converse? Kamala Harris sports Timberland boots after wearing Chuck Taylor All-Stars," titled coverage in *USA Today*.
>
> "Kamala Harris' Timberlands-Pearls Combo Has Our Vote," headlined another piece in Refinery29 picked up by Yahoo! Life.[69]

Source: Amy Kremer. Twitter. @AmyKremer. September 16, 2020.

The *Federalist* story included a smart tweet by conservative activist Amy Kremer, who as of this writing has more than 83,000 Twitter followers.

Maybe one day Yahoo Finance will meet Yahoo Life and compare notes, but this is what happens when critics lose their minds.

Chapter Four

THE WAY IT WAS

The American news landscape has changed dramatically over the past several decades. It's less trusted, more opinionated, and less profitable. Television broadcasts especially, once rooted in objective, factual reporting, are now dominated by public displays of personal opinions and perspectives. Commentary has become a commodity.

According to Gallup, in 1980, 70 percent of Americans had either a "great deal or a fair amount" of trust that the press would report the news "fully, fairly and accurately."[1] It was an era when Walter Cronkite, who anchored the *CBS Evening News* from 1962 to 1981, was widely perceived as the most trusted public figure in America.[2]

What a difference a few decades make. According to Gallup, only about 40 percent of the American people in 2020 trusted the press, a plunge of thirty percentage points from 1980.[3] In fact, according to *Columbia Journalism Review*, in 2019 the press was the least trusted institution in America compared to trust in the military, law enforcement, universities, the Supreme Court, the executive branch, and Congress.[4]

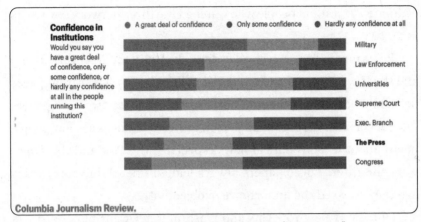

Source: "Poll: How Does the Public Think Journalism Happens,"
Columbia Journalism Review, Winter 2019.

A June 2021 survey conducted in forty-six countries by the Reuters Institute for the Study of Journalism found that American media are the least trusted in the world.[5] Only 29 percent of the American people trust the media, the survey found, the very bottom of the international barrel. (Finland is first, with 65 percent saying they trust their media. Canadian media, for comparison's sake, enjoy a 45 percent level of trust.) The American media rank lower than the media in Poland, Peru, Mexico, and Kenya! Most reporters when they hear this will think, "There's something wrong with the American people." Most Americans think, "There's something wrong with the media."

In 1980, when Ronald Reagan was elected president, 52 million Americans watched the national news on ABC, NBC, and CBS.[6] These three networks held a virtual monopoly on where people could watch national news. CNN was new, having been launched in 1980. FOX and MSNBC did not yet exist.

As for that network news monopoly, over time, viewers who depended on ABC, NBC, and CBS for their news went elsewhere; today, network viewership has plunged, from 52 million in 1980 to an estimated 21 million people who watched the three network newscasts in 2020.[7]

Print media has seen similar dives. In 1980, the *New York Times* and the *Washington Post* dominated political news. Their front pages defined what was considered newsworthy. If those two newspapers did not consider an event or a person as news, chances are few people heard about it. For political news especially, the *Post* and the *Times* were the filter. These papers always leaned liberal, but forty years ago they stressed the importance of objectivity.

Outside of New York City and Washington, DC, print newspapers went into a thirty-year decline, due in considerable part to the rise of the internet. The total estimated circulation of U.S. daily newspapers was roughly 60 million from 1964 to 1992, and then it started to drop, falling by half to below 30 million in 2018.[8]

Circulation at the *New York Times* peaked in 1994 at 1.18 million.[9] By 2019, circulation dropped to less than 500,000.[10] But the *Times* got an unexpected bump on its digital platform.

Resistance to Donald Trump found an electronic home at the *Times*. According to CNBC, in November 2016, following Trump's win, the *Times*' subscriptions grew by 132,000 paid subscribers to its news products—a growth rate tenfold of what it was during the same period the year prior.[11] The "Trump bump" helped to catapult digital subscriptions at the *Times*—to a record-breaking 7 million in 2020; the *Times* says it's confident that digital subscription numbers will reach 10 million.[12]

"Every time I hear [Trump] tweet about the 'failing @nytimes' or use the shopworn sobriquet 'fake news,' I also hear the *ka-ching* of the so-called Trump bump," said former *Times* executive editor Jill Abramson.[13]

Trump also gave cable news a boost. From his candidacy announcement in 2015 to his White House exit, Trump was the driving force behind record ratings and profits for CNN, FOX News, and MSNBC.[14]

A 2017 report from Harvard Kennedy School's Shorenstein Center on Media, Politics, and Public Policy analyzed news coverage of Trump's first one hundred days in office: "Trump is a journalist's dream. Reporters are tuned to what's new and different, better yet if it's laced with controversy. Trump delivers that type of material by the shovel full. Trump is also good for business. News ratings were slumping until Trump entered the arena." Or as former CBS chief executive officer Les Moonves put it, "[Trump] may not be good for America, but [he's] damn good for [us]."[15]

If Trump coverage fuels ratings, it's no surprise that the Harvard Kennedy School report found that the first hundred days of Trump's presidency dominated media coverage. Trump received three times the amount of coverage received by previous presidents.[16]

The media's obsession with Trump reached far beyond his first days in office. An analysis published in the *Columbia Journalism*

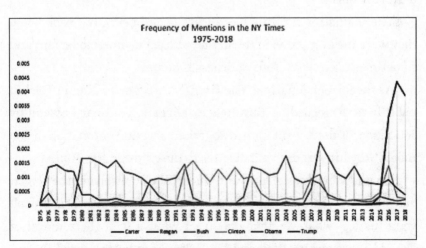

Source: Musa al-Gharbi, "The New York Times' Obsession with Trump, Quantified," *Columbia Journalism Review*, November 13, 2019.

Review found that "the quantity of coverage devoted by the print media to Donald Trump is without historical precedent." The article quantified the *New York Times'* obsession with Trump.[17]

According to the analysis, "in 2018, 'Trump' was the fourth most used word in the *New York Times*. On average, Trump was directly mentioned two to three times in every article, and indirectly mentioned an additional once or twice." The article goes on to note the spike in *Times* subscriptions.[18]

From a business point of view, *ka-ching* is great news for the *Times*, allowing it to pay its staff and keep its news bureaus open. From a fairness point of view, it has been a disaster. As former *Times* executive editor Jill Abramson points out, paying subscribers count on the *Times* to oppose Trump.

Indeed, the same Harvard Kennedy School report found that during the first hundred days of his presidency, Trump received "unsparing coverage for most weeks of his presidency, without a single major topic where Trump's coverage, on balance, was more positive than negative, setting a new standard for unfavorable press coverage of a president."[19]

The mainstream media has always been liberal, but back when they were the only game in town, they at least claimed to be fair, and sometimes tried to be. Today fairness is quaint.

As the former, longtime *New York Times* reporter Martin Tolchin put it in 2020 regarding Tara Reade's allegation of sexual assault by Joe Biden, "I don't want an investigation. I want a coronation of Joe Biden." Tolchin wrote that in a letter to the editor of the *Times*.[20]

It's really hard to get a letter to the editor published in the *Times*, but the *Times'* editors found Tolchin's worthy of publication. "I don't want justice, whatever that may be. I want a win, the removal of Donald Trump from office, and Mr. Biden is our best chance," Tolchin wrote.[21]

Tolchin was a former reporter when his letter was published, but his anti-Trump sentiment captured what many reporters who covered Trump were thinking—this guy needs to be gone.

WHEN PRESIDENT FRANKLIN ROOSEVELT IN 1933 held the first of his "fireside chats" on a device called the radio,[22] political communications changed in an instant. A mere half century removed from the late 1800s, when presidential candidates thought it was undignified to campaign and ask people for votes, technology allowed FDR to speak to all the American people at once. Technology will always determine how we communicate with one another.

As cable news emerged, especially FOX News and MSNBC in the mid-1990s, political consumers were able to digest just the news they wanted to hear. They didn't have to listen to news that didn't appeal to them.

In 2001, when I became White House press secretary, what NBC anchor Tom Brokaw, CBS anchor Dan Rather, and ABC anchor Peter Jennings reported on the evening news mattered. Viewership was down from its Reagan-era levels, but they were still the news programs with the most viewers.

During the campaign in 2000, I can't remember what the particular news item was, but I recall talking to Dan Bartlett, the campaign's rapid response leader, about some bit of information that he was able to get onto FOX News, and our reaction was, that's good, but it's not good enough. The news can't just be on FOX because not enough people will know about it, I thought in 2000.

There was no social media in the early years of the Bush presidency. No Facebook. No Twitter. No YouTube. No Instagram. Definitely no TikTok. The influence of mainstream media was shrinking, but you still had to work through them to get out the news.

The idea of a government employee in 2001 taking a video on a government camera and releasing it on a government website would have been derided as "propaganda" by everyone in every newsroom everywhere. With the advent of YouTube in 2005, such a practice became common. The Obama White House regularly released its own videos and photos, to widespread acceptance and acclaim by Obama supporters, especially younger people.

Today, every politician everywhere releases their own videos on numerous platforms, successfully going around the press.

During the Obama presidency, the media's decades-long circulation and viewership erosion was about to meet a technological, social media–driven explosion that would enable elected officials everywhere to circumvent the traditional media. Similarly, the new platforms allowed the average citizen to share his or her views with government officials, along with their friends and followers, without going through a filter controlled by the press. Rather than viewers simply *receiving* the news as they had for decades, viewers were now *interacting with* and *responding to* and *sharing* the news themselves on their own social media accounts. On the flip side, social media gave news organizations instant feedback on stories, and social media sharing capabilities enabled the media to reach broader audiences. Ultimately, this erosion of mainstream news channels and explosion of social network platforms changed everything about the media and how news is shared and consumed today.

When I was press secretary, the only way to go viral was to have the flu. Today, who doesn't want to go viral? After all, why write a letter to the editor that you hope some editor somewhere will print, and edit, when you can let it rip yourself, for all to see?

Viewership and readership habits have broken down. New media organizations that didn't have to incur the massive costs of printing and delivering a hard copy newspaper were launched. The quality, quantity, and speed of political coverage changed. The internet ushered in an era of online publications. News was broken and disseminated at breakneck speed. Online political publications—notably *Politico* in 2007—sought to change the field of political reporting. As *Politico* editor Carrie Budoff Brown wrote in 2018, "Washington journalism needed to be faster, edgier, and a lot more fun to read. The internet and the rise of social networks were fundamentally changing the way readers consumed news, but political coverage had not kept up. We stood up a homepage that year that reflected the quick metabolism of our newsroom, with tons of blogs, brash headlines, and scoopy stories."[23]

The rise of online publications like *Politico* has both improved and damaged politics. *Politico* certainly has exposed to the public many of the behind-the-scenes moments and tidbits that reporters previously knew about but didn't see fit to cover. Almost everything politicians do is now exposed to the light of day. But the pressure to perpetually produce breaking news and the commoditizing of commentary have changed what it means to be a political reporter, and it has distorted how the American people get the news.

Make no mistake, *Politico* alone didn't do that. Technology did. And technology can't be stopped, nor should it be, but the qualitative harm done by it should not be ignored. The pressure that editors put on reporters to cover news is immense. The need for reporters to come up with "fresh" material can be overwhelming. The very definition of "breaking" news has changed. It's been diluted. Minor items are now considered "breaking."

In the days when the networks were king and the *New York Times* and the *Washington Post* prevailed, an era I do not want to return to, there was a predictable twenty-four-hour news cycle.

News would break at ten in the morning, for instance, but the American people, for the most part, did not hear about it until 6:30 p.m., when the network news aired. A news story might make it on the radio, if you were listening, or it might make an afternoon daily newspaper when those existed, but if you didn't watch TV, you likely didn't hear about the day's news until you received your morning paper the next day. There were exceptions for genuinely major news stories when Brokaw, Rather, or Jennings would break into daytime TV to report news of great consequence, but that was rare. When it happened, people stopped to pay attention. News mattered.

Today, as any CNN viewer knows, everything is "breaking news," always right on time, at the top and bottom of every hour. It's hard to know what matters anymore. Every bit of news and every update appear on dozens of websites, updated frequently throughout the day. By the time the 6:30 p.m. news airs, most reporters think the news is stale.

Prior to the round-the-clock news era, news was more deeply thought about, digested, and edited before it was shared. Reporters had time to reflect and call sources. They had more time to put the news into a fuller, more robust, less sensational context. Reporters still wanted to break news, but they didn't have to rush as much as they do now. It was a slower, more thoughtful era.

It was still a liberal media era with very few alternative outlets, but it wasn't anything like it is today. Most reporters back then shunned publicity. They wanted their reporting to be the news. Now many reporters bask in publicity—and criticism—knowing it will drive more clicks and, for some reporters, lead to a surge in social media followers, fame, and even fortune.

It also was a time when reporters covered big-picture issues that mattered. There wasn't enough time on the network news or a large enough news hole in the newspapers for Mickey Mouse minutiae to matter. News had impact. A major story would last for days, in contrast to now, when most stories surge to dramatic heights, only to vanish and be forgotten in a day or two. I suspect it also was a more fulfilling time to be a reporter. They were freer to think; today most just have to crank it out.

To use a baseball analogy, reporters before the internet were not play-by-play announcers, tweeting or reporting their reflections numerous times a day. Their job was to cover the full game and to report the results to the American people. They didn't have to recount every inning, and certainly not every pitch. They reported on the big things. *Politico*, twenty-four-hour cable stations, online reporting, and social media changed that.

Reporters now dwell on every pitch. An anonymous quote from a midlevel staffer whom no one outside the narrowest political circles has ever heard of can dominate political coverage for a day or two. Medium-level White House officials who may or may not have been in a meeting are routinely quoted, especially if their quote is juicy enough. Stories that are boring to most Americans became important to the *Politico*-reading Washington press corps.

Sometimes *Politico* covered news to settle scores or send warning shots.

On the first day of Joe Biden's presidency, he had a serious message for his appointees. "I'm not joking when I say this: If you ever work with me and I hear you treat another colleague with disrespect, talk down to someone, I will fire you on the spot. No ifs, ands or buts," Biden said at a virtual swearing-in ceremony for presidential appointees.[24]

Politico covered his remarks and added, "(Serious question on our minds this morning: Does this standard apply to how mid-level press aides treat reporters?)"[25]

As I read that story, I thought to myself, I'm sorry, but why do readers care how midlevel aides treat you? And how is this news? Yes, you should be treated well. If there is a problem, complain to the press secretary, who I hope will handle it. But do *Politico*'s readers really need to learn about how midlevel Biden aides handle the needs of the White House press corps?

It's not even an inside-the-Beltway story, I thought. It's an inside-the-White-House-driveway story.

In this instance, this obscure tidbit led to the resignation of White House deputy press secretary TJ Ducklo because of the way he berated a *Politico* reporter who was working on a story to which Ducklo objected. For the press and the White House staff, it *was* a story that mattered. Ducklo's resignation may have been newsworthy, but when I read *Politico*'s first cryptic reference ("Does this standard apply to how mid-level press aides treat reporters?"), I instantly knew *Politico* was firing a warning shot with a silencer that could only be heard by a few people inside the West Wing.

It's an example of how electronic news and social media have led to coverage of items that are not relevant to most people, and detract from the substantive, critical issues facing our country. It shows how people in Washington sometimes have a coded way of talking with one another that most Americans cannot understand.

Early in 2021, *Politico* included a story about the political leanings of the new sign interpreter hired by the Biden White House.

UNEXPECTED HEADLINE—"President Biden's First White House Sign Language Interpreter Has Ties to the Far Right," Time: "[W]hen Press Secretary Jen Psaki began her briefing on Monday by announcing that American Sign Language (ASL) interpreters would now be present at all White House news briefings, many deaf and hard of hearing Americans celebrated this historic first.

"But it turns out the first ASL interpreter chosen was not such a change from the previous Administration after all. Heather Mewshaw, who Psaki introduced on Monday as 'today's interpreter, Heather,' also manages a conservative group of ASL interpreters who provide sign language accompaniments to right-wing videos. Some of these videos have featured vaccine misinformation, conspiracy theories about the 2020 election and the Jan. 6 riots at the Capitol, and false claims about Michelle Obama being transgender."[26]

How and why is that news? Why are the political leanings of an ASL signer overshadowing her commendable contribution to the deaf community? What's next? If one of the faithful stenographers who works at the White House transcribing the president's statements is a socialist, do I really need to know that?

Today, government officials and the media that cover them are bombarded with insider, cover-every-pitch internet publications. *Politico* launched Playbook as an insider's guide to the latest happenings in politics in 2007.[27] It provided quick coverage of news at the White House and Capitol Hill and included a handy crib sheet summarizing the coverage from many mainstream media outlets.

Then, in 2016, *Politico*'s Mike Allen and Jim VandeHei left to launch *Axios*, a competitor to *Politico*.

In 2021, akin to assistant coaches who went on to become head coaches after working for University of Alabama's head football coach Nick Saban, other *Politico* alumni founded *Punchbowl* (Punchbowl is the Secret Service name for the Capitol). *Punchbowl* does the same thing and covers the same people and news as Playbook and *Axios*, albeit with a focus on Congress.

Back at *Politico*, a new team took over Playbook, launching the day before Joe Biden's inauguration. The new team advertised themselves by declaring, "We aim to be essential to your understanding of the incoming Biden administration, obsessive about politics on the Hill and mischievously scoopy about people in power. We know Playbook is the first thing that hundreds of thousands of you read every morning, and we aim to guide you efficiently through what you need to know, what you need to read and who you need to watch."[28]

Obsessive? Mischievously scoopy? Most reporters I know are already obsessive. They don't need a reason to be more so.

Reporters are also faithful readers of everything they can get their hands on. They crave information. The problem today is that there's too much of it. Reporters, who often are on Twitter, where they read tweets from other reporters, live in a world where news is old if it happened an hour or two ago. They hear from and talk to other reporters too much, as they devour information from live television, social media, the latest internet site, or some other form of communication.

A fierce, self-repeating, fast-moving bubble of same-mindedness surrounds today's reporters. They're too plugged in to too narrow a space. It's how they lose their focus on the big things that matter to the American people. It also might explain why so few reporters thought Donald Trump would win in 2016. They're so focused on one another's thoughts and daily minutiae that they miss larger, more important societal trends. They spend too much time reading the tweets of their colleagues and not enough time listening to—and respecting—the voices of the American people, especially those who don't tweet.

To be fair, these instant news outlets do cover legitimate, bigger stories. A yearlong investigation undertaken by *Axios*, for example, broke the news about Congressman Eric Swalwell's (D-CA) entanglement with a Chinese spy.[29] But journalists would do better if they dedicated more attention to significant, impactful stories and less attention to inside-the-Beltway minor happenings, especially stories about personalities and personnel.

I don't know anyone in America who really cares who the conference chairman is for the Democrats or Republicans in the House of Representatives. Most people don't know what a conference chairman does. (They're ostensibly in charge of developing and distributing communication messages for members of their party to use in their speeches and other public comments.)

But in 2021, when Wyoming congresswoman Liz Cheney was deposed from her conference chairmanship by her colleagues due to her opposition to Trump, it was huge news everywhere. The press loved the story. It involved Trump. It involved a Cheney who took on Trump. It showed Trump's domination over the GOP. It received massive attention.[30]

I suspect that most Americans read the stories and shrugged. It was just more palace intrigue.

The Media Research Center summed up the Cheney coverage in a tweet showing that on ABC, CBS, and NBC, it clocked in at a hefty thirty-two minutes and fifty-three seconds. The coverage that the networks gave to the Cheney drama dwarfed coverage given to President Joe Biden's troubles at the time. The worst inflation since 2008 received one minute and forty-three seconds of airtime, and the record-breaking number of encounters at the southern border during the previous month wasn't covered at all.[31]

The internet also profoundly changed how the media operates due to the dramatic financial loss in advertising dollars, particularly for newspapers. According to a 2020 study by the Pew Research Center, "Newspaper revenues declined dramatically between 2008 and 2018. Advertising revenue fell from $37.8 billion in 2008 to $14.3 billion in 2018, a 62% decline."[32]

Television networks also have suffered a long-term decline in advertising revenue as their advertising customers pursued digital advertising instead.[33] When you're no longer the only game in town, your bottom line suffers.

The rise of alternative outlets and the mainstream media's need to find money led independent author and journalist Matt Taibbi to wisely observe, "In the course of the thirty years I spent in this job, the core commercial strategy of the news media has changed dramatically. Specifically, we've gone, especially at the national news media or international news media level, we've shifted from trying to go after one big audience to instead looking at multiple smaller audiences and trying to capture and dominate those. And this has essentially led us to going from trying to sell a very broad product that appealed to everybody and that allowed everybody to speak the same language to instead going to a format where we're essentially selling division."[34]

In the 1980s, 1990s, and through the early 2000s, the TV networks and cable TV shows tried to appeal to a mass audience and they were more conscious of serving the needs of most Americans. Although much of the media was liberal, they did not want to appear too biased and risk antagonizing a portion of their audience.

That's why, for example, in FOX's early days, it aired *Hannity & Colmes*, which featured conservative Sean Hannity *and* liberal Alan Colmes debating the news of the day. Similarly, MSNBC's political talk show *Equal Time* was hosted by liberal Paul Begala and conservative Ollie North. I was a regular on that show during the 2000 presidential campaign. Now Ollie North wouldn't be welcome anywhere near MSNBC, nor would he want to go there.

Conservatives Pat Buchanan, Robert Novak, Tucker Carlson, and Newt Gingrich were among the hosts of CNN's *Crossfire*, along with liberals Tom Braden, Michael Kinsley, Geraldine Ferraro, James Carville, and Paul Begala (again).

Imagine the reaction of CNN viewers today if Tucker Carlson or Newt Gingrich appeared regularly there. CNN's viewers would demand these conservatives be canceled in a nanosecond. Same problem at MSNBC. It's partially the same story at FOX, although it's important to note that liberal commentators like Juan Williams and Geraldo Rivera at FOX have thrived and been welcomed.

Just look at the newsroom rebellion at *Politico* in January 2021, when conservative Ben Shapiro was invited to be a guest writer. More than one hundred *Politico* staffers melted down in a letter to management objecting to the decision to give Shapiro a platform.[35] They threw an absolute fit over the temporary presence of one mere conservative writer.

In 2001, more important, network anchors and reporters purported to be fair and neutral.

As a press secretary on Capitol Hill for much of this time, I knew they were largely liberal, but at least most reporters would tell you it was their job to tell the news straight, without demonstrating favoritism for one side or another. At least that's what they claimed, despite the fact that journalism schools were graduating legions of Democratic voters into their ranks.

FOX News, recognizing the huge opening on the right for viewers who agreed that the news was dominated by liberals, launched in 1996 to tremendous success and popularity with its rightward lean.

In 2019, Pew Research asked people what their main source of news was. Then they asked people what party they belonged to. The decades-long partisan breakdown of the media is overwhelming. According to the 2019 survey, of those whose main source of political and electoral news is the *New York Times*, 91 percent identify as Democrats. Just 7 percent of *Times* readers by this measure are Republicans.[36]

MSNBC's viewers are 95 percent Democrat; NPR is 87 percent Democrat; CNN comes in at 79 percent Democrat.[37] According to Pew, FOX News viewers are 93 percent Republican and just 6 percent Democrat.[38]

The network news shows on ABC, CBS, and NBC are mostly watched by Democrats. ABC is 53 percent Democrat, CBS comes in at 55 percent, and NBC is 57 percent. (ABC viewers are 44 percent Republican; CBS's are 41 percent and NBC's are 38 percent.)[39]

So when Republicans, conservatives, and Donald Trump complain that the mainstream media are "left-wing" or "liberal," they're right—especially when measured by viewership.

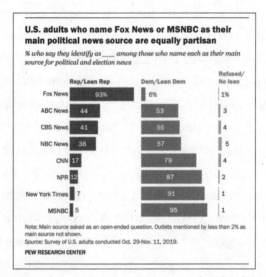

U.S. adults who name Fox News or MSNBC as their main political news source are equally partisan

% who say they identify as ___ among those who name each as their main source for political and election news

	Rep/Lean Rep	Dem/Lean Dem	Refused/ No lean
Fox News	93%	6%	1%
ABC News	44	53	3
CBS News	41	55	4
NBC News	38	57	5
CNN	17	79	4
NPR	12	87	2
New York Times	7	91	1
MSNBC	5	95	1

Note: Main source asked as an open-ended question. Outlets mentioned by less than 2% as main source not shown.
Source: Survey of U.S. adults conducted Oct. 29-Nov. 11, 2019.
PEW RESEARCH CENTER

Source: Pew Research Center, "Americans' Main Sources for Political News Vary by Party and Age," Survey of U.S. Adults Conducted October 29–November 11, 2019.

BEYOND THE TECHNOLOGY-DRIVEN FACTIONALIZATION OF the media, outward displays of ideology show how much the media has changed. Take CNN's Jim Acosta, for example.

Jim Acosta was a CNN White House reporter for all four years of the Trump presidency. He made a name for himself, not by covering the news, but by sharing his opinions on live TV. In one of his most notable moments, he instructed White House officials what President Trump's immigration position should be, based on Acosta's personal point of view. It was groundbreaking opinionizing from a White House reporter. Not even the late Helen Thomas, who was an opinionated columnist when I was press secretary, went as far as Acosta.

In August 2017, the White House point man on immigration, Stephen Miller, entered the White House briefing room to explain the details of President Trump's merit-based immigration proposals. Acosta objected. On live TV, of course.

"What you're proposing or the president's proposing here does not sound like it's keeping with American tradition when it comes to immigration. The Statue of Liberty says, 'Give me your tired, your poor, your huddled masses yearning to breathe free.' It doesn't say anything about speaking English or being able to be a computer programmer," Acosta opined.

Miller explained that for an immigrant to become naturalized, there already existed a longtime requirement that they had to speak English. But Acosta kept arguing and sharing his thoughts about what our nation's immigration policy should be.

"So, you're saying that that does not represent what the country has always thought of as immigration coming into this country. That sounds like some national park revisionism. The Statue of Liberty has always been a beacon of hope to the world for people to send their people to this country and they're not always going to speak English, Stephen," Acosta lectured.

The two antagonists argued with each other for a few minutes more.

"This whole notion of, well, they have to learn English before they get to the United States, are we just going to bring in people from Great Britain and Australia?" Acosta demanded.

To that Miller replied, "Jim, actually I am shocked at your statement. That you think that only people from Great Britain and Australia would know English. It actually reveals your cosmopolitan bias to a shocking degree that in your mind ... that you think that only people from Great Britain or Australia would speak English is so insulting to millions of hardworking immigrants who do speak English from all over the world. Jim, have you honestly never met an immigrant from another country who speaks English outside of Great Britain and Australia? Is that your personal experience?"[40]

Why would a reporter be so comfortable sharing his or her opinion about what America's immigration laws—or any law—should be? The answer: because today newsrooms increasingly welcome reporters who share their ideologies. CNN, knowing most of its viewers were anti-Trump Democrats, didn't seem to mind it a bit.

A 2019 report by the nonprofit, nonpartisan RAND Corporation examined the presentation of news information over time and across media platforms. The report noted that "[o]ver time, and as society moved from 'old' to 'new' media, news content has generally shifted from more objective event- and context-based reporting to reporting that is more subjective, relies more heavily on argumentation and advocacy, and includes more emotional appeals. These changes were observed across platforms, appearing least significant in the evolution of print journalism and most stark in comparisons of broadcast news with prime-time cable programming and of print journalism with online journalism."[41]

Bill Plante was a longtime CBS reporter, having joined the network in 1964, later becoming CBS's senior White House correspondent. He had a front-row seat in the briefing room when I was press secretary. He retired in 2016.[42] Appearing on CNN in March 2017, Plante had a word for the wise. Noting how contentious the relationship was between the Trump White House and the White House press corps, he advised his former colleagues not to let their feelings show.

"The important thing for reporters covering this is not to get involved personally in disputing this or disputing how we feel about the claim. I see tweets from people, and no names of course, who are offended by what's going on. Well, if you are offended by what's going on, you should keep it to yourself," Plante said.[43]

Many White House reporters did not want to keep it to themselves. They wanted to share their feelings and their advocacy. They wanted to tweet about it. They wanted to shout it from the rooftops. Most news organizations were happy to let them. Old-time reporters recognized their industry was changing before their eyes. Liberal ideology and anti-Trump animus exploded on Trump's watch in a way that is without precedent in modern journalism.

Writing for the *Atlantic* magazine, journalist McKay Coppins noted as Trump left office, "the Trump era has been especially rewarding to a certain class of Washington reporter. As the White House beat became the biggest story in the world, once-obscure correspondents were recast in the popular imagination as resistance heroes fighting for truth, justice, and the American way. They were showered with book deals, speaking gigs, and hundreds of thousands of Twitter followers. They got glow-ups to accompany their new cable-news contracts, and those glow-ups were covered in glossy magazines. Along the way, many of them adapted their journalism to cover an unusually mendacious and corrupt president (much to the delight of their new fan bases)."[44]

They sure did adapt their journalism. Instead of reporting what Trump said, matched by what Democrats said in opposition, many reporters took sides. And it wasn't Trump's side they took. Coppins noted the reporting of *New York* magazine's Olivia Nuzzi, a frequent, vocal antagonist to Trump. She would be the first to admit she wasn't neutral toward him. Knowing the liberal profile of her magazine's readers, Nuzzi told Coppins, "It didn't really require any special bravery to report honestly and critically on Donald Trump," and, "I could write in a piece, 'Donald Trump is the biggest asshole to ever live and he is a terrible human being and a shitty president and, like, he's ugly' . . . and nobody would be mad at me except the same people who are mad at me anyway for existing."[45]

That's a startling thing for a White House reporter to admit and it's a distressing sign of what's happened to journalism today. Nuzzi admitted to Coppins that so long as she was brutal to Trump, her magazine and her readers would think she was doing a good job. No fairness. No balance. No two sides. Just flat-out opposition. Nuzzi followed that up with an even braver admission.

"'On a purely social level, I don't know that reporting critically on Joe Biden will feel as safe for reporters,'" she told me. "'You're not going to get yass queen–ed to death.'"[46]

That's journalism today. Beat up Trump all you want—your readers and editors will thank you. Criticize Biden? That gets uncomfortable really fast. Especially, heaven forbid, "on a purely social level."

The sad truth is, Nuzzi's right. Reporters went easy on Biden throughout the campaign and well into his administration because, as Nuzzi admitted, on a purely social level, the press didn't want to be critical of him. The old notion that a reporter's job was to report the news "without fear of favor" turned into soft coverage of Biden to protect, in part, a reporter's "social level." After all, if writing a tough story about Biden meant a reporter might lose Twitter followers, it might not be worth it.

Good for Coppins. He's like truth serum. He has a way of getting reporters to open up and acknowledge how biased they are.

Coppins continued: "One cable-news anchor told me that praise from anti-Trump celebrities on Twitter has become like a 'narcotic' for some of his colleagues. 'It's important to people that George Takei likes their monologue,' the anchor said, requesting anonymity to speak candidly about his peers (and presumably to avoid alienating George Takei)," Coppins wrote.[47]

Even Jim Acosta turned himself in to Coppins.

According to the Coppins story, Acosta justified the double standard by attributing it to what Acosta called "professional solidarity." Acosta added, "If being at the White House is not an experience that might merit hazard pay then perhaps it is going to be approached differently."[48]

Hazard pay? There you have it. Could there be no clearer admission by a reporter that he is out of touch with half the country? Is it any wonder these reporters, experts at understanding what is happening in Washington, have so little knowledge about what is happening in America?

For a reporter to say he deserves hazard pay for having the privilege of covering a president from the rarefied air of the White House is the perfect illustration of how these reporters feel about the 74 million Americans who voted for Trump.

From their cut-from-the-same cloth, vote-overwhelmingly-the-same-way, oppose-Trump-all-the-time insider bubble, being fair and neutral would obliterate their more important desire to enjoy the social level so many reporters hold so dear, marked by an overwhelming moral opposition to Donald Trump and most Republicans. It has led today's reporters to become happily biased, thinking they're saving society from a threat that they and their like-minded readers and viewers can see, even if half the country disagrees. The "Trump half" of the country remains an item of curiosity to them, a subject worthy of occasional reporting, to help people "understand" why some people veer from the accepted political orthodoxy of newsrooms dominated by college-educated Democratic voters.

The media has changed from what it used to be. They've lost popularity, lost credibility, and lost the trust of the majority of the American people. They're in denial and that's not a good place to be.

Chapter Five

SUPPRESSION

Each and every day, there's news that doesn't make *the news*. It's information that you don't get to see.

Some stories are left on the cutting-room floor because too few people care about them. Other stories are left on the cutting-room floor because conservatives care deeply about them.

In newsrooms run by mostly college-educated Democratic voters whose readers and viewers are mostly college-educated Democrats, news stories about good guys with guns who stop bad guys with guns are hard to find. Similarly, stories about the "invisible hand" of capitalism that lifts people out of poverty and into the middle class are often nowhere to be found. It's not often that we read stories about the people who are in America illegally who commit crimes, including murder. Seldom does the mainstream media cover extremist, narrow-minded, condescending statements made by fringe, left-wing figures, while they often cover similar statements made by the fringe right. These events exist. They're just not reported by many mainstream news outlets.

What happens when one side of the country is regularly ill-informed and misled? What happens when important news is suppressed?

Sometimes these stories are touched on by the press, and then forgotten about, but if the controversy involves a Republican, or especially Donald Trump, they turn into feeding frenzies.

Just ask Joe Biden about news that wasn't extensively covered. A prime example of subjective news is how the national news media pursued—or more accurately, *didn't* pursue—the possibility that, in January 2017, then–vice president Biden might have involved himself in the investigation of President-elect Trump's incoming national security advisor, Michael Flynn.

At the time, the media was swirling with stories about whether Flynn's contact with Russian officials prior to his taking office had violated the Logan Act. The Logan Act is a 1799 law that prohibits private citizens from negotiating with a foreign power.[1] Flynn was under investigation by the Department of Justice for lying to the FBI, and for possible violations of a federal law pertaining to his work as a lobbyist.

The Obama administration had electronically monitored and listened to the phone calls Flynn had with Russian officials. As incoming national security advisor, his phone calls were routine and appropriate, but the U.S. government spy agencies keep track of what the Russians do. Any conversation anyone in the Trump administration had with Russians was viewed as suspect by Trump critics, who were sure the only reason Trump won in 2016 was Russian interference in the U.S. election.

On January 5, 2017, President Obama convened a meeting in the Oval Office to discuss how to handle Flynn. Obama was worried that Flynn might be a Russian asset, and he wanted to know if he should share sensitive intelligence information with Flynn.[2] In attendance with Obama were FBI director James Comey, National Security

Advisor Susan Rice, Deputy Attorney General Sally Yates, and Vice President Biden.

Even though he didn't attend the meeting, Peter Strzok, then FBI deputy assistant director, took handwritten notes about the meeting, presumably based on what Comey relayed to him afterward. Strzok's notes state that Biden, identified by the notation "VP," raised the topic of the "Logan Act." Strzok's notes also indicate that Biden said, "I have been on the intel committee for ten years and I never."[3]

Source: "Flynn Team—Strzok Notes Filing," Scribd, June 24, 2020.

It sounds like Biden saw something that he thought was unprecedented and possibly criminal.

It's important because presidents and vice presidents are supposed to stay out of criminal investigations. Decisions about prosecutions are to be made by Justice Department officials with no involvement from the White House. (In 2021, President Biden said anyone who didn't cooperate with the January 6 select committee should be prosecuted. He later apologized, saying he shouldn't have said it.) This deference is part of what makes the Justice Department independent.

Both Rice and Comey deny that Biden suggested prosecuting Flynn under the Logan Act. In sworn testimony before the Senate Judiciary Committee, Comey said, "I would remember because it would be highly inappropriate for a president or vice president to suggest prosecution or investigation of anyone. And that did not happen."[4]

The statements of Comey and Rice contradict the meeting notes. The conflicting reports normally would make reporters suspicious. Instinctively, they would ask questions, such as, Did Biden suggest the Logan Act be used against Flynn? Why did Biden bring it up? What *was* Biden talking about? And why did Comey and Rice deny it? Or were Strzok's notes wrong?

Did the media push to find out? No.

The lack of curiosity by the media was glaring. Perhaps there was nothing there. Perhaps there was. But isn't the press supposed to ask tough questions? Aren't they supposed to dig for the truth? When it came to collusion, the media dug into everything that made Trump and his people look bad. It seldom occurred to the press corps to ask hard questions of Obama officials, especially Joe Biden, about their role in what turned out to be one of the biggest, emptiest nonscandals in history.

If a sitting vice president urged or suggested the prosecution of an incoming national security advisor, it would be huge news. Asking Biden about it was obvious to conservative reporters, although they didn't have much access to Biden during the 2020 campaign. But for the mainstream reporters who were granted access to Biden, asking him about his role in the prosecution of Flynn was not their priority. They seldom tried to hold Biden to account.

During the 2020 presidential campaign, Biden was asked by ABC's George Stephanopoulos and by MSNBC about the role he played in the Justice Department's investigation of Flynn. Stephanopoulos, to his credit, asked Biden in May 2020, "What did you know about those moves to investigate Michael Flynn and was there anything improper done?"[5]

Biden replied, "I know nothing about those moves to investigate Michael Flynn."

Stephanopoulos briefly pressed Biden and then moved on.

One month later, Strzok's notes were declassified. Did the press seize on them to demand that Biden explain why he floated the Logan Act, despite telling Stephanopoulos that he knew nothing about Flynn's investigation?

The conservative press did. The mainstream media yawned. Two days after his interview with Stephanopoulos, Biden appeared with Lawrence O'Donnell on MSNBC, where O'Donnell asked him, "Mr. Vice President, what was your involvement in the investigation of Michael Flynn and the FBI investigation of Michael Flynn?"[6]

Biden answered, "I was never a part or had any knowledge of any criminal investigation into Flynn while I was in office, period. Not one single time." Except he *did* have a part in and knowledge about how to handle Flynn when he attended that January 5 meeting in the Oval Office with the deputy attorney general. Biden at best misled or misremembered. At worst, he lied. In all cases, it should have been a major story.

The mainstream press, however, couldn't have cared less. Reporters opted to pass instead of pursue the story. How simple it would have been for a reporter to ask Biden, "What did you mean when you mentioned the Logan Act in the Oval Office with the deputy attorney general? Were you suggesting to the Justice Department a possible violation of the Logan Act by Flynn? Were you suggesting to the Justice Department a possible pathway to prosecute Flynn? Do you deny mentioning the Logan Act? Why do notes show that you raised it?"

The press didn't pursue it because they knew where it would lead.

In a race against Donald Trump, the last thing the mainstream media wanted to do was pursue a line of questioning that would help Trump. Most reporters didn't want to hand Trump an issue to use against Biden. They *wanted* Trump to lose. So the media dropped it. That's what happens when the press suppresses information. That's why some stories turn into feeding frenzies, and some vanish.

Story lines that are made to vanish are a real problem for our democracy. The media is supposed to be our watchdog, holding *everyone* to account. I don't blame Democratic voters who believe Joe Biden can do nothing ethically wrong because the press glosses over or ignores his ethical lapses, so how are they to hear about them? The conservative media covered his actions. The mainstream media didn't. Ask an MSNBC or CNN viewer about this and they'll say it never happened. Ask a FOX viewer and they'll know all about it.

Biden didn't have to account for his actions because the mainstream media didn't make him. They didn't dig. They didn't demand answers. They didn't do to Biden what they normally do to politicians whose spoken word about ethical conduct is contradicted by a written document.

Which brings me back to the Steele Dossier.

In September 2020, the Justice Department released information showing that a "key source of allegations against the president [Trump] had been previously investigated as a possible Russian asset."[7]

According to the *Washington Post*, "In a letter to Senate Judiciary Committee Chairman Lindsey O. Graham (R-SC), Attorney General William P. Barr said the individual whose information was used to assemble much of a dossier of allegations against the Trump campaign had been the subject of a national security investigation between 2009 and 2011, because FBI agents suspected he might be working for Russia."[8]

"The individual's identity has been kept secret for years," the *Post* story continued, "but people familiar with the case said it is Igor Danchenko, a lawyer born in Ukraine who worked at a Washington think tank when he came under suspicion by the FBI for his Russian contacts. Danchenko's lawyer has acknowledged he was a source of Christopher Steele's."

In other words, in an effort to show that Donald Trump was *working with* Russia, the Clinton campaign worked with someone who had been suspected of *spying for* Russia.

At least the *Post* reported the Justice Department's finding. Much of the media, including ABC News, MSNBC, and NBC, did not. CNN gave the story one minute of coverage. FOX News gave it forty-three minutes.[9]

When the Steele Dossier could be used to make Trump look bad, much of the press played it up. When evidence came out showing how bogus the Steele Dossier was, the press played it down. They also played down the fact that it was the Clinton campaign that worked with Russia, via the Steele Dossier, to impact the campaign. If you asked today, I suspect the left half of the country still believes the Steele Dossier was a reliable document that told the truth about Trump.

Because that's how a biased press too often do their jobs.

IN SEPTEMBER 2017, THE SENATE Judiciary Committee held a hearing to question Amy Coney Barrett, who was nominated to become an appellate court judge. Three years later, she would go on to become a Supreme Court justice. At the 2017 hearing, she was asked two shocking questions by two Democratic senators.

"Do you consider yourself an orthodox Catholic?" Senator Dick Durbin (D-IL) asked her.

"When you read your speeches, the conclusion one draws is that the dogma lives loudly within you," Senator Dianne Feinstein (D-CA) exclaimed. Feinstein added, "And that's of concern when you come to big issues that large numbers of people have fought for years in this country."[10] Conservatives were outraged. The mainstream media didn't much care.

Since when in America is it a problem to be religious? What litmus test are these Democratic senators trying to establish by poking into a nominee's faith?

In this country, people are free to exercise their religion. So long as government officials don't try to turn their religious beliefs into laws that govern everyone, our society is better for it. Religion is a deeply important part of the American character. It influences morality, personal behavior, and charity. It's a force for good. Religious tolerance was a hallmark of our founding and it still is today. But Durbin's and Feinstein's questions smacked of intolerance. Intolerance toward a nominee based on her faith. The media should have been outraged.

If Barrett were Muslim, and two Republican senators asked questions like Durbin's and Feinstein's, I have no doubt the media would have howled in objection. It's none of their business, the press would say. It's anti-Muslim and bigoted, many would charge. A feeding frenzy would have ensued.

Indeed, in May 2021, during a Democratic debate in Virginia's lieutenant governor contest, a moderator, ABC7-WJLA anchor Dave Lucas, asked a Muslim candidate, Delegate Sam Rasoul, "Can you assure Virginians, if you're elected, that you'll represent all of them, regardless of faith or beliefs?"[11]

The *Washington Post* made the question the story. Unlike the mild treatment the paper extended to Durbin's and Feinstein's questions about Barrett's Catholicism, the *Post* was alarmed about Lucas discussing Rasoul's Muslim faith.

The *Post*'s headline was "A question about candidate's Muslim faith roils Democrats' debate for Virginia lieutenant governor." The story highlighted the problem with the question. "After the debate, the state Democratic Party's chair and several of the candidates called the question inappropriate, with some social media commenters demanding an apology from Lucas."[12]

One reason Democrats get away with questioning Barrett's Catholic faith is that the mainstream media doesn't object. Neither Durbin nor Feinstein was surrounded by reporters in a Senate hallway demanding to know why they asked those questions. There weren't immediate cries in the mainstream media for them to apologize to Barrett. Editorial pages didn't decry their intolerant interrogations.

For Americans who watched CBS, NBC, or ABC News, they weren't even told about the offensive line of questioning. These three networks didn't consider the Democrats' questions out of bounds or newsworthy.

CNN gave the story about ninety seconds of coverage, almost all of it Feinstein herself in a live interview explaining why she asked the question. FOX News was highly critical of Durbin and Feinstein, giving the story twenty-one minutes of airtime.[13]

The *New York Times* ran two opinion pieces on the line of questioning faced by Barrett, and the paper ran one news story about it—from Feinstein's and Durbin's point of view. In a story headlined, "Some Worry About Judicial Nominee's Ties to a Religious Group," the *Times* story glossed over Feinstein's and Durbin's intolerant questions and focused instead on Barrett's membership in a religious group, People of Praise. Belonging to that group, the *Times* wrote, "could raise legitimate questions about a judicial nominee's independence and impartiality."[14]

It was just another day in America's subjective world of journalism, where Republicans are held to account, but Democrats like Durbin and Feinstein aren't.

Remember the feeding frenzy and intense scrutiny during the 2020 presidential campaign over President Trump's alleged interference in the U.S. Postal Service? The one in which Trump was accused of ordering the removal of postal boxes so Democrats couldn't vote by mail? That nonscandal received massive coverage. But an actual scandal involving a presidential candidate and the U.S. Postal Service didn't.

In July 2017, the postal service's Office of Special Counsel (OSC) found that the USPS had violated the Hatch Act, which prohibits federal employees from working for or against political figures.[15] Specifically, the OSC found that the USPS had improperly coordinated with a postal workers' union that supported Hillary Clinton's 2016 presidential campaign. The USPS granted ninety-seven postal workers time off to take part in political activities that supported the Clinton campaign.

According to the *Washington Post*, "The U.S. Postal Service engaged in widespread violations of federal law by pressuring managers to approve letter carriers' taking time off last fall to campaign for Hillary Clinton and other union-backed Democrats."

"High-level postal officials had for years granted employees' requests for unpaid leave, leading last year to an 'institutional bias' in favor of Clinton and other Democrats endorsed by the National Association of Letter Carriers, one of the largest postal unions," the *Post* wrote.[16]

Now *this* was interference in the election to help a candidate, Hillary Clinton. These were *actual* violations of the law. Based on how easy it was for the press to launch into a feeding frenzy when questions were raised about Trump and the postal service, you would have thought the press would have done something similar when it was learned that postal workers violated the law to help Hillary. As you know by now, that of course didn't happen.

To this day, the *New York Times* has never covered the story.[17]

Neither has ABC, CBS, or NBC. CNN ran one story on its website about the postal service's improper actions on behalf of the Clinton campaign, but the cable outlet put nothing on the air.[18] FOX News, on the other hand, gave the story six minutes and thirty seconds' worth of coverage.[19]

If you think you're starting to see a pattern, you're right. Stories that make Republicans look bad often receive intense, instant mainstream media coverage. Stories that make Democrats look bad are often ignored, minimized, or buried, especially when Donald Trump is president.

In June 2020, the *New York Times* reported,

> An Ohio lawmaker was fired from his job as a physician on Thursday after asking at a hearing this week if the high rate of coronavirus cases among African Americans was because "the colored population" did not wash their hands as well as other groups.
>
> State Senator Stephen A. Huffman, a Republican and a doctor, made his remarks on Tuesday during a hearing of the Senate Health Committee about whether to declare racism a public health crisis. They came as he speculated about reasons black people might be more "susceptible" to Covid-19.
>
> "Could it just be that African Americans or the colored population do not wash their hands as well as other groups or wear a mask or do not socially distance themselves?" he said. "Could that be the explanation of why the higher incidence?"[20]

His racist remarks were inappropriate, wrong, and newsworthy. Flash forward less than a year later. Following Senator Tim Scott's (R-SC) nationally televised response to President Biden's address to

Ohio Lawmaker Asks Racist Question About Black People and Hand-Washing

State Senator Stephen A. Huffman, a Republican and a doctor, speculated publicly about why "the colored population" has been disproportionately affected by the coronavirus.

Source: Trip Gabriel, "Ohio Lawmaker Asks Racist Question About Black People and Hand-Washing," *New York Times*, June 11, 2020.

a joint session of Congress, Lamar County (Texas) Democratic Party chairman Gary O'Connor wrote in a since-deleted Facebook post, "I had hoped that Scott might show some common sense, but it seems clear he is little more than an Oreo with no real principles."[21] (Senator Scott is Black.)

An Oreo. You can't get much more racist than that. Under pressure from Texas governor Greg Abbott, O'Connor deleted his post, apologized, and offered to resign—although the Lamar County Democratic Party refused to accept his offer. If the public didn't know about Senator Scott being called an "Oreo," it's because most of the nonconservative press didn't cover it, unlike the coverage for a relatively obscure Republican state senator in Ohio who made a racist statement.

The *New York Times* covered the Ohio Republican's bigotry. It did not cover the Texas Democrat's.[22] It was the same story with many other mainstream media outlets. CNN, ABC News, the *Washington Post*, the Associated Press, and *USA Today* covered the Ohio Republican state senator's remarks.[23]

The *Washington Post*, *USA Today*, MSNBC, ABC, CBS, and NBC failed to cover the Democratic county chairman's "Oreo" accusation.[24] CNN covered the Oreo remark, but downplayed it. When a Republican says something racially tinged about a Democrat, it gets covered. When Democrats say something racially tinged, they often get a pass.

In April 2017, state senator Frank Artiles, a Republican from Miami-Dade County in Florida, crossed the line during a conversation with two other state senators when, according to the *Miami Herald*, he used the "n-word" to describe a group of Florida lawmakers. Days later, he resigned.[25]

Calling Tim Scott an "Oreo" didn't make the *New York Times*, but the Florida state senator's remarks did.

"A Florida state senator who unleashed an expletive-laden rant over drinks with two other lawmakers this week, uttering a racial slur for black people and other vulgarities, resigned from his position on Friday," the *Times* told its readers.[26]

It doesn't matter how low or obscure an official you need to be for the *Times* to cover your remarks if you're a Republican who says something inappropriate. But if you're a Democrat who makes racist statements, the *Times* knows how to look the other way.

Just ask Hunter Biden.

In June 2021, the British newspaper the *Daily Mail* reported that the president's son "used the n-word multiple times in conversation with his white, $845-per-hour lawyer, his texts messages reveal."[27]

> The shocking texts may prove embarrassing for his father President Joe Biden, who just last week gave a speech decrying racism on the 100th anniversary of the Tulsa massacre, and has sought to portray racial justice as a top priority for his administration.
>
> The president's son joked in a January 2019 text to corporate attorney George Mesires about a "big penis," and said to the lawyer: "I only love you because you're black" and "true dat n***a."

Conservative media in the United States ran with the story and gave it extensive coverage. The mainstream media ignored it. A few days later, the *Daily Mail* followed up with another story about the younger Biden.

> Hunter Biden referred to Asians as "yellow" in a 2019 text conversation with his cousin.
>
> Caroline Biden, President Joe Biden's niece, was texting Hunter discussing setting him up with her rich, model friends.
>
> In the January 2019 conversation she asked her cousin: "Do you want foreign or domestic. I can't give you f***ing Asian sorry. I'm not doing it."
>
> The president's son replied: "Domesticated foreigner is fine. No yellow."[28]

"The slur, uncovered from Hunter's abandoned laptop, is particularly distressing as it comes amid a surge in racist attacks against Asian-Americans," the paper reported.

Same pattern. Conservative media picked up and echoed the story. The mainstream media ignored it. The same mainstream media that rushed to print unverified, unsubstantiated anti-Trump information refused to apply similar standards to coverage of President Biden's son.

If the *Daily Mail* had reported it had evidence that Donald Trump Jr. or Eric Trump used racist terms in their texts or emails, I have no doubt the mainstream media would have run stories about it and demanded answers from the Trump White House and the Trump sons. But if you didn't know about Hunter Biden's emails, it's because the mainstream media suppressed the news.

In October 2017, the Democratic National Committee was hiring. They had job openings in their growing technology department.

According to an email obtained by the conservative *Daily Wire*, sent by DNC Data Services manager Madeleine Leader, "As you may have heard, we are rebuilding the Technology Team into a robust well-oiled machine that can tackle all elections from the Presidential down to Dog Catcher and School Board. What's more important is that we are focused on hiring and maintaining a staff of diverse voices and life experiences. . . . I personally would prefer that you not forward to cisgender straight white males, since they're already in the majority."[29]

How nice. And discriminatory.

We have a job for you, unless you're straight. Unless you're white. Unless you're male. If you're all three, the DNC technology division is definitely not the place for you. At least one manager there will discriminate against you. If the data services manager at the Republican National Committee put out an email saying the RNC was hiring, unless you're gay, a minority, or female, I guarantee you there would have been a front-page, lead the evening news, social media uproar that likely would have led to the resignation of the chairwoman of the RNC.

Because that's how it works. If a Republican makes an intolerant, discriminatory statement, the press leap into action. They are instantly offended, turn up the volume on their activist voices, and follow a formula: First, cover the story extensively. Next, extract comments that express outrage. Then, once enough outrage exists, identify a scalp—preferably a scalp as high ranking as possible. Finally, pressure this high-ranking leader into resignation. But if you're a Democrat who makes an intolerant, discriminatory statement, the press too often lets it go.

Narrow-mindedness, bigotry, and fringe behavior exist on the left, the right, and from people who couldn't care less about politics. But our nation is not well served when much of the media pretend the problem is only from the right. When the press ignores behavior like this on the left, they paint a false picture of America. They cause Democrats to falsely believe these problems are found exclusively on the right and they cause the right to distrust the media since the media doesn't tell the full story.

If the Democrats view the world through a false window, it's because it's a deceptive window created by the media.

In this instance, the DNC said the email didn't represent its views. And that was that. The *New York Times* didn't cover bigotry at the DNC. The *Washington Post* mentioned it in a column by a conservative opinion writer, but its news pages ignored it. ABC, CBS, and NBC paid no attention. FOX News did four stories about it over four days.[30] If the American people didn't hear about the DNC's discriminatory email against straight white men, it's because the mainstream media didn't report on it.

If you get all of your news from mainstream reporters, you will fully believe that Democrats are more tolerant, kinder, wiser, more compassionate in their policies, and more accepting of others. Republicans are less educated, less informed, and prone to bigotry once you scratch below the surface. The media too often protect readers and viewers from narrow-minded Democrats. How else do you explain why remarks of obscure Ohio and Florida Republican officials were extensively covered, while the bigotry expressed by the Texas and DNC Democrats was ignored?

Maybe the DNC bigotry wasn't a story because the staffer who sent the email wasn't a high-ranking official and she wasn't speaking on behalf of the DNC. Should the media, after all, treat an incident seriously when the person in question is not well known, and when the organization where she works instantly states that the staffer was not speaking for them?

The media did exactly that—and went into full feeding frenzy—when the offender was an obscure, young, Republican Capitol Hill staffer who mused on Facebook about the demeanor of President Obama's daughters at a presidential event in 2014. That November, at the annual presidential pardoning of two turkeys prior to Thanksgiving, the president's daughters appeared on camera. They were not very interested in the event. Like most teenagers, they looked bored, not pleased to attend their father's turkey pardoning, which he had done for five previous years.

"[T]ry showing a little class," Elizabeth Lauten, communications director for Representative Stephen Lee Fincher (R-TN), wrote on Facebook. "Rise to the occasion. . . . Dress like you deserve respect, not a spot at the bar. And certainly don't make faces during televised, public events."[31]

All hell broke loose.

The amount of media coverage given to an (until then) unknown, midlevel congressional aide, who worked for a congressman in his second term, was astounding. It was a full-blown feeding frenzy. All three networks covered Lauten's Facebook post. Over the first two days of the story, CBS News gave the story a massive six minutes of coverage. NBC was almost five minutes. ABC came in at a little more than three minutes. Together, these three news programs did eight segments on an unknown aide's social media message. CNN gave Lauten's story thirty-six minutes, dedicating fourteen stories to it over two days. MSNBC clocked in at twenty-two minutes. The *New York Times* covered it.[32] The *Washington Post* covered it, running six stories and opinion pieces about it! FOX News barely did. They gave it just over one minute of coverage.[33, 34]

Lauten, of course, was forced by the media to resign. As the formula calls for, the press wanted a scalp and they got one.

There is a long and healthy tradition in the press corps of not criticizing young children of the president. It's one of the few remaining civil and decent allowances left in politics. But when President

Trump's teenage son, Barron, was criticized, the press didn't do for Barron what they did for Sasha and Malia Obama.

Where was the similar outrage when Food Network host John Henson tweeted on Father's Day that Barron's father might not actually be Donald Trump? "I hope Barron gets to spend today with whoever his dad is," Henson, a regular critic of the president on social media, tweeted.[35] The defense of the Trump family by the media was limited and muted, compared to the outrage and intense coverage given to defending the Obama girls.[36] The mainstream media's hypocrisy in these instances is stunning.

The media basically suppressed the news about Barron Trump while they went into overdrive to inform the nation about Elizabeth Lauten's Facebook feed.

In early 2019, a wonky health publication called the *Milbank Quarterly* published a story detailing an effort by the Coca-Cola Company to influence the decisions of the Centers for Disease Control and Prevention (CDC) in areas pertaining to obesity and sugar intake.[37] The publication reported on a series of emails from Coca-Cola officials who sought to influence the CDC's decision-making process. *Milbank* obtained the emails through a Freedom of Information Act request. The report was instant news in the mainstream media.

- "Coca-Cola tried to influence CDC on research and policy, new report states," according to *Politico*.[38]
- "Coca-Cola emails reveal how soda industry tries to influence health officials," wrote the *Washington Post*.[39]
- "Old emails hold new clues to Coca-Cola and CDC's controversial relationship," reported CNN.com.[40]

Two years later, the *New York Post* reported that a conservative group also used the Freedom of Information Act to obtain emails concerning a different entity that lobbied the CDC about an urgent matter—COVID-19 and when schools could reopen.

"The American Federation of Teachers lobbied the Centers for Disease Control and Prevention on, and even suggested language for, the federal agency's school-reopening guidance released in February," the *New York Post* reported.

"The powerful teachers union's full-court press preceded the federal agency putting the brakes on a full re-opening of in-person classrooms, emails between top CDC, AFT and White House officials show. The emails were obtained through a Freedom of Information Act request by the conservative watchdog group Americans for Public Trust and provided to The Post."[41]

Based on how the mainstream media jumped all over an American corporation for seeking to influence the CDC, one might think media reaction to the powerful teachers' union lobbying to keep schoolrooms closed would be intense. As you know by now, one would be wrong.

CNN didn't tell its viewers about the teachers' union lobbying the CDC. Neither did *Politico*.[42] The *Washington Post* buried the story with a brief mention at the bottom of a much longer story about numerous other COVID-19 related matters.[43] For the mainstream media, it was mostly crickets.

Corporate lobbying of the CDC is suspect and newsworthy. Union lobbying of the CDC is perfectly fine. News about it is suppressed.

THEN THERE ARE THE SCANDALS. Everyone knows that throughout American history, Democratic and Republican congressmen have been involved in various scandals, followed by indictments, resignations, and convictions. Well, maybe not everyone.

As the Media Research Center pointed out in August 2018,

Republican congressman Chris Collins of the Buffalo suburbs was indicted for insider trading and then lying to the FBI. ABC, CBS, and NBC played this story to the hilt, with 18 minutes and 24 seconds of coverage in just the first 24 hours. CBS devoted the most coverage, pounding away for 7 minutes and 6 seconds. ABC came in second, offering 5 minutes and 41 seconds, and NBC was right behind, with 5 minutes and 37 seconds.

On August 21, prosecutors indicted California Republican Congressman Duncan Hunter on wire fraud and campaign finance violations charges. The morning and evening newscasts on ABC and CBS spent a total of 4 minutes and 44 seconds covering the story in the first 36 hours. In contrast with Collins, Hunter was "lucky" that there was breaking anti-Trump news—the conviction of former Trump campaign chairman Paul Manafort and longtime Trump confidante and lawyer Michael Cohen's pleading guilty to charges he violated campaign-finance laws.

It thrilled the networks that these two men, Collins and Hunter, were the first congressional endorsers of Donald Trump for President. That multiplied the "newsworthiness" for them.

Now wait a minute! Why, that's such a loaded, unsubstantiated conclusion!

Except it isn't. Look what happens when a Democrat is indicted. And tried. And convicted. And sentenced.

These very same three networks, these champions of public integrity, were bored to tears by the indictment and trial of Democratic Congressman Chaka Fattah of Philadelphia. During the year and a half between his 2015 indictment and 2016 conviction and sentencing for misappropriating hundreds of thousands of dollars of federal, charitable, and campaign funds, the

ABC, CBS and NBC morning and evening programs offered a measly 68 seconds of "news."

In other words: Collins received 18 times as much coverage as Fattah in just one day. But wait. It gets worse.

There's Rep. Corrine Brown of Florida, who was sentenced to five years in prison in 2016 for using an alleged children's charity called One Door for Education as a personal slush fund for herself and several aides. She used it for more than $300,000 in personal expenses, including tickets for NFL games and a luxury box for a Beyoncé concert. "Brazen barely describes it," the judge, Timothy Corrigan, said of Brown's sham charity. Never heard of her? There's a reason.

Network coverage: Zero. Zilch. Nada.[44]

In 2021, Brown's conviction was overturned and she was granted a new trial, but that has no bearing on the paltry coverage of her 2016 conviction.[45]

On Labor Day 2020, Democratic presidential nominee Joe Biden hosted a virtual campaign event with the AFL-CIO (American Federation of Labor and Congress of Industrial Organizations). He gave a speech off a teleprompter and then took several questions from workers. A young woman named Rebecca Vedrine asked the first question. She talked about the number of people who want to join unions and then asked Biden, "What will your administration do to help give them that chance?"

Her softball question was met with silence. Biden didn't know what to say. He waited. He paused. He breathed deep. And then he said, "Move it up here."[46]

He was talking to the teleprompter operator. Somehow, the Democratic nominee for president of the United States had the answer to the question loaded onto his teleprompter, which means the Biden campaign had the question in advance. If the campaign didn't have the question in advance, how could Biden's response to it already be loaded on the teleprompter? What a farce. You might think the Biden press corps would expose Biden.

The Trump campaign did. They tweeted about Biden needing a teleprompter to answer questions from a friendly audience. So did I, urging the press corps to dig into this story.

I worked for Elizabeth Dole when she ran for president in 1999. Before her candidacy began, Dole accepted a paid speech from a group to speak at an event during which the questions Dole would take, along with her answers, were prepared ahead of time. The event had nothing to do with Dole's campaign but when a columnist at the *Washington Post* heard about it, he criticized Dole.[47] The issue of her "being scripted" remained a controversy that played out across the press throughout her presidential run.

Did the press treat Biden the same as they did Dole? Of course not! Did the press make Biden's reading the answer to a "spontaneous" question an issue at all? No. They ignored it. They suppressed the news.

ABC, CBS, and NBC paid no attention. Neither did the *New York Times* and the *Washington Post*. On CNN, conservative commentator Michael Smerconish showed the clip and pointed out how easy the Biden press corps was on Biden.[48] That was the only coverage CNN viewers knew about. FOX News and other conservative outlets gave the story plenty of attention.[49]

You would think that a candidate who would go on to become the oldest president in American history might get asked why he needed to have his answers written out for him. Why couldn't he answer such an easy question without a script? How many other times did seemingly spontaneous events turn out to be scripted? What occasions? Which questions? You might think late-night comedy shows would make fun of a candidate who couldn't answer questions without the answers appearing on his teleprompter. It *is* the stuff of mockery.

But not when Joe Biden does it. The press knew that if they made this an issue, it would feed into one of the Trump campaign's biggest criticisms of Biden—that he was old, weak, and slow on his feet. Three days later, Biden spokesman TJ Ducklo appeared live on FOX News' *Special Report* with host Bret Baier.

"Has Joe Biden ever used a teleprompter during local interviews or to answer Qs & As with supporters?" Baier asked Ducklo.

"We're not going—this is straight from the Trump campaign's talking points—and what it does is try to distract the American people," Ducklo said. Baier kept pressing Ducklo for a yes or no answer. Ducklo dodged and finally added, "I am not going to allow the Trump campaign to funnel their questions through FOX News and get me to respond to that."[50]

Normally, when reporters see a spokesman act so defensively and repeatedly refuse to answer a legitimate question, their antennae go up. They dig in. They demand answers. It can make a spokesperson uncomfortable. Not for the Biden campaign, and not for the press that covered him. In campaign 2020, there was no way the Biden press corps would dig into a story that would help Trump and hurt Biden. Instead, they let it go. It just wasn't news. Readers and viewers who didn't read or watch conservative media weren't told about it. That's the biased state of journalism today. Suppression is a form of activism and it was a routine habit of reporters who covered Biden during his 2020 campaign.

On February 21, 2020, following Biden's defeats in Iowa and New Hampshire during the Democratic presidential primary, the *New York Times* broke what you might think would have been a major story about Biden.

"In at least three campaign appearances over the past two weeks,

Joseph R. Biden has told a similar story as he tries to revive his campaign in states with more diverse voters. On a trip to South Africa years ago, he has said, he was arrested as he sought to visit Nelson Mandela in prison," the *Times* reported.

According to the *Times*, Biden told an audience in South Carolina, "This day, 30 years ago, Nelson Mandela walked out of prison and entered into discussions about apartheid. I had the great honor of meeting him. I had the great honor of being arrested with our U.N. ambassador on the streets of Soweto trying to get to see him on Robben Island."[51]

The part about being arrested was a lie. A 100 percent lie. Biden, who needed the Black vote to maintain his candidacy, lied to get it. The *Times*, to its credit, caught him. What did the rest of the media do? Not much. There was no feeding frenzy. There was little demand for answers. There were a few questions, but by and large, Biden got a pass from the mainstream media. Every conservative in America knows that's exactly how it works.

Elizabeth Lauten and her Facebook post about the Obama girls were subjected to more media scrutiny than Joe Biden.

Once again, mum was the word at ABC and NBC. CNN waited a week to cover the story. When they did, it was only because Biden was live on the air as a guest. CNN's John Berman initially pressed Biden on the fact that "you did say 'arrest' three times, why?" but after Biden's long-winded answer, explaining he was "separated," not "arrested," Berman swiftly moved on and that was that. There was no follow-up. There was no questioning of Biden's motive for lying. Biden's explanation was enough.[52]

Four days after the *Times* story, CBS News held a candidate's debate with Biden and six other Democrats. Norah O'Donnell and Gayle King were moderators.

Did they ask Biden about his "arrest"? Did they follow up on the *New York Times* story? Biden was standing onstage with nowhere to go if they decided to press him. No, the CBS moderators didn't ask. They gave Biden a pass. Not a word was mentioned.[53] No questions were asked.

If this were baseball, the Democrats would get to start every inning with a man on second base. Republicans would start every inning with two outs. Pretending that suppression, deception, snobbery, and bias don't exist, the Democrats would declare they're better athletes.

In August 2020, Biden conducted an interview with the National Association of Black Journalists and the National Association of Hispanic Journalists. CBS News' national correspondent Errol Barnett asked the seventy-seven-year-old candidate if he had ever taken a cognitive test to show he was mentally sharp. "Please clarify, specifically, have you taken a cognitive test?" Barnett asked.

"No, I haven't taken a test. Why the hell would I take a test?" Biden said. Biden then told Barnett, "Come on, man! That's like saying . . . before you got on this program, did you take a test whether you're taking cocaine or not. What do you think? Huh? Are you a junkie?"

Barnett, an African American reporter, stood his ground despite Biden's offensive use of a stereotype suggesting that Black people were "junkies."[54] It was a rude and odd thing for Biden to say. The kind of thing you might think would become a major news story. If a Republican said what Biden said, accusations of racism would fly instantly. But once again, the Biden press corps let it slide.

CBS News, whose reporter asked the question, gave the story more than two minutes of play. NBC News, ABC News, and CNN didn't air the story. The *New York Times* buried the news in a lengthy story about all kinds of other political items.[55] FOX News gave it extensive coverage.[56]

And then, again, there was Hunter Biden.

Three weeks before the 2020 election, the *New York Post* dropped a bombshell. It reported, based on an email that was on a laptop computer purported to belong to Hunter, that the then vice president lied when he said he had never spoken to Hunter about the younger Biden's business dealings.

"Dear Hunter, thank you for inviting me to DC and giving an opportunity to meet your father and spent [*sic*] some time together," wrote Vadym Pozharsky, an adviser to Ukrainian energy company Burisma, in an email to Hunter. The email was dated April 17, 2015.[57] Biden was the vice president then and Hunter served on Burisma's board of directors. *This* should have been a feeding frenzy.

Vice President Biden's own son had what appeared to be proof that his father was lying. The lie raised questions not only about Joe Biden's honesty, but about his ethics. The father denied he was involved in his son's business affairs, but if he was telling the truth about Burisma, why did this email exist? What other business matters was he involved in as vice president? What else might he be hiding?

That line of questioning is typically part of the usual journalistic formula when the media catch a politician in a lie. The press say they take lying seriously and they demand answers. Except when the apparent liar is Joe Biden, who at that moment was running against Donald Trump. Covering this story would have put Biden on the defensive. It would have helped Trump, something the mainstream press was loath to do—especially that close to Election Day.

Then things got worse.

Not only did the mainstream media ignore the story and attack the *New York Post* for reporting it, but social media giants Twitter and Facebook suppressed the *Post*'s story. They banned it from being shared, posted, or linked to. It was an unprecedented attack *on* the free press, an attack apparently welcomed by many *in* the free press.[58]

The public is instantly and aggressively told the news when it's the GOP who, in the eyes of the mainstream media, does wrong. Conversely, when a news story alleges wrongdoing by a Democrat, it too often goes away, with the press taking a pass on pursuing leads that might connect the dots. Readers deserve the full, broad scope of the news, not a narrow adaptation that caters to a left-leaning readership and viewership. Republicans have grown accustomed to intense, skeptical media scrutiny of everything they do. It strengthens them to know their actions will be the subject of severe questioning, so they'd better be prepared.

Democrats typically don't have to endure that type of treatment, and that's a problem. Democrats tend to look at the press as an ally, knowing they often can be counted on to carry their message with little to no scrutiny. Or when something goes wrong, Democrats can take solace that the news will seldom be turned into a feeding frenzy. If reporters were fair and neutral, if they told the news fully, accurately, and fairly, the American people would be better informed and the press more trusted. But unfortunately, readers and viewers of the mainstream media don't know what they are missing. Instead, they are mostly presented with a narrow, sanitized version of events. Everything else is right-wing and suspect, meaning it isn't fit to print.

Chapter Six

VIEWERSHIP VIEWS

The press loves to take polls about politics.

For this book, I decided to take a poll of my own.

I hired Frank Luntz, one of America's best-known pollsters and public opinion experts, to poll viewers of CNN and FOX News, along with readers of the *New York Times*.[1] Something told me I would find major differences among Americans who rely on these three sources.

What I found is that FOX viewers are from Mars. CNN viewers and *New York Times* readers are from Venus. The differences are stark.

CULTURE AND MORALITY

Let's start with a few easy cultural questions. I asked, "Do you fly or display the American flag at your home?" Most FOX viewers (67%) said yes. *New York Times* readers (62%) came in a close second. Only half of CNN viewers (50%) said the same.

"Would you attend a gay wedding?" I asked. This time the answers were the reverse. Most *Times* readers (79%) said they definitely or probably would attend a gay wedding. CNN viewers (71%) said yes, while a slim majority of FOX viewers (51%) said they'd attend.

"Do you stand for the National Anthem?" The good news is that pretty much everyone stands, although the differences are predictable.

Almost all FOX viewers (86%) said they always stand for the anthem. Most CNN viewers (77%) said the same. *New York Times* readers (72%) also said they always stand. Having been to a lot of baseball games, I figured most Americans do stand, but I wondered what people thought about those who don't.

"Do you consider it disrespectful to America for athletes or celebrities to kneel for the National Anthem?" I asked. Big gaps started to emerge. Most FOX viewers (81%) said it's disrespectful to kneel during the National Anthem. That figure drops like a rock for CNN watchers and *Times* readers. A minority of CNN viewers (45%) and *Times* readers (44%) said it's disrespectful to kneel.

No wonder stories about kneeling during the National Anthem are covered so differently across these three media outlets. At FOX, kneeling during the National Anthem borders on disgraceful behavior. On CNN and at the *New York Times*, it's perceived as a powerful, peaceful gesture, and a pretty okay thing to do.

"Is America the greatest country on earth today?" I had the pollsters ask. That was a yes among FOX viewers and a maybe/maybe-not for those who rely on CNN and the *New York Times* for their news. FOX viewers (59%) said America is definitely the greatest country on earth. The figure drops to 46% among *New York Times* readers and 41% of CNN viewers.

What about systemic racism? I wondered. "Is America a systemically racist country today?" I asked. That was a no for FOX viewers and a big yes at the other two outlets. About half of FOX viewers (50%)

said probably or definitely no to that question, while a small minority of CNN viewers (13%) and a tiny number of *Times* readers (7%) said America is definitely not or probably not a systemically racist country. A majority of *Times* readers (51%) said American *is* definitely a systemically racist country today.

No wonder the 1619 Project—an effort to show that the true origins of the United States were not in 1776, but in 1619, when slaves were brought to Virginia, whereby everything that made America exceptional is based on slavery—found a happy home at the *New York Times*.

That also helps explain why so many *Times* readers canceled their subscriptions over Senator Tom Cotton's "Send in the Troops" op-ed. When a company's customers feel so strongly about something, it's not—from a business point of view—a good idea to let them see something they disagree with, especially on a topic as sensitive as race. The *Times* knows who its readers are, along with what they think and what they want.

HISTORY QUIZ

In the poll, I wanted to have a little fun with American history and test people's knowledge of events. I started easy. "What year was the Declaration of Independence signed?"

FOX viewers came in first. A solid majority of FOX viewers (82%) knew it was 1776. Most CNN viewers (77%) said the same and the *Times* came in last, with 72% correctly answering 1776. Interestingly, 7% of *Times* readers said it was signed in 1619. There's a little bit of karma in that, if you ask me.

"Who was the primary author of the Declaration of Independence?" I wondered. I gave people multiple-choice answers that included Thomas Jefferson, Benjamin Franklin, George Washington,

Alexander Hamilton, James Madison, Samuel Adams, Abraham Lincoln, John Jay, and Paul Revere. This is getting fun, I thought.

This time, CNN viewers came in first, with most (61%) saying it was Thomas Jefferson. FOX viewers finished second with 56% saying the same, while 48% of *Times* readers correctly said it was Jefferson. George Washington came in a respectable, but still wrong, second place for *Times* readers, with 16% picking him.

My final history question was a tough one. "Who was the primary author of the Constitution?" In what should be a dismaying result for U.S. history teachers, everyone lost this round. Forty-four percent of FOX viewers said Jefferson. A plurality of *Times* readers (33%) and a slightly smaller plurality of CNN viewers (31%) also said Thomas Jefferson was the primary author of the Constitution. They're all wrong. He didn't write a word of it. James Madison did, a fact known to a minority of readers and viewers everywhere. A small number of CNN viewers (24%), however, did give the right answer, while *Times* readers (17%) came in second and FOX viewers (15%) picked up the rear. Definitely not a good result for historians.

By the way, 6% of CNN viewers said Samuel Adams wrote the Constitution, which makes me wonder what they were drinking.

ELECTIONS, BURNING FLAGS, AND POLICY

The poll also asked participants a few questions about some of the most important issues in the news. The answers reinforced one of the most vexing matters facing journalism today. The public knows what it believes, and it chooses media outlets that reinforce its beliefs.

"Is it racist to require a driver's license or other official government ID in order to vote?" I asked. A majority (55%) of *Times* readers said it is definitely or probably racist to require an ID. A minority

(30%) said it is not. CNN's viewers were more balanced, but a plurality (47%) thought it's racist and a smaller number (37%) said it's not. The story at FOX is the opposite, where a small number of viewers (27%) said it's racist, while a large number of viewers (66%) said it's definitely or probably not racist.

I wish I could poll reporters on that question. I strongly suspect that reporters, way out of line with the U.S. population, would say it's probably or definitely racist to require ID to vote. Most reporters would call it a voting "restriction" instead of a provision to protect the integrity of elections.

The flip side of the ID question is a predictable but more nuanced answer. "Does requiring a driver's license in order to vote promote voter integrity, ballot security, and election accuracy?" I asked. Majorities everywhere said yes, but by differing degrees.

A slender majority of CNN viewers (53%) said requiring a license definitely or probably promotes voter integrity and ballot security. A bigger majority (65%) among *Times* readers agreed, while an overwhelming majority of FOX viewers (79%) said requiring an ID to vote promotes voter integrity and ballot security.

Most Americans recognize that it is helpful and appropriate to have provisions that protect ballot integrity written into law. Most Americans understand there has to be a reasonable balance between a system in which voting is easy because there are no rules and a system in which voting is hard because there are too many rules. As usual, the smart solution is somewhere in the middle.

But if you think we live in a systemically racist country and that requiring an ID to vote is a racist act, you're going to view changes in election procedures differently. You'll call them "restrictions." You also will fit the profile of a *New York Times* reader.

In 2019, a story about Stacey Abrams, the 2018 Democratic

gubernatorial candidate who lost in Georgia, caught my eye. In an interview on PBS, she told host Margaret Hoover that she "wouldn't oppose" allowing noncitizens the right to vote in local elections.[2]

I do oppose allowing noncitizens a vote, and have always remembered Abrams's interview.

Most people aren't familiar with Abrams's permissive comments because most of the media didn't report them. It's hard to imagine a more outside-the-mainstream position than allowing people who aren't American citizens to vote in American elections, regardless of whether the elections are local, municipal, or otherwise. Abrams's statement should have been prominently covered as an example of how the Democrats are going too far in abandoning traditional beliefs. The only major outlet to cover the story was FOX News, which gave Abrams's position four minutes of coverage. CNN and MSNBC did not cover it. Neither did the *New York Times*, the *Washington Post*, or *USA Today*.[3]

Abrams doesn't stand alone in her position. A small but growing number of American cities and towns have begun to allow noncitizens the vote. Several candidates running for mayor of New York City in 2021 advocated allowing noncitizens the right to vote in New York's municipal contests.[4] According to the New York *Daily News*, "'As mayor, Shaun [Donovan] will implement a number of policies to improve the lives of New York City immigrants, including making sure that the right to vote in municipal elections is not just reserved for citizens,' said Jeremy Edwards, spokesman for Shaun Donovan, a former top official in the Obama White House and Bloomberg administration."[5] Sure enough, in December 2021 the New York City Council passed a law allowing legal noncitizens the right to vote in New York City elections.[6]

Ballotpedia reports that ten municipalities across the United States allowed noncitizens to vote in local elections as of March 2020.

Nine were in Maryland. The other was San Francisco, California.[7] Two cities in Vermont, Winooski and Montpelier, changed their laws in 2021 to allow legal-resident noncitizens the right to vote in their local elections.[8]

It's a growing movement. So I asked about it. "Should noncitizens who live in America be allowed to vote in elections?"

A small majority of *New York Times* readers (52%) said definitely or probably yes. Only 33% of *Times* readers said noncitizens should not get to vote. CNN viewers were evenly split, with 43% saying yes and 43% saying no. For FOX viewers, noncitizens should not have the right to vote. The majority (64%) said no to allowing noncitizens the right to vote, while 29% said yes.

Keep your eye on the issue of noncitizens voting. Often, once these kinds of liberal causes are started by a few liberal true believers, they keep going and find a catalyst in the left-leaning media, which is either for them or noncritical of the effort, even though most Americans think voting in American elections should be reserved for American citizens.

In November 2016, the *Washington Post* headlined a story: "In flag-burning comments, Trump again plays to the voters that elected him."[9] President-elect Trump had tweeted that anyone who burns the American flag should be prosecuted for an illegal act.

The full tweet read, "Nobody should be allowed to burn the American flag—if they do, there must be consequences—perhaps loss of citizenship or year in jail!"[10]

The story continued: "[T]he president-elect's outburst underscored a key aspect of his three-week-old transition: He is continuing to cater to his base—the largely white, working-class voters that propelled him to the White House—with relatively few overtures to the majority of voters who cast ballots against him."[11]

His base? I remembered thinking at the time. I bet most people think burning the flag should be illegal. So I asked about it. "Should burning the American flag be illegal?" was the question on my poll. Majorities everywhere said yes.

A large majority (68%) of FOX viewers said burning the flag definitely or probably should be illegal. A strong majority (63%) of CNN viewers agreed, and a majority of *Times* readers, too, (59%) said burning the flag should be illegal. So much for Trump catering to his base. Making flag burning illegal enjoys widespread support.

What about guns? I wondered. "Does the Constitution guarantee a citizen the right to bear arms?" I asked. While the numbers differed, majorities everywhere accurately said yes. FOX viewers overwhelmingly (88%) said yes, while CNN viewers strongly said yes (84%), and *Times* readers mostly said yes (70%).

I asked about abortion, too. "Does the Constitution guarantee a citizen the right to have an abortion?" The results were interesting. Majorities everywhere said no. *Times* readers were most inclined to see a constitutional guarantee, but it's still a narrow minority (48%) of the paper's readership. A minority of CNN viewers (40%) said there was a constitutional guarantee to an abortion, while an even smaller minority of FOX viewers (32%) said abortion is a right guaranteed by the Constitution.

Perhaps those who took the poll were literalists who know that the right to an abortion is the result of a 1973 Supreme Court case, *Roe v. Wade*, that found a constitutional right to privacy, which the Court said included abortion.

It's notable, however, that most Americans say the Constitution guarantees the right to bear arms but not a right to have an abortion. Many news stories seem to have it the other way around.

One of the reasons our country is so divided is that our press is so divided. Readers and viewers can reliably get much of the news they want by reading and watching the outlets they want. At the same time, people long for one place to go to get the news straight. But as liberal bias took root throughout the media decades ago, FOX and other conservative outlets successfully spun off. If the mainstream media had been doing its job well, conservative media never would have been able to break away in the first place. By failing to play it straight, the mainstream media created the fractured environment we're now in.

Earlier I described a Pew Research Center poll showing that the only people who think the press understand them are college-educated Democrats. There's an intelligentsia among the media, a form of snobbery, that think of themselves as smart, caring, and well informed. Bigotry, hatred, and violence, they think, are things practiced by Republicans, not Democrats and certainly not liberals, who care about their fellow humans. Happily housed among the mainstream media, biased reporters have a hard time imagining how someone thoughtful or well educated could be for Trump, or be pro-life, or oppose illegal immigration. Allowing noncitizens the vote and respecting those who kneel during the National Anthem is a sign of sophistication and understanding. Raising taxes is "patriotic." Government spending is an "investment."

America consists of so much more than college-educated Democrats. It's about time for the media to recognize that fact.

Chapter Seven

CNN

I don't know what has happened to CNN.

CNN was once a typical liberal TV network, with a newsroom full of college-educated, mostly Democratic voters who—for much of my career—were dedicated to covering news the old-fashioned way, meaning they tried to be fair to both sides and avoided obvious and blatant pursuits of agendas. The early days of reporting at CNN were in keeping with CNN founder Ted Turner's vision that at CNN, "the news is the star." It also reflected the stance of former CNN president Jonathan Klein, who vowed to double down on straight reporting during his tenure (2004–10) and told the *New York Times*, "We are not about fomenting an agenda."[1]

Those days are over.

Today, CNN and its anchors pretend to be objective when, instead, it's a news organization with its thumb firmly on the scale. MSNBC also has its thumb on the scale, but it's overt about it. MSNBC's news programming and opinion shows are anti-Republican, anti-Trump, and progressive. MSNBC wears their bias on their sleeve. CNN wants it both ways. Its reporters and anchors like to think of themselves as objective, while instead they're driving an anti-Republican, anti-Trump agenda.

Thanks to that agenda, CNN has erred repeatedly. In addition to sometimes reporting the news straight, it too often aired false stories, especially anti-Trump stories, that they later had to retract, or sometimes reverse direction on and pretend they never aired in the first place. I guess they hoped no one would notice. (I did.) They routinely fed a diet of anti-Republican messaging to their predominantly Democratic viewers that reinforced for these viewers reasons to believe that Republicans are largely a group of antidemocratic racists (they're not) who suppress the rights of minorities (they don't), are inclined toward violence (not true), and want COVID to spread (that's false), and that Donald Trump colluded with Russia to win the 2016 election (he didn't). For Democrats who watch CNN, it's hard to blame them for the views they hold when their source for many of those views is so wrong so often.

For two years, I was a CNN contributor. From 2011 to 2013, I regularly appeared on CNN, where I was paid to give my opinions about major events of the day. While many of the anchors on the air then remain on the air now, I don't recognize the place anymore. In 2012, CNN anchors were driven to provide viewers with news, with a slant to the left, especially when it came to which stories were selected to make it on the air, but they seldom if ever overtly told viewers what viewers were supposed to think.

That changed with the election of President Trump in 2016. The change was also inspired by the growing divisions in America in which TV viewers increasingly watch news programs that reflect the views they want to hear.[2] Knowing how largely Democratic its viewers are, CNN changed its reporting habits to increasingly reflect the bias of its viewers. CNN is now the place to go to get the news from an overwhelmingly opinionated, Democratic point of view. It's the place to go for Republican guests to be regularly interrupted by CNN's anchors, while Democratic guests are given the floor. It's the place where almost half their "Republican" contributors said they would vote for Joe Biden in 2020.[3]

According to a report by the *Washington Free Beacon*, prior to the 2020 election, "There are now at least six Republican [contributors] at CNN who say they will vote for Biden in November, making up 40 percent of the network's Republican roster. In contrast, only 8 percent of self-identified Republican voters nationwide say they will vote for Biden."[4]

As the *Free Beacon* notes, "the disparity illustrates how CNN viewers get a distorted view of how typical Republicans are reacting to news of the day. Tim Graham, a longtime media watchdog critical of the network, said that the message being pushed is that the 'only good Republican' is one who opposes [President Trump]."[5]

In its desire to air anti-Trump information, CNN too often let down its guard, putting information on the air that never should have been reported in the first place. But at CNN, if the news was anti-Trump, it got a bump.

As Glenn Greenwald wrote in a January 2019 article for the *Intercept*, "It's inevitable that media outlets will make mistakes on complex stories. If that's being done in good faith, one would expect the errors would be roughly 50/50 in terms of the agenda served by the false stories. That is most definitely not the case here."[6]

Look no further than CNN's get-Trump Russia collusion coverage, where CNN led the league in the number of "blockbuster" collusion stories it later retracted. As I discussed earlier, CNN broke the news and then retracted it about Donald Trump Jr. being told in advance about Hillary's emails, prior to WikiLeaks releasing them.

- CNN broke the news—and retracted it—alleging that a Senate committee was investigating former Trump supporter Anthony Scaramucci's ties to a Russian bank.[7]
- CNN broke the news—and retracted it—saying that then–FBI director James Comey in 2017 would contradict President Trump's claim that Comey told him three times that Trump was not under investigation by the FBI.[8] Trump was accurate. Comey did tell him that. CNN was wrong.
- CNN broke the news—and retracted it—alleging that the FBI had wiretapped former Trump campaign manager Paul Manafort before and after the 2016 election. A report by the Justice Department inspector general stated that the CNN story was wrong and that no wiretap was sought for Manafort.[9]
- CNN broke the news in 2018 alleging that former Trump attorney Michael Cohen would tell federal investigators that then-candidate Trump knew ahead of time about the 2016 meeting Trump's staff held at Trump Tower with a Russian who claimed to have dirt on Hillary Clinton.[10] CNN billed its reporting as a "collusion bombshell."[11] Cohen's lawyer, Lanny Davis, later told reporters he could not confirm that Cohen would say that, and apologized for it, since he was the original anonymous source who spread the rumor in the first place.[12]
- CNN alleged, during a "Reality Check" segment on their show *New Day*, that "[t]he [Steele] dossier was initially funded by Republicans who were opposing then-candidate Trump and was then picked up by folks associated with the Democratic campaign."[13] Of course, that's false, but for this one, CNN refused to retract it.

During the GOP presidential primary in 2015 and 2016, the *Washington Free Beacon*—a conservative website funded largely by a major Republican donor—hired a research firm, Fusion GPS, to dig up damaging information about several Republican candidates, including Trump. The *Free Beacon* called off the research in May 2016 when it looked as if Trump would secure the Republican nomination.[14] One month earlier, the Clinton campaign and Democratic National Committee had begun paying the same research firm for information on Trump, and it was this research—funded by the Democrats—that became the infamous Steele Dossier.[15]

If someone, almost anyone, had dirt on Trump and his possible connections to Russia, CNN was the place to air it. No one received more airtime on CNN to air their dirt than Trump critic and attorney Michael Avenatti.

Described by *Los Angeles* magazine in 2021 as "disgraced" and a "three-times convicted felon,"[16] Avenatti, who was sentenced in July 2021 to thirty months in prison for attempted extortion,[17] appeared on various news shows an incredible 254 times from March 2018 through early 2019, according to the Media Research Center.[18] CNN led the league with 122 interviews, followed by MSNBC at 108, while FOX had him appear just twice, according to the MRC. During the intense period of March 2018 through early May 2018, as the Stormy Daniels allegations against Trump heated up, Avenatti appeared 59 times on CNN.[19] In contrast, Congressman Adam Schiff (D-CA) appeared only 10 times over the same period. Every single Republican in the Senate, if you add them all up, appeared on CNN just 34 times during these months, 25 fewer interviews than Avenatti.[20]

CNN booked Avenatti to talk about Stormy Daniels and collusion more than they booked the entire Trump administration to talk about COVID.

Avenatti's 122 live appearances over one year easily beat the 68 interviews by Department of Health and Human Services secretary Alex Azar, CDC director Dr. Robert Redfield, Surgeon General Jerome Adams, Dr. Anthony Fauci, Dr. Deborah Birx, and the HHS director of coronavirus diagnostic testing, Dr. Brett Giroir, *combined*, during the entire first year of the COVID outbreak.[21]

CNN's anti-Republican agenda goes beyond Trump. The Georgia Senate runoff in January 2021 was a red-hot race with control of the U.S. Senate on the line.

When Democrat Raphael Warnock won, Christian Sierra, a CNN media coordinator, tweeted:

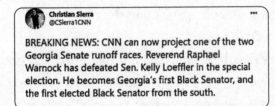

Christian Sierra
@CSierra1CNN

BREAKING NEWS: CNN can now project one of the two Georgia Senate runoff races. Reverend Raphael Warnock has defeated Sen. Kelly Loeffler in the special election. He becomes Georgia's first Black Senator, and the first elected Black Senator from the south.

Source: Christian Sierra. Twitter. @CSierra1CNN. January 6, 2021.

First elected Black senator from the South? Only if you ignore the existence of Senator Tim Scott, from South Carolina, who was elected in 2016, five years before Warnock. Scott is a Black Republican. The CNN tweet has now been deleted.

The day after Joe Biden was sworn in as president, CNN broke an exclusive story that quoted an anonymous official, hyped as a source with direct knowledge of the new administration's COVID-related work.

"We are starting to get a clearer picture of what exactly the Biden White House is inheriting from the Trump administration when it comes to COVID, when it comes to the vaccine distribution," CNN's MJ Lee reported. "Sources with direct knowledge telling CNN within hours of Biden being sworn into office, that there simply was no vaccine distribution plan under the Trump Administration. One source telling CNN, quote, there is nothing for us to rework. We are going to have to build everything from scratch. Another source said that it was further affirmation of complete incompetence—the fact that the Biden team will have to essentially start from square one."[22]

No questions asked. From the anonymous White House official's lips to the ears of CNN viewers, CNN regurgitated what it was told, without ever stopping to wonder if it might not be true.

CNN hyped the story and ran with it all day long, until it was contradicted by Dr. Anthony Fauci, who told reporters in the White House briefing room, "We certainly are not starting from scratch because there is activity going on in the distribution."[23] CNN's story vanished in a flash.

The story may have vanished but its impact did not. People inclined to believe the worst about Trump and Republicans continue to believe these false stories. Like the proverbial horse out of the barn, a retraction is often too little, too late. The damage is done and a one-time retraction to an often-repeated false story isn't enough to undo the harm done to the truth. I suspect that if you asked CNN viewers today if Trump left Biden a plan for vaccinations, most viewers would say he did not, even though Dr. Fauci says he did.

As soon as I saw the story, I tweeted, "Why is CNN granting anonymity to whoever gave them these quotes? The Trump Admin is gone. No one will lose their job. The info is not classified. If the media wants more credibility, make these sources go on the record."[24] But once again, CNN gave someone anonymity and airtime because their anti-Trump quote was too good to pass up. It didn't matter that it was too good to be true. CNN ran with it, at least until they were contradicted by Fauci. They bought it hook, line, and sinker. Until Fauci corrected them and then they stopped reporting it.

You would have thought after the many retractions CNN previously issued, all due to accepting the word of anonymous sources with an anti-Trump agenda, they would have been more careful in the new administration. But no. The catnip of airing anti-Trump stories remained strong at CNN, even after Trump was gone.

CNN's bias was on display before the arrival of Donald Trump and it will be on display well after he is gone.

In 2008, Republican senator Ted Stevens was put on trial by the Justice Department for corruption.

In 2017, Democratic senator Bob Menendez was put on trial by the Justice Department for corruption.

According to an analysis by *NewsBusters*, "When it came to reporting on [Republican] Stevens, CNN rarely missed a day, and often updated viewers on the status of the trial multiple times in the same day. In the first three weeks of his trial (Sept. 20, 2008 to Oct. 11, 2008), CNN aired 36 stories about Stevens, compared to only 7 for [Democrat] Menendez in the exact same time period (Sept. 5, 2017 to Sept. 26, 2017)—a six-to-one disparity."

"If CNN journalists thought that the Stevens trial was worth covering, there's no reason why they shouldn't be covering Menendez—other than the obvious partisan bias," *NewsBusters* stated.[25]

Remember President Trump's trip to Japan in November 2017, the one in which CNN fabricated the koi fish feeding crisis? Judging from CNN's coverage of another event on that trip, you might think CNN had it in for Trump.

During the same trip, Trump delivered remarks to U.S. and Japanese business leaders in Tokyo—encouraging them to expand their auto plants in the United States: "When you want to build your auto plants, you will have your approvals almost immediately. When you want to expand your plants, you will have your approvals almost immediately." Trump went on to say: "And in the room, we have a couple of the great folks from two of the biggest auto companies in the world that are building new plants and doing expansions of other plants."[26]

How did CNN cover Trump's attempts to create jobs for American factory workers?

With derision, mockery, and bad reporting.

Source: Daniel Shane, "Trump asks Japan to build cars in the U.S. it already does," CNN Money, November 6, 2017.

CNN's original story, which was reprinted across several news outlets, began:

> President Trump wants Japan Inc to "try" building vehicles in the U.S.
>
> "Try building your cars in the United States instead of shipping them over. Is that possible to ask? That's not rude. Is that rude? I don't think so," Trump told executives from automakers including Toyota (TM) and Mazda (MZDAF) during a trip to Japan on Monday.
>
> Japanese automakers, however, already have huge factories in the U.S. that churn out millions of cars each year.[27]

The CNN story failed to tell its readers that Trump was aware that Japanese auto companies already made cars in the United States or that he called for *expanding* their U.S.-based plants. CNN later corrected its story by dropping the snide "It Already Does" headline and added context to its story by making clear that Trump was referring to the expansion of existing Japanese plants in the United States. Yet most of the news outlets that ran the original story did not run the subsequent corrections.

Reporting is supposed to be facts first. At CNN during the Trump years, it was agenda first. And CNN's agenda was to make Trump and Republicans who support him look bad.

ONE PARTICULAR ANCHOR AT CNN had a problem. Chris Cuomo, the former anchor of *Cuomo Prime Time*, is the younger brother of New York's former Democratic governor Andrew Cuomo. CNN had a policy of Chris not covering Andrew because of the obvious journalistic conflict of interest. That is, until the management of CNN yielded to the entertainment side of the news business and let Chris interview his brother, in what passed for sycophantic, soft journalism, the type that would make any serious news reporter cringe.

In May 2020, when Governor Cuomo was seemingly riding high and fighting COVID, despite disputes over the deaths of elderly New Yorkers in nursing homes, Chris hosted his brother on his show for a softball interview, where the hard-hitting anchor held up a gigantic nasal swab to tease his governor brother about the size of his nose, generating chuckles on the air.[28]

Source: *Cuomo Prime Time*, CNN, May 21, 2020.

While journalist Cuomo went easy on politician Cuomo, the CNN anchor targeted Florida governor Ron DeSantis and his handling of COVID in Florida.[29] In July 2020, Cuomo questioned the validity of COVID case data released by the Sunshine State.

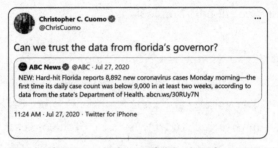

Source: Chris Cuomo. Twitter. @ChrisCuomo. July 27, 2020.

Less than six months later, in January 2021, New York's Democratic attorney general, Letitia James, released an investigation showing that New York State underestimated the number of deaths in nursing homes by as much as 50 percent.[30] Governor Cuomo was suddenly on the defensive and in big political trouble at home.

What did CNN's Chris Cuomo do next? Did he put out a tweet asking if data from New York's governor could be trusted? No. He returned to CNN's conflict of interest policy and stopped interviewing his brother. How convenient. The blurring of news and entertainment worked well for CNN when a Democratic governor could be puffed up. Doesn't CNN realize how promotional and nonjournalistic they become when they practice such an overt double standard?

CNN should not have waived its conflict of interest policies in the first place. Allowing Chris Cuomo to promote his brother added to CNN's woes as a news outlet that favors one party over another. To be clear, CNN lowered its journalistic standards because CNN's audience liked it. The brother-to-brother interviews were amusing and fun to a largely Democratic audience, so CNN's management chose pleasing its viewers above maintaining journalistic integrity.

To CNN's credit, other shows on the cable outlet did cover Governor Cuomo's nursing home controversy, but one week later, when a former Cuomo aide, Lindsey Boylan, alleged that the governor had kissed her on the lips and sexually harassed her, CNN went virtually silent.

According to the Media Research Center, "After over 24 hours of silence, CNN decided to acknowledge on Thursday Lindsey Boylan's sexual harassment claims against *Prime Time* host Chris Cuomo's brother Governor Andrew Cuomo (D-NY) . . . with only 96 seconds over two news briefs. Worse yet, neither brief came on any of CNN's evening or primetime shows."

In contrast to CNN's 96 seconds, MSNBC gave Boylan's allegations 9 minutes, while FOX News dedicated 137 minutes to coverage of her allegations.[31]

After a second woman accused the New York governor of sexual harassment, CNN gave the accusations heavy coverage. But why did it take two accusations to get CNN's attention?

But the problem didn't end there. Guess who, again, crossed the line from journalist to activist? His brother the anchor, that's who.

In May 2021, the *Washington Post* broke a story revealing that "CNN anchor Chris Cuomo advised his brother, New York Gov. Andrew M. Cuomo, and senior members of the governor's staff on how to respond to sexual harassment allegations made earlier this year by women who had worked with the governor, according to four people familiar with the discussions."

The story continued, "Cuomo, one of the network's top stars, joined a series of conference calls that included the Democratic governor, his top aide, his communications team, lawyers and a number of outside advisers, according to the people familiar with the conversations, who spoke on the condition of anonymity to describe the private sessions."[32]

Results of an investigation released in August 2021 by Attorney General James into the sexual harassment allegations against Governor Andrew Cuomo confirmed that CNN anchor Chris Cuomo was brought in as part of a team to "control and direct" the governor's response.[33]

When CNN was confronted with its anchor crossing the line from journalist to overt political adviser, its spokesman issued a statement saying what reporter Cuomo did was "improper" but that he would face no disciplinary action.[34] Later, in December 2021, after the actual texts sent to and from Cuomo were publicly released, CNN had enough and fired its star anchor.[35]

CNN is also the place to go to hear the personal opinions of its reporters, regularly shared on the air, as if their opinions are news.

In July 2020, the government reported that the nation's gross domestic product (GDP) dropped by an annualized rate of 32.9 percent—a historic drop as the coronavirus shut down businesses and forced millions out of work.[36] It was the worst drop ever recorded.

Four months earlier, in March, Congress passed and Trump signed into law the $2 trillion Coronavirus Aid, Relief, and Economic Security (CARES) Act. As part of the CARES Act, an unemployed worker was permitted to claim a $600 a week cash payment in addition to any other unemployment compensation for which the worker was eligible through July 31.[37] The assistance was unprecedented; comparatively, the American Recovery and Reinvestment Act of 2009 provided the unemployed with a $25 weekly boost.[38]

According to the *Washington Post*, "The typical unemployed American was receiving about $930 a week from late March to late July 2020."[39] That translates to $48,360 on an annual basis. Add it up and many of those unemployed made more in public assistance than they did in their jobs.

How much money someone should get for being unemployed is a fair debate. Pay them too little and there will be a hole in the social safety net. Pay them too much and they will have an incentive not to work. But at CNN, there were no two sides to this debate.

CNN correspondent and anchor Julia Chatterley joined fellow CNN anchors John Berman and Alisyn Camerota on CNN's *New Day* to discuss the devastating GDP report.

After discussing the GDP numbers and rising weekly unemployment claims, Chatterley decided to give her opinion about what policy makers should do. "If ever I could give you an excuse for needing to extend those enhanced jobless benefits, this is it," she said.[40]

She didn't say, "According to Democrats, this is the excuse they need." She didn't say, "According to some economists, this is what is best." She simply said that the unemployed should continue to receive extra payments. It was her opinion. There was no discussion on whether that might disincentivize people from working. No discussion about two sides to an issue.

There was the Democratic side and the CNN side. They were identical.

Julia Chatterley is a sharp reporter. I wish she had simply reported how devastating the GDP news was. I don't know why she felt the need to veer off and give her opinion about federal legislation. When reporters and anchors, as opposed to contributors or analysts, give their opinions, they taint the news. It's not hard to report both sides, saying, "Democrats claim the GDP report is further proof that the enhanced unemployment checks should continue, while Republicans warn continuing them will keep people out of work."

I miss those days. That's how most reporting used to be.

A few days later, after the additional benefits expired, CNN returned to the topic, with anchor Poppy Harlow declaring, "The bottom line is it's totally unacceptable that Congress has still not reached a deal after the additional $600 in unemployment benefits per week for millions of Americans ended on Friday."[41] Once again, an opinion. At least Harlow interviewed former senior Trump economic adviser Kevin Hassett, who made the case against incentivizing people to remain unemployed. Harlow told Hassett she disagreed with his position, again expressing her opinion, but at least she let Hassett make a case.[42]

The additional $600 in federal aid, above and beyond state aid, was never extended. Five months later, in December 2020, Congress and President Trump agreed to a new measure providing an additional $300 in federal aid for the next eleven weeks.[43] Despite CNN's gloom-and-doom discussion about failing to extend the $600 supplement, three months after that CNN report, GDP rose by a record-setting annualized rate of 33.4 percent in the third quarter, and the unemployment rate dropped from 10.2 percent in July,[44] when CNN aired its report, to 6.7 percent in December,[45] when Congress compromised and provided the additional $300 in funds for the unemployed.

Christine Romans, CNN's chief business correspondent, is a serious-minded reporter. She, too, sometimes can't resist telling viewers what positions they should hold. Shortly after Biden took office in 2021, the Department of Labor reported there were 900,000 new claims for first-time unemployment benefits.[46]

"This new administration inherits a really difficult job situation," Romans reported. "The president has a pretty robust plan here. $1.9 trillion he'd like to pass. More stimulus checks. Rental assistance. Money for state and local governments."[47] And then she abandoned neutral journalism and took sides.

"Beware the deficit hawks. You can see the deficit and the debt, the national debt exploded under the Trump administration, even before coronavirus. The debt exploded. You will start to hear people in Washington say, oh, we don't want to spend too much money because of the debt. This is not the time for that kind of talk right now when you look at these job numbers," she concluded.[48]

The fact that so many CNN reporters are so comfortable giving their opinions is deeply troubling. These aren't even CNN's night-time anchors like Anderson Cooper, Chris Cuomo, or Don Lemon, who, despite viewing themselves as serious anchors, regularly give their opinions. These are reporters. These are people who used to say, "Republicans argue and Democrats claim." Reporters at CNN used to bring the public the news so the public could form its views. Now too many of them tell us what views we are supposed to hold.

A common thread in these reporter editorials is that Republicans are wrong and Democrats are right. If the GOP point of view is accepted, these reporters are telling viewers, people will be hurt. The undertone is constant—Republican politicians are misinformed, misguided, factually wrong, and uncaring about the little guy. The undertone to these opinions is that normal Americans should agree with the Democrats. It's a pejorative point of view that permeates much of CNN's coverage.

Jeff Zeleny is CNN's chief national affairs correspondent. He got his start in journalism at the *Des Moines Register* and then went on to cover politics for the *Chicago Tribune* (where he won a Pulitzer Prize), the *New York Times*, and ABC News.[49] He's a nice guy. He's also the former *New York Times* reporter who asked President Obama during his hundredth-day press conference the now-infamous question, "During these first one hundred days, what has surprised you the most about this office? Enchanted you the most from serving in this office? Humbled you the most? And troubled you the most?"[50]

I didn't criticize him for that question. Early on in administrations, there are certain "soft" questions that make sense, especially asking a new president how he likes the place. After Trump's defeat in 2020, Zeleny watched Trump leave the White House during Christmas for his home at Mar-a-Lago in Palm Beach, Florida.

Zeleny tweeted:

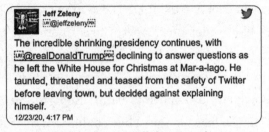

The incredible shrinking presidency continues, with @realDonaldTrump declining to answer questions as he left the White House for Christmas at Mar-a-lago. He taunted, threatened and teased from the safety of Twitter before leaving town, but decided against explaining himself.
12/23/20, 4:17 PM

Source: Jeff Zeleny. Twitter. @jeffzeleny. December 23, 2020.

It's one more sign of how journalism descended during the Trump years into slashing opinion-giving, taunting, and mockery conducted by actual reporters who once believed their job was to play it down the middle. It's another indication of how deceptive and biased journalism has become.

But when it comes to letting an opinion rip, CNN's White House correspondent John Harwood takes the cake.

In July 2020, Trump retweeted a tweet by TV personality Chuck Woolery. Woolery's tweet read, "The most outrageous lies are the ones about Covid19. Everyone is lying. The CDC, Media, Democrats, our Doctors, not all but most, that we are told to trust. I think it's all about the election and keeping the economy from coming back, which is about the election. I'm sick of it."[51]

Trump's retweet was preceded by an effort carried out by White House aides to diminish the reputation of Dr. Anthony Fauci, the director of the National Institute of Allergy and Infectious Diseases, by releasing to some media outlets a list of statements made by Fauci early in the COVID crisis that turned out to be wrong.

A Trump-versus-Fauci fight was brewing. The press loved it.

At CNN, the morning anchor, John Berman, turned to Harwood to explain to viewers what was going on.

"The difference between Donald Trump and Anthony Fauci is this, and yes, both have said different things at different times about the coronavirus," Harwood reported. "Anthony Fauci has changed his position on some things like mask-wearing and whether people needed to change their behavior. We've been watching the clips all morning, but it's the difference between someone who is experienced, who is capable, who is public service spirited, who is adjusting his views in response to facts for the benefit of his fellow citizens, with someone, I'm talking about the president now, who doesn't know what he's doing, not honest, and cares about no one else but himself."[52]

Harwood wasn't finished sharing his opinions with CNN viewers.

"There's no other conclusion you can reach, but the incompetence of the Trump White House has lit the country on fire," Harwood stated.[53]

In December 2020, after a group of House Republicans announced their support of a lawsuit that challenged the results of the November election, Harwood "reported":

What's happening here is a demonstration of the low quality of the House of Representatives Republican caucus. It's pathetic. These are people who their lone remaining conviction seems to be simply preserving themselves in office. They're too weak to stand up for the principle of democracy. And so at the behest of Donald Trump[,] who psychologically and emotionally can't handle the fact that he lost the election, they're stepping up and signing this effort to throw out the results in these battleground states. . . . And I would add in particular though, the attorney general of Georgia doesn't say this, they're mad that they lost the election because of the votes of non-white people.[54]

They're not supposed to teach this kind of nasty, biased, look-down-your-nose-at-Republicans stuff at journalism school, but they do practice it at CNN.

House Republicans are "low quality." Their actions are "pathetic." And by the way, they're a bunch of racists who are mad at "non-white people." It's hard to tell what the difference is between Harwood and the spokesman for the Democratic National Committee. Harwood didn't even bother to attribute his remarks to Democrats who criticized Trump's criticisms of Fauci. Harwood simply made the accusations himself. He did the same thing when he described GOP House members who supported the lawsuit.

What Harwood did is not reporting. Instead, it's him delivering his biased, anti-Republican conclusions. It's his opinion. Harwood's views are superior to other people's points of view, especially House Republicans, and that's why he's on the air. To let people know his opinions. It's delivering for the resistance, on what's supposed to be a news show, by someone who is supposed to be a reporter. Sadly, it's what too much of journalism has turned into. Reporters give their opinions on shows watched mostly by Democrats and designed to appeal to Democrats who want partisan takedowns. No one does it better than Harwood.

On Trump's final day in office, Harwood tweeted that the change from Trump to Biden would be marked by going from "lies to truth, ignorance to knowledge, amorality to decency, cruelty to empathy, corruption to public service."

How in good conscience can an organization that purports to be a serious news outfit empower someone so overtly biased in the role

> **John Harwood** ✓
> @JohnJHarwood   •••
>
> Trump—>Biden
>
> lies—>truth
> ignorance—>knowledge
> amorality—>decency
> cruelty—> empathy
> corruption—>public service
>
> 10:39 AM · Jan 20, 2021 · Twitter for iPhone

Source: John Harwood. Twitter. @JohnJHarwood. January 20, 2021.

of White House correspondent? Trump deserved tough but fair coverage. Harwood was incapable of providing it. Biden deserves tough but fair coverage. Harwood began Biden's tenure with a love note, more worthy of MSNBC's Chris Matthews or a liberal columnist than a hard-hitting White House correspondent. There are better uses of Harwood's time than being a White House reporter. He needs his own show. Call it the "Harwood Angle."

CNN's trash-Trump opinion-giving continued even after Trump left office.

One week after Biden became president, CNN turned to its chief climate correspondent, Bill Weir, to report on one of President Biden's executive orders banning new oil and gas leases on federal land. "Joe Biden promised to help avoid planet cooking, climate-changing fossil fuel suicide," Weir said, "and within hours of his oath, he signed an executive order for every agency in government to be guided by the best science while undoing the many results of Donald Trump's fossil fuel fetish."[55]

Fetish?

What neutral, fair-minded reporter would use the word *fetish* to describe a legitimate, decades-long policy position? Why didn't Weir say Biden had a fetish for signing executive orders? Or that Biden had a fetish to get rid of Trump's policies? It's the use of loaded words like *fetish* to describe a policy position that shows how biased reporters can be. At CNN the bias is welcome, if not encouraged.

It's one thing to share opinions. It's another to be consistent about them.

In August 2020, after Joe Biden had announced Democratic senator Kamala Harris as his running mate, Trump attacked the ticket. Referring to Harris's attacks on Brett Kavanaugh when he was nominated to the Supreme Court, Trump said Harris was "a mad woman," "angry," and "full of hatred" toward Kavanaugh.[56]

That was too much for CNN. Anchor John Berman threw a flag. "The president himself is using sexist attacks against Senator Harris," Berman concluded.[57] CNN's shows, of course, routinely used the same language against Trump.

In April 2020, during its broadcast of a combative White House Coronavirus Task Force briefing with Trump, CNN ran a series of editorialized banners along the bottom of the screen: "Angry Trump Turns Briefing Into Propaganda Session," read one chyron; "Trump Melts Down in Angry Response to Reports He Ignored Virus Warnings," read another.[58] A few months later, CNN.com ran an editorial headlined, "Trump's Powerful Message of Rage."[59]

As Republicans were on their way to taking control of the House of Representatives, thanks to the Tea Party rebellion in 2010, the media was full of stories about "angry Republicans." "Angry Voters Could Affect Both Parties" headlined one CNN story in January 2010.[60] Just before Republicans took the Senate in 2014, another CNN story read, "CNN Poll: Voters Are Angry."[61]

So it's okay for CNN to say Trump is angry; voters are angry; Trump lashes out; and Trump is full of rage, but you can't call Kamala Harris mad or angry, because that's sexist. At CNN, the double standard is the standard.

This is what's wrong with anti-Trump, anti-Republican journalism. There is nothing wrong with calling your opponent angry. It's the stuff of everyday politics. But because CNN's anchors are encouraged to have agendas, they blow the whistle on Trump and say he was being sexist when CNN itself routinely does and says similar things. Double standards like this destroy good journalism. They undermine trust from viewers and readers. What is any fair-minded person to think when they see a news show give a pass to one side while blaming the other side for using the same words? Taking sides may be good for CNN's business. It's terrible for journalism and the country.

Then there was the time that CNN anchor Brianna Keilar let the world know where she stood as Senator Rand Paul (R-KY) and Dr. Anthony Fauci faced off at a May 2021 congressional hearing.

"But Senator Paul, who is an eye doctor, approaches these hearings as if they were a WWE match," Keilar stated. "Only instead of titillating a willing crowd, he blows disinformation all over them. Nothing brings out Senator Paul's propensity to act like *an ass* [emphasis added] like a Congressional appearance by Fauci, and that's really saying something."[62]

An ass.

Such is CNN these days.

Note that many of these examples aired during CNN's daytime broadcasts. Neither Kielar, nor Harwood, nor Weir, nor Romans, nor Zeleny, nor Chatterley, nor Harlow is a nighttime opinion-show host. They're daytime reporters and anchors whose jobs used to entail telling the news straight.

Sadly, those days are over.

If newsrooms weren't so full of like-minded anti-Trump, anti-Republican journalists who see the world the same way, maybe someone would have pointed these things out to CNN so their reporting standards could be consistent. But just as they were inconsistent in favor of New York governor Cuomo, they were also inconsistent in their standards for how they treated President Trump. The CNN anti-Republican agenda doesn't only appear on the air. You can find it on CNN's Twitter page. Just ask Texas senator Ted Cruz, who noted that when he introduced legislation in 2017 to create a "Consumer Freedom" amendment as part of a health care bill, CNN dismissed it as a "so-called" Consumer Freedom amendment:

Source: CNN. Twitter. @CNN. July 13, 2017.

To which Cruz aptly replied:

Source: Ted Cruz. Twitter. @tedcruz. July 13, 2017.

CNN today wouldn't be CNN without Jim Acosta, the famous anti-Trump, publicity-seeking reporter who served as CNN's chief White House correspondent during the Trump administration. Acosta was notorious for using his seat in the White House briefing room to give his opinions about the Trump presidency.

In January 2019, Trump traveled to the U.S.-Mexico border to inspect the wall that was being built. Acosta was there, too. He tweeted a video of himself walking along the border wall in McAllen, Texas.

As Acosta walked, he reported, "As we're walking along here, we're

Source: Jim Acosta. Twitter. @Acosta. January 10, 2019.

not seeing any kind of imminent danger. There are no migrants trying to rush toward this fence ... but no sign of the national emergency that the president has been talking about. As a matter of fact, it's pretty tranquil down here."[63]

There were no migrants trying to rush toward the fence. Maybe that's because there was a fence, so they went elsewhere. I guess that never occurred to Acosta. If ever there was a Trump critic who mistakenly made the case for a Trump policy, it was Jim Acosta and his reporting from the American side of the wall.

On March 11, 2020, President Trump spoke to the nation from the Oval Office to address the coronavirus outbreak and to discuss his plans to combat the virus's growing threat. He said, "This is the most aggressive and comprehensive effort to confront a foreign virus in modern history."[64] That mild and accurate remark was too much for Acosta, who went on CNN to tell the world that Trump's use of the word *foreign* was "smacking of xenophobia."[65]

"The president referred to the coronavirus as a 'foreign virus.' ... It's going to come across to a lot of Americans as smacking of xenophobia to use that kind of term in this speech," Acosta said, appearing on *Cuomo Prime Time.*[66]

Anytime a reporter uses the vague terminology "a lot of Americans think," the reporter is really saying, "Here's what I think." It's another way that reporters slide their personal opinions onto the air, disguised as reporting.

Of course, Acosta and CNN forgot to tell their viewers that just two months earlier, CNN repeatedly called the outbreak the "Wuhan Coronavirus" or the "Chinese Coronavirus" when it first emerged. According to a video montage put together by the Media Research Center, numerous CNN anchors and reporters referred to it using those two phrases, including Christiane Amanpour, Christine Romans, Don Lemon, and Dr. Sanjay Gupta. The montage also showed numerous reporters and anchors at PBS, ABC, CBS, CNBC, and MSNBC using the same terms.[67]

It was okay for them to refer to the virus by its place of origin, but, according to Acosta, it was xenophobic when Trump used the word *foreign.*

Despite the numerous CNN reporters and anchors who used the

CNN @CNN · Feb 11

The UK coronavirus **variant** that has "swept the country" is "going to sweep the world in all probability" Sharon Peacock, director of the Covid-19 Genomics UK consortium, said on Wednesday.

Source: CNN. Twitter. @CNN. February 11, 2021.

Source: *The Lead with Jake Tapper,* February 8, 2021.

phrase "Chinese coronavirus" themselves, one week later, CNN ran a story that claimed, "After consulting with medical experts, and receiving guidance from the World Health Organization, CNN has determined that that name [Chinese virus] is both inaccurate and is considered stigmatizing."[68]

Almost one year later, a new variant of the coronavirus was found in people in both South Africa and the United Kingdom. Back at CNN, where it was inaccurate, stigmatizing, and xenophobic to call the virus the "China virus" or the "Wuhan virus," there was no similar problem calling the new strain the "South Africa variant" or the "UK coronavirus variant."

At CNN, you can call the virus whatever you want. You just can't call it Chinese.

CNN IS ALSO THE PLACE to go for left-wing guests to say whatever they want, especially if it's anti-Trump, or anti-America, with barely an interruption. Trump aides were routinely interrupted, often before they could finish a sentence. When an interviewee begins to express views that deviate from those of the CNN newsroom, CNN anchors are quick to interrupt. Why invite on guests with dissenting views if they're not even able to fully communicate those views?

Nina Turner is a former Ohio state senator, a cochair of Bernie Sanders's 2020 presidential campaign, and an unsuccessful candidate in a Democratic congressional primary in 2021.[69] She was also a CNN political commentator.

Shortly after the Democrats' 2020 convention, Turner appeared on CNN with Anderson Cooper to discuss President Trump's criticism of the Democrats. Cooper rolled the tape of Trump saying about the Democrats' convention, "They spent four straight days attacking America as racist and a horrible country that must be redeemed." Cooper then asked for Turner's reaction.

Turner told Cooper, "I mean, the country does need to be redeemed. I don't know which convention he was looking at, though, but this country definitely needs to be redeemed. This country is racist. It's rooted in racism."[70]

The entire country is racist, she said. Not just Republicans, which is a common refrain on CNN. According to Turner, the entire country is racist. The entire country must be redeemed.

Cooper sat there silently. No pushback. No interruption. He didn't even ask her if she was saying that Democrats were racist. He just let her go. For one minute and forty-five seconds, an eternity on live cable TV! Watch any show, anytime. After about thirty or forty-five seconds, guests start to get interrupted by their hosts simply because their answer is getting too long. A neutral or even curious anchor would have interrupted Turner immediately upon her declaration that "the country is racist." On CNN, that kind of criticism is shown the red carpet.

Senator Chris Murphy (D-CT), the man who said Trump's phone call with the president of Taiwan would start a war, appeared on CNN with anchor Jim Sciutto shortly after Trump went to the hospital after coming down with the coronavirus. "If President Trump can't be out there on the campaign trail for the next two weeks, then he is going to rely on his surrogates and unfortunately, one of his surrogates is Vladimir Putin," Murphy told Sciutto as part of his assessment that Russia was endeavoring to influence the U.S. presidential election in Trump's favor.

Sciutto sat there, tilting his head, nodding in agreement.[71]

On CNN, it's never too early or too late to charge Trump with collusion, in 2016 or 2020. Facts about collusion don't matter. CNN's anchors certainly won't push back.

Many of CNN's problems could be addressed if they had a more diverse newsroom. It would help them if there were people on the inside who thought differently and pushed back, raising issues with stories before they aired. I'm not referring to on-air contributors. I'm talking about editors who shape the news.

CNN made a teeny-tiny effort to do that by hiring a known Republican to join their editorial team, but, unfortunately, one Republican in particular was too much for CNN; the network came under pressure from reporters who objected to the hiring of a Trump administration Republican. Meet Sarah Isgur. She served as the Department of Justice spokeswoman for Attorney General Jeff Sessions, and had previously worked for Ted Cruz, Mitt Romney, and Carly Fiorina. In February 2019, Isgur was hired as a political editor in the CNN Washington bureau. All hell broke loose at CNN as a result.

"CNN staffers are upset and confused about the network's decision to hire a partisan political operative to oversee its 2020 campaign reporting. . . . 'It's extremely demoralizing for everyone here,' one network editorial staffer told the *Daily Beast*."[72]

According to CNN's Brian Stelter, "CNN employees are concerned, according to numerous people who reached out to me on Tuesday. They are asking what Isgur's role will be and questioning whether her sudden leap from the Trump administration to the CNN newsroom is an ethical breach."

Stelter added, "My understanding is that Isgur—who isn't starting work for a few more weeks—will be joining a group of several political editors who coordinate coverage. This entails managing teams in the field, making decisions about how to frame the day's biggest campaign stories, etcetera. There is certainly a lot of work to go around, given the crowded Democratic field of presidential candidates and the prospect of Republican primary challengers."[73]

Never mind that George Stephanopoulos moved from the Clinton administration to ABC News,[74] or that Tim Russert was a Democratic staffer on Capitol Hill before joining NBC News,[75] or that Dana Perino worked for George W. Bush before becoming a FOX News anchor.[76] None had journalistic experience before successfully moving from politics into journalism.

Nor was there a newsroom uproar when CNN hired Laura Jarrett, the daughter of top Obama aide Valerie Jarrett, as a reporter to cover the Justice Department and legal issues during the Trump administration.[77] Like Isgur, Jarrett had no journalistic experience,[78] but both were graduates of Harvard Law School. Jarrett still works at CNN.[79] Isgur does not.

Think about this. CNN hired Jarrett, a Harvard Law School graduate with no journalistic experience, the daughter of a prominent Democrat, to cover the Trump Justice Department. CNN withdrew an offer to Isgur, a Harvard Law School graduate with no journalistic experience, the spokeswoman for a prominent Republican, who used to work at the Justice Department.

How is that fair?

Nor was there a newsroom meltdown when CNN hired the communications director for one of the most prominent, controversial Democratic governors in the nation. CNN's former number two executive, Allison Gollust, was the communications director for—you guessed it—former governor Andrew Cuomo.

In a February 2013 letter to Governor Cuomo announcing her departure for CNN, Gollust wrote, "Regardless of where I am employed, you will continue to have my unwavering allegiance as an adviser and, most importantly, a friend."[80]

Unwavering allegiance as an adviser?

Gollust, whose title at CNN is executive vice president and chief marketing officer for CNN Worldwide, was also in the running to replace Jeff Zucker as the president of CNN Worldwide.

According to Dylan Byers of NBC, "Allison Gollust, a CNN executive and top lieutenant to Jeff Zucker, has emerged as the leading internal candidate to take over the network if Zucker steps down as president, two people at CNN familiar with the matter say."

Byers noted, "As Zucker's most-trusted lieutenant for decades, she has been involved in or had a front-row seat to every major decision of his tenure at the network, from international deals to talent management and programming. The CNN sources noted that she is almost always present at his side both in the office and in the field."[81]

Gollust was fired from CNN in early 2022 for using her position to provide preferential treatment to promote Governor Cuomo's image. You can't say she didn't promise everyone she would do exactly that.[82]

At CNN, hiring known Democrats is no problem but hiring a known Republican is a bridge too far.

When it's not withdrawing jobs from people whose background might upset its newsroom, CNN has an alternative way of dealing with contributors who deviate from the party line. It vanishes them.

James Gagliano served twenty-five years with the FBI. He worked on investigations and he handled crises. He also worked in undercover positions, including assignment to the FBI's elite counterterror unit, the Hostage Rescue Team (HRT), and was the senior team leader of the FBI New York Field Division's SWAT team. He was awarded the FBI's second-highest award for valor, the Medal of Bravery. In FBI parlance, he was a brick agent. He also graduated from the U.S. Military Academy at West Point and is an Army veteran.[83] He is one tough and smart dude.

In 2016, after his retirement from the FBI, CNN invited Gagliano to discuss a bombing in the Chelsea section of New York City that injured thirty-one people.[84] Inspired by ISIS and Al Qaeda, the bomber, Ahmad Khan Rahimi, of Elizabeth, New Jersey, was sentenced to life in prison one year later.[85]

CNN thought Gagliano was a sharp analyst and asked him repeatedly to go on air to discuss matters involving the FBI. After Trump was elected, CNN asked him back onto the air to discuss the growing accusations of collusion with Russia involving Trump and the Trump campaign and their counterintelligence implications.[86]

"Everything they used me for is pretty standard law enforcement stuff," Gagliano told me in an interview.[87] "It didn't really delve into the political realm." Until May 9, 2017. The day Trump fired James Comey. CNN called Gagliano at 1:00 a.m. the next day and asked him to go on the air at 5:00 a.m. He said yes.

Gagliano thought the way Trump fired Comey was wrong. "I didn't lionize [Comey], but I thought this was an awful way to treat somebody. This is just the wrong way to handle this. This is no way to treat a career public servant. This is unconscionable," Gagliano told me. That was basically Gagliano's message on the air.

Gagliano told me that CNN, that day, offered him a contract to become a contributor. Gagliano spent the entire day doing shows about the firing. As CNN's attention turned to the Mueller probe, Gagliano found himself in an increasingly uncomfortable position on the air. The anchors, he told me, kept asking him leading questions, designed to make him condemn Trump.

"I was full of condemnatory things to say about Donald Trump in the initial part of the Russian investigation," he said. "Then the [FBI agent] Peter Strzok and [FBI lawyer] Lisa Page piece comes out, and then the [FBI deputy director] Andy McCabe piece comes out."

Emails between FBI agents Strzok and Page showed that they both opposed Trump's election in 2016 and may have misused their positions at the FBI to pursue an investigation against Trump.[88]

McCabe, who worked for Gagliano when Gagliano was a SWAT team leader in New York City, was fired from the FBI in 2018 for lying under oath to the department's inspector general.

"So all these things start happening and then the whole unraveling of the FISA. Well, CNN is using me. And then the first IG [inspector

general] report comes out, and I read it cover to cover and I'm sick-
ened. Until the IG reports came out and until more was divulged, I
was a supporter of the FBI. As more and more came out, as I read
more and more of the text exchanges, as I read more and more of the
IG report, I became convinced I've got to take a position and criticize
the FBI here. I have to call this straight.

"Once I started doing that, I got moved off of those issues,"
Gagliano told me.

Instead of putting a decorated, retired FBI agent on the air to talk
about a growing scandal at the FBI, CNN moved him away from the
Trump/FBI story and had him do crime stories instead, often on their
sister station, Headline News. Gagliano wondered why. "Of course, the
obvious thing in your mind is, they don't like what you're saying. We
demand diversity in everything these days, except for thought.

"They stopped using me on Trump stuff . . . but because I looked
at what the FBI had done and what some members of the intelligence
community had done, I said, 'this was wrong.'"

As Gagliano found himself covering shootings and other crime
stories,[89] he was essentially replaced on the air by Josh Campbell, a
former FBI agent and top aide to James Comey.[90] CNN hired him
from the FBI public affairs office to become a CNN contributor.
CNN later hired McCabe as well.[91]

In contrast with Gagliano, Campbell routinely defended Comey
and the FBI against Trump. With a diminished voice on CNN,
Gagliano took to Twitter and op-eds to make his points.

After New Orleans Saints quarterback Drew Brees, since retired,
initially said he would stand for the National Anthem, Gagliano
tweeted that he stood with Brees.[92] CNN didn't approve. According
to Gagliano, an executive at CNN, Rebecca Kutler, called him to say,
"Your job at CNN is to be a law enforcement analyst."

"But you don't use me," Gagliano told Kutler.

Gagliano pointed out to Kutler the anti-Trump tweets and statements issued regularly by other CNN contributors, including Preet Bharara, Sam Vinograd, and Asha Rangappa.

"You need to watch your social media," Kutler told Gagliano.

I called Kutler to hear her side of the story, but she told me she couldn't talk about it and referred me to CNN's media relations department. I emailed Lauren Pratapas, CNN's vice president for communications, but she did not reply.

Despite how Gagliano was treated, he looks back at his time at CNN fondly. He remains grateful to have been hired by the network. "CNN gave me an amazing opportunity," he told me. "I was proud to be at CNN."

The retired FBI agent concluded in his interview with me, "I liked being in a place where everybody doesn't think like me. I just didn't want to be at a place where nobody thought like me. It was always an away game for me. If I gave them my unfiltered opinion, and it didn't fit within the editorial focus of what they were looking for, they would bat it down. If you bash Trump, you can be political. If you bash the GOP and talk about how evil they are, you can get political. But if you dare push back the other way, you're just not going to get airtime."

Chapter Eight

THE NEW YORK TIMES

Sometimes, people spill the beans from the most unexpected places.

> Though [Executive Editor Dean] Baquet said publicly that he didn't want the Times to be the opposition party, his news pages were unmistakably anti-Trump, as were the [Washington] Post's. Some headlines contained raw opinion, as did some of the stories that were labeled as news analysis.[1]

This revelation was not written by a conservative critic of the *New York Times*. Instead, it was penned in 2019 by former *New York Times* executive Jill Abramson, who held the newspaper's top editor post from 2011 to 2014. When the former highest-ranking editor of the *Times* admits the paper is biased, you know there's a problem.

Fifteen years earlier, another executive editor of the *Times* acknowledged that the paper's front page was excessively opinionated. Appearing at the National Press Club in Washington, DC, on

February 9, 2004, Bill Keller, the paper's executive editor at the time, noted, "The fact is, what goes into—what we publish on the front pages of the *New York Times* today—a fair amount of it would have been regarded as excessively opinionated twenty years ago."[2]

At the time, Keller's reference to "twenty years ago" would have been 1984—nearly forty years ago now. Over the past forty years, the lines between fact and opinion at the *New York Times* have become increasingly blurred. Editorial points of view are camouflaged as analysis. Commentary permeates coverage. The shift from objectivity to subjectivity is not unique to the *Times*; today, all too often, it's just the way of mainstream journalism. What is rare is for two top editors to publicly speak out about their newspaper's bias and admit that raw opinion is part of what the news pages offer.

Many journalists won't admit it, but it's good to see the people at the top of the *Times* say it. Given the *Times'* prominent place at the top of mainstream journalism, when the *Times* launches a trend, other media outlets follow. If it was acceptable for headlines and stories to contain "raw opinion" at the *Times*, it quickly became acceptable for the practice to extend to all kinds of mainstream media outlets everywhere. If it was acceptable for news pages at the *New York Times* to be "unmistakably anti-Trump," it quickly became acceptable for that to be the case in other places, too.

To me and millions of others, it's why objective journalism at the *New York Times* and elsewhere is broken.

Once a symbol of journalistic integrity, the *Times* is now a place where editors and writers are fired if a story doesn't sit well with the paper's resistance readership. Internal dissent boils over in a newsroom filled with young writers who perceive their words as instruments of change. Objectivity bends to advocacy. News stories often adhere to a narrative dedicated to championship of the left and vilification of the right. Meanwhile, accuracy, objectivity, and fairness suffer.

TODAY, THE *TIMES* NEWSROOM IS under assault by a younger generation of staffers who approach the news with an activist angle. This generation questions whether objectivity is appropriate if being objective means giving a platform to—and inadvertently legitimizing—views these writers perceive as dangerous (their definition of dangerous is highly elastic).

As 2020 ushered in the pandemic and racial unrest, the *New York Times* newsroom was smoldering with tension between those loyal to upholding balanced, cover-all-sides journalism and this new generation of reporters who argued that objectivity and balance must yield to subjectivity, especially on matters pertaining to so-called social justice. On June 3, 2020, the *Times* ran an op-ed that ignited these tensions, and anger inside the newsroom boiled over.

That was the day the *Times* published online an op-ed written by Senator Tom Cotton (R-AR) headlined "Send in the Troops." The op-ed was based on the riots that broke out in the aftermath of George Floyd's murder.

Cotton wrote:

> Some elites have excused this orgy of violence in the spirit of radical chic, calling it an understandable response to the wrongful death of George Floyd. Those excuses are built on a revolting moral equivalence of rioters and looters to peaceful, law-abiding protesters. A majority who seek to protest peacefully shouldn't be confused with bands of miscreants.
>
> But the rioting has nothing to do with George Floyd, whose

bereaved relatives have condemned violence. On the contrary, nihilist criminals are simply out for loot and the thrill of destruction, with cadres of left-wing radicals like antifa infiltrating protest marches to exploit Floyd's death for their own anarchic purposes.

These rioters, if not subdued, not only will destroy the livelihoods of law-abiding citizens but will also take more innocent lives. Many poor communities that still bear scars from past upheavals will be set back still further.

One thing above all else will restore order to our streets: an overwhelming show of force to disperse, detain and ultimately deter lawbreakers.[3]

The reaction to this perfectly reasonable point of view was instant and tumultuous.[4] The *Times* newsroom melted down, which tells you how different the *Times* newsroom is from much of America. *Slate* magazine characterized the reaction of the *Times* staff as an "Open Revolt" and pointed out that publication of the op-ed resulted in the "highest-ever number of cancellations in a single hour," which again tells you how different *New York Times* readers are from much of America.

The *Slate* story pointed out that many reporters at the *Times* thought their lives were in danger because the paper printed Cotton's op-ed:

Seemingly countless *Times* employees on both the news and opinion sides were tweeting some variation of the following, directly criticizing their own paper.[5]

I'll probably get in trouble for this, but to not say something would be immoral. As a black woman, as a journalist, as an

American, I am deeply ashamed that we ran this. —Ida Bae
Wells (@nhannahjones) June 4, 2020

Source: Ashley Feinberg, "Newsroom Breaks Into Open Revolt After New York
Times Publishes Call for Military Crackdown," Slate.com, June 4, 2020.

As the *Slate* story noted, "This sort of mass, public pushback from
the *Times'* own employees is wholly unprecedented. Previously, *Times*
executive editor Dean Baquet had chastised reporters for so much as
clicking 'like' on a tweet that criticized a colleague. But after countless
stories of unrest at the *New York Times* and complaints from younger
reporters falling on deaf ears, it seemed *Times* reporters had reached
a breaking point."[6]

Indeed. Later that night, *Times* staffers put out a statement
through the NewsGuild of New York, the union representing many
Times journalists, criticizing *Times* management for its "irresponsible
choice" in publishing a message that "promotes hate."[7]

After initially supporting the decision to publish the op-ed, the
paper went into full retreat. The loudest, most liberal voices support-
ing suppression of opinions was winning—at a newspaper ostensibly
dedicated to the free expression of multiple points of view.

Cotton's piece was rescinded and withheld from the *Times'* print edition. James Bennet, the editorial page editor, resigned amid the furious backlash. Jim Dao, Bennet's deputy, was reassigned at the paper. Two days after publishing the op-ed online, the *Times* canceled itself, adding an "Editor's Note" to Cotton's column that read:

> After publication, this essay met strong criticism from many readers (and many Times colleagues), prompting editors to review the piece and the editing process. Based on that review, we have concluded that the essay fell short of our standards and should not have been published.[8]

This was not the first time that the *Times* had tucked its tail and scrambled to placate its liberal newsroom and readership. One summer earlier, an objective headline stirred outrage and rebellion within the *Times* newsroom. In August 2019, two back-to-back mass killings took place—one in El Paso, Texas, and the other in Dayton, Ohio. The El Paso shooting killed twenty-two people. The killer confessed he wanted to target Mexicans. The shooting in Dayton killed nine.[9]

The next day, President Trump addressed the nation from the White House, declaring, "These barbaric slaughters are an assault upon our communities, an attack upon our nation, and a crime against all of humanity. We are outraged and sickened by this monstrous evil, the cruelty, the hatred, the malice, the bloodshed, and the terror. . . . The shooter in El Paso posted a manifesto online consumed by racist hate. In one voice, our nation must condemn racism, bigotry, and white supremacy. These sinister ideologies must be defeated. Hate has no place in America."[10]

The *New York Times* headlined Trump's speech "Trump Urges

Unity Vs Racism." It was a fair description of the president's speech. The left went nuts. Not against Trump. Against the *New York Times*.

Congresswoman Alexandria Ocasio-Cortez (D-NY) tweeted, "Let this front page serve as a reminder of how white supremacy is aided by—and often relies upon—the cowardice of mainstream institutions."

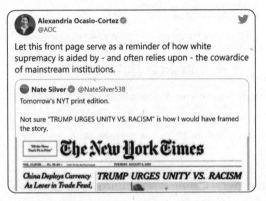

Source: Alexandria Ocasio-Cortez. Twitter. @AOC. August 5, 2019.

Former presidential candidate Senator Cory Booker (D-NJ) jumped into the act, saying lives depended on the *Times* doing better.

Source: Cory Booker. Twitter. @CoryBooker. August 5, 2019.

A newsroom rebellion was under way.

Wajahat Ali tweeted, "I write for the NYT. This is a terrible headline."

Source. Wajahat Ali. Twitter. @WajahatAli. August 5, 2019.

The complaints were pouring in, fast and furious from the left. Given the *New York Times* readership, not to mention the ideological leanings of its own newsroom, left-wing complaints are taken seriously. If they aren't, subscribers will cancel their subscriptions, as Joan Walsh, a CNN political contributor and the national affairs correspondent[11] for the liberal *Nation* magazine, did.

Joan Walsh ✔ @joanwalsh · Aug 5, 2019   •••
I canceled my subscription. I know a lot of folks will tell me I'm wrong. I will miss it. But I can't keep rewarding such awful news judgment. "Trump Urges Unity Against Racism" is almost as bad as their full-page Comey letter coverage just before 2016 election. Nobody learns.

Source: Joan Walsh. Twitter. @joanwalsh. August 5, 2019.

Other liberals jumped in to attack the *Times*.

When the criticism comes from the *Wall Street Journal* editorial page or FOX News, the *Times* ignores it since so few of its readers read or watch those outlets. But when the left-wing outlets like the *Nation* and *HuffPost* raise the alarm, the *Times* hears it loud and clear.

Source: Yashar Ali. Twitter. @yashar. August 5, 2019.

New York Times executive editor Dean Baquet was trapped. He either had to stand by an accurate headline or cave to the pressures of liberal staff and subscribers. Given where he works, Baquet had no choice. He caved. And with that capitulation, another piece of the journalism's bedrock crumbled.

Fifty-nine minutes after the first headline hit and the meltdown began, the *Times* headline was changed to "Assailing Hate But Not Guns."[12] The meltdown, however, could not be stopped.

Jack Shafer, *Politico*'s senior media writer, pointed out, "Scores of Twitter users, including *Philadelphia Inquirer* columnist Will Bunch, called for *Times* Executive Editor Dean Baquet to resign and at last count, the hashtag #CancelNYT had appeared in 16,000 tweets."[13]

Shafer added, "The fury uncaged by the five-word *Times* headline had less to do with the language used and more to do with the political validation that liberals and lefties have come to demand from the news media they consume. . . . They want every column-inch of copy in the *Times* to reinforce and amplify their resistance values, right down to the headlines. Anything perceived as even a minor deviation from that 'mission,' they seem to think, requires the mass cancellation of subscriptions and calls for the executive editor's resignation."[14]

As Baquet characterized it during the August 2019 town hall called to deal with the newsroom furor, "It was a fucking mess."[15]

As the *Times'* own media columnist, Ben Smith, put it in a 2021 piece, "The *Times'* unique position in American news may not be tenable. This intense attention, combined with a thriving digital subscription business that makes the company more beholden to the views of left-leaning subscribers, may yet push it into a narrower and more left-wing political lane as a kind of American version of *The Guardian*—the opposite of its stated, broader strategy."[16]

The *New York Times* had to decide if they would stand up for the diverse thought, thorough debate, and exchange of ideas that at least some of their subscribers expect, or give in to the most vocal group, tuck its tail, and run. They headed for the hills without hesitation. A younger, more activist generation of reporters learned that if you complain loud enough, and if you claim you are somehow in danger, management will buckle.

In my interview with President Trump, he told me how the *Times* was "excoriated" over the headline. "They had a meltdown."

"I think they [the *New York Times*] are so—they're both a victim, and it also brings them I guess success, but I think they're so chained to the people that read it I'm not sure they can write the truth even if they want. Look, we have fifty percent. They have fifty percent. I think that they are—I'm not sure they have a choice. In just that incident, when I saw that story, I was thrilled by the fact that the title was so good—and they got killed by it. It became a major story. So I'm not sure they can write the truth, and that's a very bad thing for the country," Trump told me.

IN MANY WAYS, WHAT HAPPENED at the *Times* is an extension of a movement that has swept across college and university campuses— with college students demanding that campus leadership shield them from labels, words, or ideas they perceive as offensive. "Safe spaces" were created to protect students from triggering or uncomfortable language and "microaggressions," or language that indirectly and unintentionally "discriminates." Liberal college students, with the support of liberal faculty members and liberal college administrators, began to shun the virtues of open debate. If someone claimed they were "hurt" by someone else's opinion, the "victim" needed to be protected by college authorities.

As safe spaces spread, and as the "rights" of the aggrieved to punish people whose opinions they didn't like took hold on campuses across America, a lesson was learned: If you complain the right way, you can silence those with whom you disagree. Students graduated from college expecting authorities around them, especially employers, to conduct themselves the same way college administrators and faculty conducted themselves. A new generation of reporters, especially at a flagship paper like the *Times*, demanded their bosses and editors act as if they were on a college campus, where liberal points of view are the norm, and conservative voices, like Tom Cotton's, are silenced or not allowed.

In November 2019, the Northwestern College Republicans invited former attorney general Jeff Sessions to give a speech at Northwestern University. Students and community members protested. As reported by the university's newspaper, the *Daily Northwestern*, "Students on Tuesday protested Northwestern College Republicans' decision to host former Attorney General Jeff Sessions, chanting outside Lutkin Hall before attempting to interrupt Sessions' talk by climbing through open windows and pushing through doors."[17]

Sounding a lot like the newsroom at the *New York Times*, the campus paper quoted a student protester saying, "There's a difference between having a sustained dialogue and listening to other opinions and accepting hate speech and fascism. That's the difference with the Trump administration. There are other viewpoints, but when your actions and your words are actively killing and oppressing people, we can't accept that."[18]

I see. Conservative speech should not be allowed, in person or in writing. What happened next, however, should trouble anyone who supports tough, fair-minded journalism.

The *Daily Northwestern* apologized for covering the protests. It apologized for covering the news!

Referring to the presence of Sessions on campus as a "traumatic event" (just like *Times* journalists stating the presence of a Cotton op-ed put them in danger), the paper wrote, "We recognize that we contributed to the harm students experienced, and we wanted to apologize for and address the mistakes that we made that night—along with how we plan to move forward.

"One area of our reporting that harmed many students was our photo coverage of the event. Some protesters found photos posted to reporters' Twitter accounts retraumatizing and invasive. Those photos have since been taken down."[19]

The paper also apologized for calling protesters and asking for their comments.

What a mess. No one apologized to the former attorney general for trying to shout him down and deny his right to address his hosts. Instead, journalists apologized to protesters for covering their protests.

Many journalistic organizations, including the *New York Times*, were critical of the student paper for its apology.[20] Student journalists are supposed to be taught to cover the news without fear or favor, but even that standard is threatened by a growing generation of activist reporters who increasingly are finding they have more power than their editors. There is not much difference between a university paper apologizing to its readers for covering a protest and the *New York Times* apologizing to its readers for publishing an opinion piece about violent protests. The biggest difference is that no one at the student paper lost his or her job, which can't be said for the staff of the *Times*.

In an interview, Senator Cotton told me, "The *Times* is not objective. It's not dedicated to providing its readers with an intellectually diverse set of views."

Cotton continued: "Every year, elite prestigious universities are turning out new graduates who are indoctrinated in things like critical race theory or critical gender theory, and they're very dogmatic about it. More than anything, it's dogma from which heretics are not allowed to defend, even on the left. And those people go on to populate newsrooms. . . . It's strange to me that the *New York Times*, too, is the place where the senior leadership has most often and most flagrantly caved to left-wing pressure from their workforce. Because after all, the *New York Times* is the most prestigious landing place for left-leaning journalists in America."

Reflecting on why his op-ed caused such a dramatic and tumultuous revolt inside the *Times* newsroom, Cotton told me, "The editorial page of the *New York Times* is like the Holy of the Holies for leftist intellectuals in America. I think that's one reason why my op-ed was particularly offensive to them. It didn't run in the *Wall Street Journal*. It didn't even run in the *Washington Post*. It ran in the Holiest of the Holies. I marched into the Holy of Holies and desecrated their sacred space on the issue of greatest import and sensitivity to the left, which is identity politics."[21]

The trend against objectivity in journalism is deeply worrisome.

Paola Boivin is a professor of journalism at the Cronkite School of Journalism and Mass Communication at Arizona State University. She spent her career covering sports and now teaches young people how to become journalists.[22]

"When I first got into journalism it was very much about accuracy and objectivity. . . . [Objectivity] has gotten a little tricky for the old-school like me," she told me in an interview.[23] "I've learned a lot from the students. We're being challenged if the objectivity that my generation knows is how we should still report the news. I think much of the younger generation is arguing that objectivity is sort of a falsehood. We all come in with some biases and [the students say] that the priority should be truth and fairness over objectivity."

Boivin said if a sportswriter's Twitter bio says "Go Yankees" or demonstrates any type of bias, it's a journalistic problem. "At Cronkite, we very much send the message that they can't show any allegiances for sports teams while they're working at Cronkite as a sports reporter."

She said a hot topic of debate is whether students should be allowed to have "Black Lives Matter" or "Blue Lives Matter" in their Twitter bios. She described it as a good and healthy debate.

"We used to have very strict rules at Cronkite about what your social media handles should look like when you're reporting for us. We now have changed that to 'there's not going to be a punishment if you do something' but it's more a recommendation. You can put what you want, but also be aware that when you're applying for jobs, they'll look at your social media accounts, so we're offering guidance about how they should handle it. For some students that matters, but for others, their concerns and issues are more important to them."

Remember the tweet by Ron Fournier, the former chief White House correspondent for the Associated Press? He wrote, "Most journalists get into the business to make things better, to force change, to move the needle."[24]

Add it up.

Some reporters believe their concerns and issues are more important than neutrality or objectivity. Fournier says people become journalists to force change and to move the needle. The media is descending into a new world in which it's increasingly hard to separate advocacy from journalism. It's a growing debate inside newsrooms. Some veteran reporters are trying to resist this shift, while many younger reporters believe it's their mission, especially concerning issues they define as "social justice."

Appearing on CNN in March 2018, Rebecca Schneid, then co-editor in chief of the Marjory Stoneman Douglas High School newspaper in Parkland, Florida, said, "I think that, in its own right, journalism is a form of activism."[25]

Josh Kraushaar, the senior national political columnist of *National Journal Daily* and *National Journal* politics editor,[26] wisely replied, "Journalism isn't activism; it's presenting the facts, honestly and objectively. It's this mentality that's killing trust in our profession."

This little dustup, which involved a high school student who, in my opinion, is entitled to wide latitude as she forms her thoughts, sparked a broader debate among older journalists.

Longreads jumped into the debate with a story exploring where journalism ends and advocacy begins. In the piece, the *Washington Post*'s Wesley Lowery was quoted as saying, "Even beyond big, long investigations, journalists perform acts of activism every day. Any good journalist is an activist for truth, in favor of transparency, on the behalf of accountability. It is our literal job to *pressure* powerful people and institutions via our questions."[27]

The debate over activism is a slippery slope that leads straight to bias.

When Bill Keller said the *New York Times* front page was "excessively opinionated," whose opinions do you think the *Times* represented? College-educated, cosmopolitan, mostly Democratic voters, that's who. On Manhattan's Upper West Side, that tends to mean that Republicans, especially those from rural areas and the South, are seen mostly as a group of poorly educated, gun-toting, tobacco-chewing, narrow-minded Christians who really need to learn the facts so they can improve themselves. The *Times*, after all, certainly wasn't the place for readers to go for conservative, pro-gun, or pro-life opinions in its news stories.

A study published in a 2018 edition of the *Journal of Expertise* found that the writing staffs of the *New York Times* and the *Wall Street Journal* overwhelmingly hail from elite schools—with nearly 52 percent of *Times* writers and 54 percent of *Journal* writers having attended elite universities. The study authors, *Psychology Today* editor in chief Kaja Perina and University of Arkansas assistant professor Jonathan Wai, examined the education backgrounds of 1,979 employees working at the *Times* and the *Journal* in 2016. In their findings, the authors noted the elite schooling background of not only writing staffs but of the newspapers' employees as a whole (staff writers, editors, contributors, and other newspaper staff included) with approximately 44 percent of *Times* employees and nearly 50 percent of *Journal* employees having attended elite schools.

According to the study, "Almost half of the people who reach the pinnacle of the journalism profession attended an elite school and were likely in the top 1% of cognitive ability. This means top 1% people are overrepresented among the NYT and WSJ mastheads by a factor of about 50."[28] Within the study sample, the authors found that the Ivy League schools were well represented—with roughly 20 percent of overall employees and 28 percent of the editors and writers group having attended them.[29]

If anyone has been on the campus of an Ivy League school in the last few decades, or the campus of any so-called elite university, they know these universities are not very welcome places for conservative students, or conservative thought. Neither is the *New York Times* newsroom.

Remember that Pew survey that showed of those who said their main source of political and election news was the *New York Times*, 91 percent considered themselves Democrats or lean Democrat?[30] The current top editor at the paper knows how lopsided the readership is at the *Times*.

At the heated *Times* newsroom town hall meeting in August 2019 to address the controversial "Trump Urges Unity Vs Racism" headline, Baquet made an appeal for the *Times* to remain an "independent newspaper." Baquet then added, "What I'm saying is that our readers and some of our staff cheer us when we take on Donald Trump, but they jeer at us when we take on Joe Biden." Baquet also went on to say that the *Times* needed to try to understand the forces that led to the election of Donald Trump. "And that means trying to understand the segment of America that probably does not read us."[31]

At least Baquet acknowledges the reality of his customers' purchasing habits. By the "segment of America that probably does not read us," Baquet is referring to Trump voters. According to Pew, just 7 percent of those who say the *Times* is their main source for political or election news consider themselves Republicans or lean Republican.[32]

Despite its ideological bias, the *Times* remains deeply influential. It often sets the national news agenda, the tone, and the pace for much of what the rest of the media report, especially ABC, CBS, NBC, CNN, and MSNBC. What appears on the front page of the *Times* in the morning is often covered by much of the media throughout the day. This is the media's bubble. After voting overwhelmingly for Democratic candidates as journalism students, it's a comfortable and easy bubble for like-minded college-educated journalists to belong to. It's an intellectual bubble. It's a cultural bubble. It's the "social level" bubble *New York* magazine White House correspondent Olivia Nuzzi referred to when she told the *Atlantic* that, on a social level, reporting negative things about Biden wouldn't feel as safe, compared to reporting negative things about Trump.[33]

I've subscribed to the *Times* since I was in college. I still subscribe. Not every story in the *Times* is biased.

The *Times*, after all, broke the story about Hillary Clinton's use of a private server for her government emails while serving as secretary of state.[34] The *Times* broke the story in 2010 of Senator Richard Blumenthal (D-CT) falsely claiming he served in Vietnam.[35] And the *Times* broke the story detailing the sexual harassment claims against New York governor Andrew Cuomo by former aide Charlotte Bennett.[36]

With its large staff and budget, the *Times* still digs for scandal, and when it finds it, the paper knows how to blow its whistle.

In several instances in this book, I cite reporting done by the *Times* or the *Washington Post* or other media outlets, and I praise it. Not every story is wrong or biased. But too many are.

Day in and day out, the news pages of the *New York Times*, especially in the Trump era, represented a powerful anti-Trump point of view. For decades, day in and day out, the *Times*' news pages have portrayed Democratic policy positions as obviously beneficial while portraying Republican policy positions as obviously abnormal. And when Democrats and Republicans fight, it's easy to see with whom reporters and editors agree.

In 2010, the Senate Judiciary Committee heard from President

Obama's nominee to the Supreme Court, Elena Kagan. As has been the decades-long practice for nominees of both parties, Kagan refused to answer questions about how she would vote on matters that could come before her.

"Kagan Follows Precedent by Offering Few Opinions," read the *Times* headline.

Kagan Follows Precedent by Offering Few Opinions

By CHARLIE SAVAGE and SHERYL GAY STOLBERG   JUNE 29, 2010

Source: Charlie Savage and Sheryl Stolberg, "Kagan Follows Precedent by Offering Few Opinions," *New York Times*, June 29, 2010.

Eight years later, President Trump nominated Brett Kavanaugh to the Supreme Court. Like Kagan, Kavanaugh followed the decades-long practice of not answering questions about Supreme Court cases. But this time, the *Times* headline scoffed: "Kavanaugh Ducks Questions on Presidential Powers and Subpoenas."

Kavanaugh Ducks Questions on Presidential Powers and Subpoenas

Source: Michael Shear, Adam Liptak, and Sheryl Stolberg, "Kavanaugh Ducks Questions on Presidential Powers and Subpoenas," *New York Times*, September 5, 2018.

Democrats follow precedents. Republicans duck questions. Two very different headlines for two Supreme Court nominees saying essentially the same thing.

Beyond the wildly disparate headlines, a comparison of the *Times* articles reveals equally disparate word choices. Whereas the *Times* article about Kagan's confirmation hearings uses softer language to explain how Kagan "deflected" questions and "declined" to say where she stood on a variety of issues,[37] the *Times* article on Kavanaugh's hearings utilizes harsher vocabulary to report that Kavanaugh "dodged" questions and that he "refused" to say where he stood on various matters.[38] "Deflecting" is softer than "ducking" and "declining" is more polite than "refusing."

This subtle (or not so subtle) change in word choice is anything but accidental. By choosing certain words, reporters can write a story to support one side's point of view—or to oppose the other side. Word choice is a handy window into a reporter's bias.

Every day, numerous stories in the *Times* make conservatives shake their heads, wondering why the paper makes so many mistakes, so often in ways that are derisive of Republicans, conservative thought, or Donald Trump. In June 2020, President Trump finished a speech to the graduating class of the U.S. Military Academy at West Point. As he left the stage, he walked noticeably slowly down a ramp.

The *New York Times* sprang into action.

"Trump's Halting Walk Down Ramp Raises New Health Questions," ran a *Times* headline.

It's a good thing Trump didn't actually fall.

But Joe Biden did.

In March 2021, seventy-eight-year-old Joe Biden, the oldest president in American history, fell three times while walking up the ramp to Air Force One.

The *Times* covered that story, too.

Biden is 'doing 100 percent fine' after tripping while boarding Air Force One.

Source: *New York Times*, March 19, 2021.

According to the *Times*, Trump's nonfall raised questions about his health, but Biden's actual fall did not. The *Times* wasn't alone. According to the Media Research Center's *NewsBusters*, CNN and MSNBC combined dedicated fifty minutes to Trump's slow walk.[39] In contrast, CNN dedicated a mere fifteen seconds[40] to Biden's fall while MSNBC gave it just one minute.[41]

The headline about Trump wasn't the event; it was what the Democrats were saying about it. The headline about Biden wasn't the event, either. It was what the Democrats were saying about it.

Trump was unforgiving of the coverage his slow walk got. In our interview, he told me the steps were wet, his shoes were slick, and he knew how punishing the coverage would be if he took a tumble.

"I said to the general, get ready to hold my hand, my arm because I'm not going to fall here. . . . I took these little steps going down the ramp. That was a massive story. It totally overrode the speech. I think that was my best speech. . . . They killed me on that.

"It showed me and a lot of people how corrupt they are. When you look at these things you realize how dishonest they are," he added.

In a 2018 profile of Campbell Brown, the former NBC and CNN journalist who became a Facebook executive, the *Times* described a project Brown was working on as "far right conspiracy programming" because the project said that Palestinians paid out $400 million in pensions to terrorist families.[42]

It's a fact that the Palestinian Authority rewarded the families of terrorists who were killed or captured with large financial payments. In what world was this a far-right conspiracy? In the world of the *Times* reporter, Nellie Bowles, and her editors, that's who.

Two days later, the paper corrected the story.

"An earlier version of this article erroneously included a reference to Palestinian actions as an example of the sort of far-right conspiracy stories that have plagued Facebook. In fact, Palestinian officials have acknowledged providing payments to the families of Palestinians killed while carrying out attacks on Israelis or convicted of terrorist acts and imprisoned in Israel; that is not a conspiracy theory."[43]

In the fall of 2018, Supreme Court nominee Brett Kavanaugh's hearing in the United States Senate was derailed by allegations of sexual harassment against Kavanaugh. As the attacks on Kavanaugh mounted, the *Times* assigned more reporters to the case, including Emily Bazelon, a staff writer for the *New York Times Magazine* and a senior research scholar at Yale Law School. She is also a former senior editor of the left-wing magazine *Slate*.[44]

Bazelon is also on Twitter, where, when she heard about Kavanaugh's nomination, she posted a since-deleted tweet:

"As a @YaleLawSch grad & lecturer, I strongly disassociate myself from tonight's praise of Brett Kavanaugh. With respect, he's a 5th vote for a hard-right turn on voting rights and so much more that will harm the democratic process & prevent a more equal society."

Source: Emily Bazelon. Twitter. @emilybazelon. July 9, 2018.

Remember the meltdown in the CNN newsroom about hiring a known Republican? Do you think there was a meltdown in the *Times* newsroom about assigning a known opponent of Kavanaugh's nomination to cover the fight over his nomination? Of course not. Did *Times* editors think how this assignment might look to half the country, or to anyone who thinks fairness is important and bias in journalism is a problem?

Of course not.

Journalists and their editors think too much alike for anyone to have thought, maybe she's the wrong reporter for the job. She joined the liberal pile-on against Kavanaugh, coauthoring a story headlined, "Kavanaugh Was Questioned by Police After Bar Fight in 1985," referring to an incident in which Kavanaugh, then a junior in college, allegedly threw ice at someone. No arrests were made.[45]

After the story appeared and critics pointed out Bazelon's opinionated background, the *Times* stood by her reporting, but acknowledged they shouldn't have assigned her to the story.[46]

If Bazelon's bias isn't bad enough, there's Katie Benner. In 2021, Benner was the *New York Times'* Justice Department reporter. It's one of the most important, politically sensitive reporting jobs at the paper. Given the power and importance of Justice Department investigations, you would hope whoever the *Times* assigns to cover Justice would be especially fair-minded and impartial. It's the last place any organization should assign a reporter with an ax to grind.

Which, based on a three-thread tweet she put out on July 27, 2021, is exactly what Benner proved to have.[47]

In late July 2021, Benner covered the first hearing of Speaker Nancy Pelosi's January 6 special select committee. Benner's takeaway: In order to combat a national security threat, it was necessary to call Trump supporters "enemies of the state."

She wasn't just referring to those who rioted on January 6. Her tweets made clear she was referring to everyone who voted for Trump, which is almost half the country. "What happens if a politician seems to threaten the state. If the politician continues to do so out of office and his entire party supports that threat?"

Benner then made the case that it was up to the voters to remove these politicians from office; she put in a plug for "free and fair access to the polls," which also shows she doesn't think access to the polls currently is free or fair.

Katie Benner ✔
@ktbenner

Today's #January6thSelectCommittee underscores the America's current, essential natsec dilemma: Work to combat legitimate national security threats now entails calling a politician's supporters enemies of the state. 1/

11:06 AM · Jul 27, 2021 · Twitter Web App

157 Retweets   **168** Quote Tweets   **566** Likes

♡   ⇄   ♡   ⬆

Tweet your reply   Reply

Katie Benner ✔ @ktbenner · 5h
Replying to @ktbenner
As Americans, we believe that state power should not be used to work against a political figure or a political party. But what happens if a politician seems to threaten the state? If the politician continues to do so out of office and his entire party supports that threat? 2/

♡ 149   ⇄ 107   ♡ 216   ⬆

Katie Benner ✔ @ktbenner · 5h
This dilemma was unresolved by the Russia probe and 2 impeachments. With many Republicans denying the reality of the Jan. 6 attack, I doubt the #January6thCommittee will resolve it either. That leaves it up to voters, making even more essential free, fair access to the polls. 3/

♡ 216   ⇄ 66   ♡ 219   ⬆

Source: Katie Benner. Twitter. @ktbenner. July 27, 2021.

Benner is a dream-come-true reporter for every anti-GOP Justice Department source who now has reason to view her as simpatico with their political agenda. Who doesn't want a reporter to see the world the same liberal way they do? Republicans *are* enemies of the state—and the *New York Times* correspondent agrees. Elections *aren't* free or fair—and the *New York Times* correspondent agrees. If you're a Democrat, how delightful. It's like having liberal columnist Paul Krugman assigned to cover the Justice Department instead of a neutral, independent reporter.

After a storm of criticism broke out, Benner deleted her tweets, explaining they were "unclearly worded."

Sometimes all you can do is shake your head.

In September 2020, Tatiana Turner, a Black Lives Matter organizer, was arrested for attempted murder after driving her car into a group of pro-Trump demonstrators in Yorba Linda, California.

At National Public Radio, the story was headlined, "Woman Charged with Attempted Murder After Driving Into Pro-Trump Demonstrators."[48]

The *Los Angeles Times* headline was "Orange County rally organizer accused of running over Trump supporters faces new charges."[49]

The story was news everywhere. The liberal New York *Daily News* headline said, "California driver plows through pro-Trump rally, charged with attempted murder."[50] At the *New York Times*, it was a different story. The fact that Turner hit a pro-Trump crowd was cleaned up and suppressed.

"California Driver Charged After Striking Two Protesters, Police Say" was the *Times* headline, omitting the fact that she targeted Trump supporters.[51]

The *Times* story began, "A woman was charged with attempted murder after the car she was driving struck two people during a demonstration for racial justice in California that clashed with a counterprotest on Saturday, the authorities said."[52]

In the only reference to the pro-Trump victims, the fourth paragraph said the racial justice march "was met by a group of counter protesters, some waving 'Trump 2020' flags and wearing 'Make

America Great Again' hats."[53] The story never said these were the people she hit.

The *New York Times* is not always the place to go if you want to hear the news fully, accurately, and fairly.

Contrast the *Times*' coverage of an attempted murder against Trump supporters with the way they covered a less dangerous incident a month later, when a bus carrying Biden-Harris supporters in Texas was forced to slow down and was intimidated by a group of pro-Trump motorists.

"Vehicles flying Trump flags try to force a Biden-Harris campaign bus off a highway in Texas" is how the *Times* headlined its story, which began, "Multiple vehicles bearing Trump flags and signs surrounded a Biden-Harris campaign bus heading from San Antonio to Austin on Friday, forcing campaign officials to scrap two campaign events, according to reports by Democratic officials on Saturday."[54]

When it was attempted murder against Trump supporters, the *Times* suppressed the news. When it was intimidating Democrats on a bus, the *Times* told all. It's as if the *Times* has concluded that most of the people in America who engage in bad political deeds are uninformed, narrow-minded, intolerant Republicans. When Republicans do something wrong, the *Times* is quick to expose it. When Democrats, who really are kind and compassionate to others, engage in bad political deeds, the *Times* sometimes covers it and sometimes they don't. It's a higher hurdle to cross.

That wasn't the only bit of information the *Times* did its best to hide.

After the January 2021 riot at the Capitol, the *Times* ran a piece dismissing attempts by conservatives to compare the Capitol riot to the George Floyd protests.

"For months, Republicans have used last summer's protests as a political catchall, highlighting *isolated instances of property destruction* [emphasis added] and calls to defund the police to motivate their base in November," the *Times* story said.[55]

"Isolated instances of property destruction"? Is that what happened in the summer of 2020? Just a few isolated bits of property damage? I see.

No one disputes the legitimacy and righteousness of the peaceful protests throughout the country that called out the murder of George Floyd. Those peaceful protests were spontaneous, heartfelt, and appropriate. However, in the wake of Floyd's murder, there was a separate group of nonpeaceful looters, arsonists, and rioters who caused massive damage and destruction through violence. It was anything *but* isolated instances of property destruction.

Estimates are that the attacks that summer may become "the most costly civil disorder in United States history."[56] More than 700 police officers were injured in the first two weeks of protest, including more than 350 New York City officers,[57] 130 Chicago officers,[58] 60 United States Secret Service agents, and 40 members of the U.S. Park Police. More than 150 federal buildings were damaged.[59]

According to an article in the insurance publication *Claims Journal*, the damage caused by the riots reached "catastrophe level." The story stated, "Rioting that erupted in cities across the United States after the Memorial Day death of George Floyd in Minneapolis may rival the 1992 Los Angeles riots to become the most costly civil disorder in United States history."[60]

The *Times'* description of the widespread violence, arson, rioting, and looting that took place in the summer of 2020 as "isolated instances of property destruction" was inaccurate revisionism at its worst. It was also a fine example of activism disguised as journalism.

It's likely that most Americans, including the majority of Democrats, are unaware of how destructive the riots and looting had become, resulting in the deployment of the National Guard throughout the country.

In an effort to curb violence, at least twenty-five cities in sixteen states imposed curfews to protect their communities from looting and violence.[61] Additionally, governors in at least twenty-three states deployed their National Guard to protect their citizens, including states run by Democratic governors—California, Illinois, Michigan, Pennsylvania, Washington, and Wisconsin.[62] These Democratic governors "sent in the troops" *prior* to the *Times'* publication of Cotton's op-ed that caused the newsroom revolt. I don't recall the *Times* newsroom melting down over these *actual* deployments.

In many instances, violent rioters damaged and undermined the very community they purportedly set out to champion. In one such case, featured on National Public Radio, Chris Montana, the owner of a small Black-owned distillery business in Minneapolis, lost his livelihood to the riots.[63]

Montana told NPR, "They set multiple fires. They stole our inventory. I found cases of our booze all up and down the street. And it was the sprinkler system coming on and putting about a foot of water in the entire warehouse. That's what did most of the damage. It feels like someone punched you in the face."[64]

The NPR reporter added:

Rioting and property destruction has happened in cities across the U.S., and business owners like Chris Montana are left trying to pick up the pieces all in the middle of the worst economic crisis since the Great Depression. And they are up against some formidable odds. Bradley Hardy is an economist at American University. He has studied the economic impact of property damage and rioting on neighborhoods. Bradley looked at neighborhoods that had seen damage back in 1968. Even 20, 30 years later, Bradley says those neighborhoods never fully recovered.[65]

Community members like Montana were the actual victims of riots. So, too, were the employees of stores in Portland and Seattle that were routinely forced to close because of the near-constant violence in the streets of those cities. *They* are the people in actual danger. Reporters at the *Times* are not in danger, especially because of words that are printed in their newspaper.

At protests throughout the country in the summer of 2020, marchers chanted "silence is violence."[66] So now silence is violence. Words are violence. Opinions are violence. Heartfelt disagreement is violence. How is it violence to write about sending in the troops, as Cotton did, when it's not violence to actually send them, as numerous Democratic governors did?

How on earth did "isolated instances" slide past *Times* editors?

Maybe they feared another newsroom rebellion if they told the facts about how much destruction accompanied the 2020 protests. Maybe objectivity and truth don't stand a chance against the sentiments and opinions of those who go into news to move the needle. Or maybe the *New York Times* is not the place to find news that is full, fair, and accurate.

WHEN TRUMP TOOK OFFICE, THE *Times*' bias climbed to new heights.

In September 2018, the *Times* ran one of those "gotcha" stories, this time concerning President Trump's ambassador to the United Nations, Nikki Haley.

"Nikki Haley's View of New York Is Priceless. Her Curtains? $52,701" was the *Times*' original headline. A picture of Haley accompanied the piece so readers could see exactly whom the paper was writing about.

The story began, "The State Department spent $52,701 last year buying customized and mechanized curtains for the picture windows in Nikki R. Haley's official residence as ambassador to the United Nations, just as the department was undergoing deep budget cuts and had frozen hiring."[67]

Except that's not the full, fair, or accurate story.

As pointed out by the *Washington Post*'s media critic, Erik Wemple, buried in the middle of the *Times* story was the following statement: "A spokesman for Ms. Haley said plans to buy the curtains were made in 2016, during the Obama administration. Ms. Haley had no say in the purchase, [Haley's spokesman] said."[68] Wemple's piece was headlined "New York Times wrongs Nikki Haley with curtain headline."[69]

As the *Times* realized they blamed Haley for a decision made by the Obama administration, it scrambled to fix its headline. The cute "Priceless" headline was out. For a while, it was replaced by "State Department Spent $52,701 on Curtains for Nikki Haley's Residence," which was still unfair to Haley. That headline was then replaced by "State Department Spent $52,701 on Curtains for Residence of U.N. Envoy."[70]

Then came the correction in the form of an editor's note:

An earlier version of this article and headline created an unfair impression about who was responsible for the purchase in question. While Nikki R. Haley is the current ambassador to the United Nations, the decision on leasing the ambassador's residence and purchasing the curtains was made during the Obama administration, according to current and former officials. The article should not have focused on Ms. Haley, nor should a picture of her have been used. The article and headline have now been edited to reflect those concerns, and the picture has been removed.[71]

I remember reading the story when it came out. The spokesman's statement about the decision being made in 2016 jumped out at me. How is this a story? I thought to myself at the time. Haley had had nothing to do with it, but the *Times* put the focus on her.

Was there not a single editor at the *Times* who read the 2016 reference and didn't think, There's something wrong here? The evidence the paper needed to kill the story was right before their eyes, but they couldn't see it. The *Times* could have saved itself considerable embarrassment if its newsroom contained more people who think differently from the bubble.

Like many media outlets, the *Times'* biggest mistake of the Trump years was the amount of credibility and attention it gave to the charges that the Trump campaign colluded with Russia to steal the 2016 election, as well as the attention it gave to allegations that Trump colluded in the email account hacks of the Democratic National Committee and of John Podesta, Hillary Clinton's campaign chairman.

The *Times* also went long on coverage of the Steele Dossier, giving credibility to what turned out to be one of the most bungled, bogus stories ever reported. The paper ran more than one hundred stories that mentioned the Steele Dossier in the four years prior to the 2020 election. That's a lot of attention given to something that wasn't worth the ink it was printed with.

Even as it referred to the dossier as "unsubstantiated" and "unverified," the *Times* gave it plenty of attention. Over two consecutive days in January 2017, the paper ran eight stories focusing on the "crisis" the dossier caused for President-elect Trump.[72]

"Trump received unsubstantiated report that Russia had damaging information about him," ran one headline.

The next day, another headline read, "How a Sensational, Unverified Dossier Became a Crisis for Donald Trump."

"The consequences have been incalculable and will play out long past Inauguration Day," the *Times* wrote. The paper also referred to the dossier's author, Christopher Steele, as a "respected foreign British spy."[73]

Incalculable. Long past Inauguration Day.

What a set of understatements. Incalculable damage was done to the United States of America by a media—often led by the *New York Times*—that gave credibility to information that turned out to be purely partisan, mostly misleading, and frequently entirely wrong.

With the appointment of Robert Mueller as special counsel to investigate the collusion allegations, the *Times*, and all the media, had license to spend even *more* time on a story that was wrong from the start.

This wasn't the first time, and it won't be the last that partisans have gone to the media in an attempt to harm a political opponent. When it came to collusion, just like at CNN, if the allegations were anti-Trump they got a bump. One month later, the *Times* dropped a bombshell on the new president.

"Trump Campaign Aides Had Repeated Contacts with Russian Intelligence," screamed the *Times* headline.

The story stated:

Phone records and intercepted calls show that members of Donald J. Trump's 2016 presidential campaign and other Trump associates had repeated contacts with senior Russian intelligence officials in the year before the election, according to four current and former American officials.

American law enforcement and intelligence agencies inter-cepted the communications around the same time they were discovering evidence that Russia was trying to disrupt the presidential election by hacking into the Democratic National Committee, three of the officials said. The intelligence agencies then sought to learn whether the Trump campaign was colluding with the Russians on the hacking or other efforts to influence the election.[74]

The three journalists who wrote the story were part of *New York Times* teams that won a Pulitzer Prize for their "deeply sourced, re-lentlessly reported coverage in the public interest that dramatically furthered the nation's understanding of Russian interference in the 2016 presidential election and its connections to the Trump campaign, the President-elect's transition team and his eventual administra-tion."[75] Years later, we learned that this story, and so many others, were wrong.

In July 2020, the Senate Judiciary Committee released declassi-fied documents connected to the Russia investigation that indicated the FBI was skeptical of the dossier linking the Trump campaign to Russian intelligence. Among the released documents were notes that former FBI agent Peter Strzok—who helped lead the FBI's investiga-tion of Russian interference in the 2016 presidential election—made in the margins of the February 14 *New York Times* story. Strzok's typed annotations completely invalidated the *Times* story.

Of the *Times*' assertion that "phone records and intercepted calls" showed that the Trump campaign team had contact with Rus-sian intelligence, Strzok wrote, "This statement is misleading and inaccurate as written. We have not seen evidence of any individuals affiliated with the Trump team in contact with IOs [intelligence officials]."[76]

In another comment, Strzok noted, "We are unaware of ANY Trump advisors engaging in conversations with Russian intelligence officials."[77]

The *Times* story was wrong the day it came out. The entire narrative was wrong. But it was too late to stop it. While the FBI quietly knew the story was wrong and kept that fact to itself, the rest of the media pounced. For many reporters and countless pundits, it was the only story they wanted to talk about.

The collusion allegation dominated coverage of Trump, to the point where even after Special Counsel Robert Mueller found no evidence of Trump's collusion in the email hacks and no evidence of Trump officials colluding with Russia to interfere in the election, it was too late for the truth to catch up to the coverage.

Much of the media spent the Trump years obsessing over misinformation, disinformation, and conspiracy theories. However, very few outlets seemed concerned that they were damagingly, harmfully wrong.

As journalist and author Matt Taibbi wrote in his March 2021 newsletter, "From the much-ballyhooed 'changed RNC platform' story (Robert Mueller found no evidence the changed Republican platform was 'undertaken at the behest of candidate Trump or Russia'), to the notion that Julian Assange was engaged in a conspiracy with the Russians (Mueller found no evidence for this either), to Michael Cohen's alleged secret meetings in Prague with Russian conspirators ('not true' the FBI flatly concluded) to the story that Trump directed Cohen to lie to Congress ('not accurate,' said Mueller), to wild stories about Paul Manafort meeting Assange in the Ecuadorian embassy, to a 'bombshell' tale about Trump foreknowledge of Wikileaks releases that blew up in CNN's face in spectacular fashion, reporters for years chased unsubstantiated claims instead of waiting to see what they were based upon."[78]

How could so many reporters be so wrong, so often about something so consequential?

The reason, I suspect, is that most reporters *wanted* the collusion stories about Trump to be true. They didn't like Trump, and it showed in their copy. It showed in what they decided was news. It showed when editors didn't use wiser judgment to believe that where there is smoke, there is fire. When something is unverified and unsubstantiated, a good case can be made that it should receive little to no coverage until it *is* verified or substantiated.

But if you're anti-Trump and you think alike, act alike, and write alike, the *New York Times* is a good place to be.

And then there was "Anonymous."

If ever there was a story that showed the lengths the *New York Times* would go to get Donald Trump, "Anonymous" was it.

Miles Taylor is probably the most famous person you've never heard of, thanks to the *New York Times*. He's the author of a *Times* op-ed that appeared on September 5, 2018, under the pseudonym "Anonymous."

Taylor was a policy adviser at the Department of Homeland Security and a deputy chief of staff to the secretary of DHS when the *Times* published his anonymous opinion piece.[79] From a White House point of view, he wasn't a high-ranking official, let alone a

Opinion

I Am Part of the Resistance Inside the Trump Administration

I work for the president but like-minded colleagues and I have vowed to thwart parts of his agenda and his worst inclinations.

Source: "I Am Part of the Resistance Inside the Trump Administration," *New York Times*, September 5, 2018.

senior official at the time. (He later went on to serve as chief of staff to the secretary of DHS.)

Explaining its exceptionally rare decision to grant anonymity to an op-ed writer, the paper wrote, "The Times is taking the rare step of publishing an anonymous Op-Ed essay. We have done so at the request of the author, a senior official in the Trump administration whose identity is known to us and whose job would be jeopardized by its disclosure. We believe publishing this essay anonymously is the only way to deliver an important perspective to our readers."

At the bottom of the piece, which was sharply critical of President Trump, it said simply, "The writer is a senior official in the Trump administration."[80] If the piece had said the author was "Miles Taylor, a deputy chief of staff at the Department of Homeland Security," no one would have cared. By suppressing accurate information about the author, the *New York Times* made news. The piece hit like a flame-thrower, igniting a massive debate about the identity of the author and how brave he or she was to save the nation from Trump.

The *Times* news pages chased the *Times* op-ed page, trying to sleuth out who this high-ranking official could be.

It Wasn't Me: Pence, Pompeo and a Parade of Administration Officials Deny Writing Op-Ed

Source: Peter Baker, Maggie Haberman, and Eileen Sullivan, "It Wasn't Me: Pence, Pompeo and a Parade of Administration Officials Deny Writing Op-ed," *New York Times*, September 6, 2018.

"One by one, they came forward, almost as if in a virtual lineup. Not me, said the vice president. Nor me, said the secretary of state. Or me, said the attorney general," the *Times* reported the next day.[81]

Of course it wasn't them. It wasn't written by anyone senior, or by anyone with deep or actual insight into what was going on in the West Wing, let alone the Oval Office. In a spectacle that may be without precedent, numerous *Times* reporters peppered almost the entire cabinet and leadership team working for President Trump, asking them to plead not guilty to writing an extraordinary anonymous essay about their boss. It's amazing how the *Times* op-ed page could send the *Times* news page on such a wild-goose chase. But the *Times* must have been delighted by what it pulled off. It moved the needle. The resistance celebrated the fact that there was an underground inside the White House. Brought to you by the *New York Times*.

Except the whole thing was deceitful.

Taylor, who, after leaving DHS, campaigned against Donald Trump and endorsed Joe Biden for president, revealed himself as "Anonymous" just prior to the 2020 election, after he had written a book under the name "Anonymous."

Next time you hear that the *New York Times* has an anonymous senior source, it's worth asking, how senior is this person in reality? Are they in a position to know what's going on? Or is someone being elevated because their ideology and activism matches the ideology and activism of the paper's editors and writers? During the Trump years, anonymous sources were often wrong and senior officials sometimes weren't senior.

PERHAPS NO ONE HAS SUMMED up the changes at the *New York Times* better than Bari Weiss, the former *Times* editor who was hired to help the paper understand people in America who weren't Upper West Side liberals.

According to Weiss, she resigned from the paper because she was driven out by people who didn't want her working there. In her resignation letter, Weiss wrote that "a new consensus has emerged in the press, but perhaps especially at this paper: that truth isn't a process of

collective discovery, but an orthodoxy already known to an enlight-
ened few whose job is to inform everyone else. Twitter is not on the
masthead of The New York Times. But Twitter has become its ulti-
mate editor."

In a devastating reflection on what is happening inside the
Times, Weiss added:

> The paper of record is, more and more, the record of those living
> in a distant galaxy, one whose concerns are profoundly removed
> from the lives of most people. This is a galaxy in which, to choose
> just a few recent examples, the Soviet space program is lauded
> for its "diversity"; the doxxing of teenagers in the name of justice
> is condoned; and the worst caste systems in human history in-
> cludes the United States alongside Nazi Germany.
>
> Even now, I am confident that most people at The Times do
> not hold these views. Yet they are cowed by those who do. Why?
> Perhaps because they believe the ultimate goal is righteous.
> Perhaps because they believe that they will be granted protec-
> tion if they nod along as the coin of our realm—language—is de-
> graded in service to an ever-shifting laundry list of right causes.
> Perhaps because there are millions of unemployed people in this
> country and they feel lucky to have a job in a contracting industry.
>
> Or perhaps it is because they know that, nowadays, stand-
> ing up for principle at the paper does not win plaudits. It puts a
> target on your back. Too wise to post on Slack, they write to me
> privately about the "new McCarthyism" that has taken root at
> the paper of record.
>
> All this bodes ill, especially for independent-minded young
> writers and editors paying close attention to what they'll have
> to do to advance in their careers. Rule One: Speak your mind at

your own peril. Rule Two: Never risk commissioning a story that goes against the narrative. Rule Three: Never believe an editor or publisher who urges you to go against the grain. Eventually, the publisher will cave to the mob, the editor will get fired or reassigned, and you'll be hung out to dry.[82]

Chapter Nine

ACTIVISTS FOR A CAUSE

Sometimes reporters just give themselves away. It's almost as if they *want* their bias to show.

> Between workouts during his Hawaii vacation this week, [President-elect Obama] was photographed looking like the paradigm of a new kind of presidential fitness, one geared less toward preventing heart attacks than winning swimsuit competitions. The sun glinted off chiseled pectorals sculpted during four weightlifting sessions each week, and a body toned by regular treadmill runs and basketball games.[1]
>
> —*Washington Post*, December 25, 2008

> The contrast on display tonight was so stark, I mean those lights that are just shooting out of the Lincoln Memorial along the Reflecting Pool . . . it's like almost extensions of Joe Biden's arms embracing America. It was a moment where the new president

came to town and sort of convened the country in this moment
of remembrance, outstretching his arms.[2]

—CNN political director David Chalian, January 19, 2021

Obama's chiseled pectorals. Joe Biden's embracing arms. You have
to love journalists who know how to swoon. Time after time, when it
comes to expressing preferences for people and policies, most of the me-
dia line up behind the Democrats. It's not just their thumb that's on the
scale. Sometimes it's their entire writing hand, plus much of their body.

This bias shows up in numerous ways as reporters cover the news.
It shows up in how they decide what is and what isn't news, in how they
frame their stories, and in whom they favor or oppose in a political
campaign or policy debate.

It's become increasingly common for Democrats to only subscribe
to publications that reinforce their points of view—and there are many
publications and cable outlets that love Obama, support Biden, take
pro-choice positions, fight against climate change, push for a $15
minimum wage, and advocate on behalf of people entering America
illegally. Most mainstream reporters share similar worldviews—and
their copy too often shows it.

In all areas, journalists should be neutral. They should be neutral in
campaign coverage. They should be neutral in policy coverage. But all
too often, they are not. They have preferences and take sides. And, con-
sequently, they distort the news. When it comes to policy—the essence
of government—this bias is particularly evident in stories involving
social issues, especially abortion. It shows up in stories about eco-
nomic policy, with much of the press receptive to spending increases
but dismissive of tax cuts. And it shows up regularly in coverage of
political races, riots, and even of COVID-19.

The mother of all social issues is abortion. Pro-life Republicans have a much harder time getting the press to cover their story than pro-choice Democrats. I experienced firsthand the difference between how a pro-choice and a pro-life president is treated by the media at one of my first briefings as White House press secretary.

As I recounted in my previous book, *Taking Heat*, President George W. Bush ran on a promise that he would prohibit the use of taxpayer funds overseas to promote abortion. On one of his first days in office in 2001, President Bush issued an executive order restoring the prohibition that was in place under President Reagan and President George H. W. Bush.[3]

President Bush's reinstatement of the policy wasn't a surprise; the policy has been rescinded and reinstated along party lines since it was first announced by the Reagan administration in 1984.[4] Republicans put in the prohibition. Democrats take it out. In 1992, Bill Clinton ran on a promise to remove the prohibition and fulfilled his campaign promise by signing an executive order two days after his inauguration that allowed for the use of taxpayer dollars to promote abortion overseas.[5]

Much of the press supported what Clinton did and opposed what Bush did. They took sides in their reporting, and it was obvious. I was hit at my briefing with forty-one mostly hostile questions about Bush's action.[6] Clinton's spokesman, George Stephanopoulos, got just six questions about Clinton's action, two of them hopefully asking if President Clinton might fund additional abortions, including those for women in the military.[7]

Network news coverage that night demonstrated how the press can twist and turn a story to tell it whichever way they want, which typically means in a way that helps Democrats.[8]

"President Clinton kept a promise today on the twentieth anniversary of the Supreme Court decision legalizing abortion," ABC's Peter Jennings reported on January 22, 1993.

Flash forward eight years.

"President Bush also made antiabortion conservatives happy, re-installing a Reagan-era policy that prohibited the funding of family planning groups that provide abortion counseling services overseas," ABC's Terry Moran reported on January 22, 2001.

Clinton kept a promise. Bush made conservatives happy. Why didn't ABC News lead with the fact that Bush kept a promise, or that Clinton made liberals happy? Why not say they both kept a promise, or they both made partisans happy? Because that's not how reporting works—not then and not now. Covering it that way would be fair, and when it comes to abortion coverage especially, the press is not fair. They happily take sides.

Dan Rather at CBS was worse.

"Today with the stroke of a pen, President Clinton delivered on his campaign promise to cancel several anti-abortion regulations of the Reagan-Bush years," Rather told his audience on January 22, 1993.

Here's the same guy, Dan Rather, eight years later. "This was President Bush's first day at the office, and he did something to quickly please the right flank in his party," Rather reported.

Clinton delivered on a promise. Bush pleased his right flank. Thanks, Dan. Your bias is showing.

On January 19, 2011, a grand jury in Pennsylvania accused a Philadelphia abortion doctor of killing babies and endangering their mothers. The grand jury's report was 281 pages long, full of graphic details about the killings. The doctor was Kermit Gosnell, whose usual method of abortion was to use scissors to snip the spinal cord of babies who were born alive, in effect beheading them.[9]

According to one account from a movie made about the killings, Gosnell was America's biggest serial killer.[10]

Conservative *Washington Post* columnist George Will wrote, "No one knows how many—certainly hundreds, probably thousands—

spinal cords Gosnell snipped before the 2010 raid on his 'clinic.' Law enforcement came looking for illegal drugs. They also found jars of babies' feet, fetal remains in toilets and milk cartons, and a pervasive smell of cat feces—in a facility that had not been inspected for 17 years. Pennsylvania nail salons receive biennial inspections."[11]

Gosnell's trial for seven counts of first-degree murder began on March 18, 2013,[12, 13] although you wouldn't have known it since much of the national media ignored it. In Pennsylvania, cameras are not allowed in courtrooms, but that alone doesn't explain the lack of interest from the national press, which typically pounces on trials of a horrifying nature.

What's more, by 2013, sensationalized news coverage of trials was commonplace. Television's obsession with trials began decades earlier—from the Menendez brothers to Lorena Bobbitt.[14] The superstar of dramatic televised trials was in 1995, when former NFL star O. J. Simpson was tried for the murder of his ex-wife Nicole Brown and her friend Ronald Goldman. Trials became must-see TV, with commentary by expert contributors and wall-to-wall, minute-by-minute coverage. Cable television loves a trial, even if they can't go live from the courtroom.

Except for Kermit Gosnell's trial. Not when the issue was late-term abortion, and the victims were mostly poor, inner-city women and their babies.

CNN gave Gosnell's trial a twenty-four-second mention on March 21.[15] The network didn't cover it again until April 12,[16] when it and other national news media were shamed into coverage by social media decrying the lack of press.[17] MSNBC didn't cover it at all until April 15.[18, 19] FOX News covered it on March 21, March 24, March 25, and March 26. Coverage then accelerated beginning April 12.

What makes the failure to cover the trial odd is the fact that most of the mainstream media devoted significant attention to Gosnell's

2011 indictment. It was gruesome and was covered prominently by the networks, along with CNN and the *New York Times*.

The trial, however, became another (lack of) story.

In late March, Christopher Harper wrote a column in the conservative *Washington Times* calling out the lack of media coverage.[20] One week later, Mike Ozanian, a sports reporter at *Forbes* magazine, wrote a column pointing out that Rutgers University basketball coach Mike Rice, who was fired for his rough treatment of his players, got more media attention than the trial of Gosnell.[21]

"Gosnell apparently made a fortune running a slaughterhouse. It went unnoticed for decades. How many clinics are being run like Gosnell's in this country? Isn't it worth a look into by the media and politicians? How much of this story have you seen on the evening news? I bet not nearly as much as you have seen about Rice," Ozanian wrote.[22]

The following week, Kirsten Powers wrote a column for *USA Today* that shamed the media for its inattention to the abortion doctor's trial. She pointed out, *"The Washington Post* has not published original reporting on this during the trial and *The New York Times* saw fit to run one original story on A-17 on the trial's first day. They've been silent ever since, despite headline-worthy testimony."[23]

To drive it home deeper, Powers wryly noted, "When Rush Limbaugh attacked Sandra Fluke, there was nonstop media hysteria. The venerable *NBC Nightly News*' Brian Williams intoned 'A firestorm of outrage from women after a crude tirade from Rush Limbaugh,' as he teased a segment on the brouhaha. Yet, accusations of babies having their heads severed—a major human rights story if there ever was one—doesn't make the cut."[24] Fluke, a law student at Georgetown University who advocated for mandatory contraceptive insurance coverage, was called a "slut" by Limbaugh. He later apologized.

These three journalists were right. If newsrooms had more reporters like them, the media might start to look more like America, and therefore do a better job covering America. For college-educated, mostly Democratic thinkers, abortion should always be legal and those who oppose it are narrow-minded, intolerant backward thinkers. Who would want to rub shoulders with pro-life people in a newsroom?

As journalist David Weigel wrote in a *Slate* piece, "Let's just state the obvious: National political reporters are, by and large, socially liberal. . . . We are, generally, pro-choice. Twice, in D.C., I've caused a friend to literally leave a conversation and freeze me out for a day or so because I suggested that the Stupak Amendment and the Hyde Amendment made sense. There *is* a bubble. Horror stories of abortionists are less likely to permeate that bubble than, say, a story about a right-wing pundit attacking an abortionist who then claims to have gotten death threats."[25]

When a doctor goes on trial for a series of horrendous baby murders, the media know if they give the story attention, it will likely cause people to think twice about abortion. Covering the ongoing story, as opposed to the one-time indictment, will generate sympathy for the pro-life movement—a movement that I would say has precious few adherents in most newsrooms. Republicans often see stories like Gosnell's and think about how many more atrocities like this are out there, and doubt the media will look into it. The mainstream media, meanwhile, look at the Gosnell horror show and think it's an isolated incident. When the story line hurts Republicans, the press often dig deep and repeatedly into it. When the story line hurts the Democrats, the media know how to skip right past it, especially on social issues.

Similarly, the press lionizes one side in the abortion debate. Just ask former Democratic state senator Wendy Davis in Texas.

Wendy Davis was a state senator who in June 2013 famously filibustered a bill in the Texas Senate that would have prohibited abortions after twenty weeks. In the aftermath of the Gosnell killings, the bill also increased regulations for abortion clinics. Davis spoke in opposition to these measures for eleven hours on the floor of the state Senate, wearing pink sneakers.[26]

The media loved her for it, celebrated her, and rallied to her side. They didn't need a columnist to make them cover her that way. The coverage came naturally. It's how much of the media think when they decide what is and isn't news. Gosnell's murder trial was not news. Wendy Davis's pro-abortion filibuster was.

Calling her filibuster a "national phenomenon," CNN headlined its story about Davis's path, "From teen mom to Harvard Law to famous filibuster."[27] *Vogue* magazine profiled Davis, calling her an "overnight sensation."[28] The story oozed about her character. "Her warmth is genuine and profound, if just a hair shy of maternal." She's a "stunning blonde," *Vogue* wrote,[29] falling just short of describing her glittering pectorals.

"Wendy Davis has become a national political star and charismatic new face of women's rights," chirped the *New York Times*.[30]

In a sign of how the left's feedback loop works, Hollywood actors and actresses spoke out on Davis's behalf.[31] President Obama praised her.[32] She got a book deal. The cultural left had a new, instant heroine.[33] The press made Davis famous, and then they wrote about how she had become famous. Instantly, an unknown state senator was propelled into a soft, glowing, friendly national limelight.

The Sunday shows booked her and threw softball questions at her.

As pointed out by conservative *New York Times* opinion writer Ross Douthat, then–ABC News senior Washington correspondent Jeff Zeleny asked Davis six questions—every one of them a softball, including two questions about her shoes.

Q: Why did you decide to wear your running shoes? Let's take a look at those . . . they've kind of been rocketing around the internet.

Q: As the filibuster was going on, you were receiving a lot of support from places and people far away from Texas, from movie stars, from the president. . . .

Q: The front page of the *Fort Worth Star-Telegram* is featuring the back and forth with Governor Perry and you. He has made this very personal against you. [Shows video clip of Governor Perry's criticisms.] Is that offensive?

Q: Do you believe that SB5 [Senate Bill 5] will become law?

Q: Will you have to filibuster again?

Q: You gonna put these shoes on again, or?[34]

Zeleny could have asked Davis her thoughts on the Gosnell trial, wondering if there might be any abortion clinics in Texas that had questionable safety practices requiring greater regulation. He could have asked her how late in a pregnancy she would allow abortions. He could have asked her when life begins. He could have asked any number of questions showing there are two sides to every issue. He asked no such questions. On most Sunday shows, Republicans know they're going to get grilled and drilled. For most Democrats, it's a comparatively easy day to roll out the talking points.

Davis, it should be noted, took the fame the media bestowed upon her and ran with it—literally. She ran for governor and for Congress, raising massive amounts of money due to her media-given fame. She lost both times. Unfortunately for her, she wasn't running in a seat that was populated mostly by reporters.

How many times will the media do this to the American people? Republicans must work twice as hard to get to the same starting point as Democrats. Republicans must battle through a media filter that opposes them on most issues. For Democrats, the gates are often wide open. Being pro-choice is a solid place to start if you're a Democrat who wants to gain the favor of the national press. To paraphrase an exchange between F. Scott Fitzgerald and Ernest Hemingway, the media are different from you and me. The platitudes the press heaped upon Davis reflected their natural thinking. Who among them wasn't enthralled by her filibuster? Who didn't think she stood and fought and spoke for an issue vital to so many? And weren't her shoes pretty?

The press propped Davis up, but failed to see that roughly half the country thinks differently than they do. When the media move as a virtual block and heap praise on an unknown politician who holds a liberal point of view, especially on abortion, the media give themselves away. They lose trust. They take sides. Soft and biased coverage like this also deceives Democratic viewers who, surrounded by like-minded coverage, can't imagine how anyone, other than the most uninformed and intolerant among us, could see the world differently.

Just ask Abby Johnson.

For eight years, Johnson worked for Planned Parenthood, where she eventually served as clinic director. Johnson's experience assisting with an ultrasound-guided abortion compelled her to reevaluate her support for abortions and ultimately moved her to become a leader in the pro-life community.[35] In 2020, Johnson spoke at the Republican National Convention.

Source: NBC News, Republican National Convention livestreamed
(1:15:43 and 1:16:14 video marker), August 25, 2020.

NBC News streamed Johnson's RNC speech with its own chyron underneath reading, "Abby Johnson Opponent of Abortion Rights."[36]

As the *Federalist* pointed out, "Any number of other descriptors would have been more accurate—'pro-life activist,' 'anti-abortion spokeswoman,' 'former Planned Parenthood employee'—but the mainstream media just doesn't know when to quit."[37]

I don't recall NBC News covering a speaker who supports gun control with the chyron "opposes gun rights."

That's how media bias works. If you support what the press supports, you're part of the solution. If you support what the press opposes, you're part of the opposition. Mainstream media reporters will deny they take a stand on issues. On abortion, many of them do.

RUNNING FOR PRESIDENT IN 2020, Joe Biden made a promise to the American people, based on a faulty assumption. He said, "I will raise taxes for anybody making over $400,000. Let me tell you why I'm going to do it. It's about time they start paying a fair share of the economic responsibility we have. The very wealthy should pay [their] fair share.... I'm not punishing anybody. This is about everybody paying their fair share."[38]

How do you define "fair share"? For years, Democratic politicians have said the same thing, and the press duly quotes them. Almost half the American people have been relieved of the burden of paying income taxes, so if income taxes are raised or cut, the impact will fall disproportionately on the few people who pay them.

According to the latest information from the Tax Foundation,[39] the top 10 percent, people making more than $151,935, made 48 percent of all the money and paid 71.4 percent of all income taxes.

And the bottom 50 percent? Those with an income less than $43,614 made 11.6 percent of all the money and paid 3.4 percent of all income taxes.

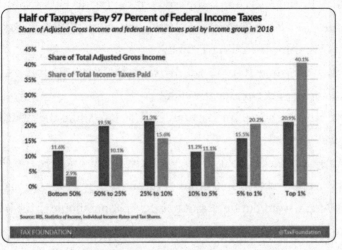

Source: "Half of Taxpayers Pay 97 Percent of Federal Income Taxes," Tax Foundation, February 3, 2021.

A simpler way to put it: Half the taxpayers pay 97 percent of federal income taxes.

But since the top 1 percent made 20.1 percent of all the money, shouldn't they pay 20.1 percent of all income taxes? Wouldn't that be fair? But they actually pay 40.1 percent of all the income taxes, which is about twice the share they made. You could say they're paying more than their fair share.

The top 10 percent made 48 percent of all the money. Wouldn't it be fair if they paid 48 percent of all the income tax? They actually pay 71.4 percent of all income taxes, so you could say they, too, are paying more than their fair share.

What about the bottom 50 percent of taxpayers? Those taxpayers, half the country, made 11.6 percent of all the money while paying 3.4 percent of all income taxes. They've mostly been forgiven the burden of paying any income tax at all. But for politicians who want more money to spend, and for their media cheerleaders, fair is never fair enough.

When President Trump proposed a sweeping tax cut in September 2017, the *New York Times* headlined one story, "Trump Tax Plan Benefits Wealthy, Including Trump."[40]

It was the same story at the *Washington Post*. "Trump's tax 'reform' looks like tax cuts for the rich."[41]

At CNN, anchor John Berman said "it looks like the wealthy do pretty well here."[42]

If only the media told the news fully, fairly, and accurately, the country would have a better understanding of how the tax code works. People would understand how few people shoulder the income tax burden.

When a politician says someone needs to pay their "fair share," the media should demand the politician define "fair share" and hold the politician's feet to the fire. The press should point out how a few people shoulder so much of the income tax burden, way out of proportion to the money they make. That would be fair coverage, but since it would blow up the Democratic argument about paying a fair share, the press won't do it. Instead, they repeat Democratic talking points about tax cuts for the wealthy and making the rich pay their fair share. The press will deny it, but because of how they tilt their stories, they actively take sides in public policy debates. It's not the conservative side they take.

In 2019, after the 2017 tax reforms and easing of federal regulations went into effect, the economy boomed. The poverty rate reached its lowest level since 1959. Income rose at one of the fastest rates on record, with the largest gains going to Hispanic, Black, and Asian households.[43] Manufacturing jobs grew at the fastest rate in twenty-three years, and the unemployment rate for Americans without a high school diploma reached the lowest point ever recorded.[44] The unemployment rate for Black and Hispanic workers reached record lows. Income inequality declined.[45]

All these gains were blown away by the COVID-19 crisis of 2020. But, if every time, a reporter replaced "tax cut for the rich" headlines with "the 2017 tax cuts helped all Americans," the news would be more accurate.

Not only does much of the media take the Democrats' side on tax policy, they often extend their pro-Democratic spin to the politics of tax cuts. Here's one take in the *Washington Post* after the 2017 tax bill passed.

"Republicans just passed a tax bill. Democrats think the GOP just signed its death certificate," opined the *Post* in an "analysis" from December 2017.[46]

The story began with quotes from two Democratic senators, Joe Donnelly (D-IN) and Claire McCaskill (D-MO), both of whom opposed the new tax law.

"Democrats have calculated that a mix of public perception and the popularity of populism has made this bill toxic to voters. They are convinced that cutting taxes for the wealthy and corporations while giving the middle class a temporary tax cut strikes the wrong tone. And polls suggest Democrats are right," the *Post* wrote.[47]

Donnelly and McCaskill are now former senators, both having lost their reelection bids in 2018. So much for those polls and that *Post* story.

Contrast the negative coverage of the tax cuts with the fawning coverage of President Biden's 2021 spending sprees. The tilt was overwhelmingly hostile to Republican tax cuts but strongly supportive of Biden's blowout spending spree, only a small portion of which went to COVID relief.

Even before Biden took office, his massive spending proposals were well received by the press.

"Biden Outlines $1.9 Trillion Spending Package to Combat Virus and Downturn," the *New York Times* headlined a story in mid-January

2021. "The president-elect plans for an initial effort to fight the coronavirus and a subsequent one to address economic recovery" was the subheadline.[48]

Unlike most of the stories about Trump's tax cut, which criticized Trump for adding to the deficit, the only mention of the deficit in this story was a statement by economists who urged Congress to "deficit spend in order to promote economic growth."[49] Note that the 2017 tax cut that many reporters derided for adding to the deficit was $1.5 trillion over *ten* years.[50] Biden's spending bill was $1.9 trillion—over *one* year.

The next day, another story in the *Times*—this time in the paper's business pages—pointed out how much money the Biden plan would spend, but it then made the case for why deficits don't matter.[51]

As the Biden plan passed Congress, the media fell all over themselves to praise the Democratic law.

"Biden Lifts Up Poor to Jolt the Recovery," read a front-page *New York Times* headline.[52]

SENATE APPROVES
$1.9 TRILLION IN AID
FOR AILING NATION

Biden Lifts Up Poor to Jolt the Recovery	Partisan Vote After All-Night Session

Source: *New York Times*, March 7, 2021.

The soft coverage continued, with another *Times* story headlined, "In the Stimulus Bill, a Policy Revolution in Aid for Children."[53]

The soft coverage persisted at the *Washington Post*. "Relief bill is most significant legislation for Black farmers since Civil Rights Act, experts say."[54]

Each of these pro-Biden headlines was a snapshot based on items in Biden's spending bill. The GOP tax bill also included items that could have merited snapshot, headline coverage. For example, the 2017 tax reform almost doubled the standard deduction for joint returns from $13,000 to $24,000,[55] a major benefit to lower-income taxpayers and families.

I don't recall many headlines in the mainstream media focused on that fact. "Tax Cut Provides Big Boost to Low-Income Families" would have been an accurate headline for the GOP tax cut. Instead, there were stories that mentioned the doubling of the standard deduction inside stories that were critical of the overall tax cut.

The 2017 tax cut doubled the maximum child tax credit from $1,000 to $2,000, another major break for lower- to middle-income families.[56] I don't recall many headlines in the mainstream media focused on that fact, either. "GOP Lifts Poor with Expansion of Aid for Children" would have been an accurate headline.

The *Washington Post* ran one analysis headlined, "Single moms are the darlings of Republicans' tax-cut speeches."[57] The story focused on how the GOP was pitching its plan as a benefit for single moms. See that? The media was full of declarative headlines about how good Biden's spending would be for the poor. When it came to headlines for the GOP, the best this one *Post* story could do was to declare that this is what the GOP claims.

Even as the press gave glowing support to Biden's proposals, the *Post* framed the story entirely from a pro-Democrat, pro-Biden, pro-spending point of view.

As Biden campaigned for his spending plans, he taunted Republicans, demanding to know what changes they would make to his spending spree, falsely labeling any Republican counteroffer "a cut." The *Post* went right along, headlining its story, "Biden to critics of $1.9 trillion relief plan: 'What would they have me cut?'"[58]

The story's lede framed everything the way Joe Biden wanted it.

President Biden mounted a strong defense Friday of his $1.9 trillion coronavirus relief plan, addressing GOP critics who say it's too big and asking, "What would they have me cut?"

"Should we not invest 20 billion dollars to vaccinate the nation?" Biden asked during a visit to a Pfizer plant in Kalamazoo, Mich. "Should we not invest 50 billion dollars to help small businesses stay open when tens of thousands have had to close permanently?"

"How many people do you know will go to bed tonight staring at the ceiling saying, 'God, what is going to happen if I don't get my job, if I don't have my unemployment check?'" Biden added.[59]

Anyone see the problem here?

Every single penny of the $1.9 trillion Biden proposed was a spending increase. Only in liberal Washington is an increase in spending less than the one Biden proposed "a cut." But in this instance, the *Washington Post* uncritically went along with Biden's false framework.

Let's say the final package approved was a $1 trillion plan. That would be a $1 trillion spending increase. *Nothing* would be cut. Not a single penny. But by accepting Biden's framework, anything less than the amount of money Biden wanted was "a cut." What nonsense. What bias. That's one reason why Washington spends so much. It's also an example of how the press's policies and preferences match the Democrats' and are inimical to GOP ideas.

Think of it this way. A future Republican president calls for a $1.9 trillion tax cut. He or she then states that anything less than that would be a "tax hike." The mainstream media would never frame the debate that way. They would jump all over the Republican president for the false framing of an issue. Biden did it and the press supported him. Republicans can't do things like that. At least not according to the media.

Over at *Punchbowl*, reporters wrote a story early in Biden's first year asking what the two parties stand for.

"Democrats, of course, will follow President Joe Biden's lead—a surprisingly progressive approach to governing that's designed to be a blend between compassion and competence," *Punchbowl News* wrote, summarizing the Democratic approach to government.[60]

A blend between compassion and competence. How nice.

The Republican Party, they continued, "used to be for fiscal discipline and balanced budgets, but they no longer are. Their 2017 tax cuts blew up the deficit, and they had no problem running up the red ink under Trump. They can't make a case for fiscal discipline anymore."[61]

I see. Biden's spending is compassionate, and I guess it doesn't increase the deficit. Republican tax cuts, which resulted in the lowest poverty levels since 1959,[62] are not labeled as compassionate, but they sure blew up the deficit. It's always good to see straightforward, neutral reporting.

Even the words used by most reporters to describe Democratic policies betray bias.

Knowing that many voters are resistant to expanding the size of government by enacting major new spending programs, Democrats shifted their rhetoric during the Clinton years from the word *spending* to the word *investment*.[63] To listen to a Democrat, you'd think they don't spend money. They invest it.

I'm sorry. An investment is when I take *my* money, put it somewhere, and get back *more* money in return.

Government spending is government spending. It's anyone's argument about whether society gets more in return as a result of government spending, but the blanket description of government spending as an "investment" is a loaded and biased use of the word.

In March 2021, Biden went to the Carpenters Pittsburgh Training Center in Pittsburgh to make the case for a new $2 trillion spending

proposal. Biden said it was aimed at rebuilding America's infrastruc-
ture, along with a list of other items the Democrats have long wanted
to spend money on.

In thirty-two minutes of remarks, the president used the word
investment thirteen times.[64] "It's a once-in-a-generation investment
in America, unlike anything we've seen or done since we built the
Interstate Highway System and the Space Race decades ago. In fact,
it's the largest American jobs investment since World War Two,"
Biden said.

A week later at the White House, the president gave follow-up
remarks urging passage of his $2 trillion spending bill. He used the
word *investment* nine times. He never used the words *spend* or
spending.[65] The press, for the most part, went right along with him.

"Biden, in Pennsylvania, Details $2 Trillion Infrastructure Plan,"
headlined the *New York Times*. The story used the word *investment*
eleven times, often quoting Biden but also using the word as the pa-
per's own description of Biden's spending plan.[66]

At the *Washington Post*, the headline was more balanced, but the
story relied on the switcheroo of words from "spending" to "invest-
ment."

"White House unveils $2 trillion infrastructure and climate plan,
setting up giant battle over size and cost of government" was the
Post headline.

The story, however, stated, "Biden's plan also includes measures
unrelated to either infrastructure or the climate, such as an approx-
imately $400 billion *investment* in home-based care for the elderly
and disabled that was a top demand of some union groups. . . . Biden's
plan lays out a large *investment* in clean-energy and environmental
priorities"[67] (emphasis added). The Democrats' talking point was car-
ried verbatim by the *Washington Post*.

Biden wasn't done spending money. Later that month, the president released details of his budget for annual domestic spending. In a story that, to the credit of the *New York Times*, repeatedly used the words *spend* and *spending*, the investment angle still found its way into print.

"Mr. Biden proposed *investing* $861 million in Central America, part of the four-year $4 billion package the administration has committed to spending to improve the economy and quality of life in the region. Another $1.2 billion would go toward *investing* in border security technology, such as sensors to detect illegal crossings and tools to improve entry ports"[68] (emphasis added).

The *Washington Post*'s coverage of the Biden budget went straight for the Democrats' favorite word. "President Biden on Friday asked Congress to authorize a massive $1.5 trillion federal spending plan later this year, seeking to *invest* heavily in a number of government agencies to boost education, expand affordable housing, bolster public health and confront climate change,"[69] read the lede (emphasis added).

The story continued, "Many of the programs Biden seeks to fund at higher levels starting in October are initiatives that President Donald Trump had unsuccessfully tried to slash while in the White House."[70] Democrats invest. Republicans slash. I see how it works.

On CNN, it was a Biden White House wordsmithing dream come true.

"President Biden is enlisting members of his cabinet to go out and sell his American Jobs Plan. It's a historic *investment* in infrastructure, climate, and technology nationwide," reported CNN *Early Start* anchor Laura Jarrett[71] (emphasis added).

"It goes way beyond just modernizing highways, roads and bridges. It also *invests* $600 billion across manufacturing, research and development in areas like climate, science and job training," CNN anchor Don Lemon told his viewers[72] (emphasis added).

"The plan calls for a $16 billion *investment* to close unused oil and gas wells," said CNN chief business correspondent and *Early Start* anchor Christine Romans[73] (emphasis added).

Punchbowl described the environmental spending in Biden's infrastructure plan as "a package that includes the most significant green *investment* in decades"[74] (emphasis added).

My point here is not that reporters have abandoned the use of the words *spending* or *spend* to describe Democratic policies. They do use those terms. But objective journalists shouldn't take a page out of the Democratic spin book to replace the word *spend* with the word *invest*.

Republicans are also calculated in their word choices. For example, when rich people die, their assets could be subject to estate and inheritance taxes. Republicans, who think it's wrong for people to pay taxes while they're alive and then pay taxes again on the same money when they're dead, tried to rename the estate tax. It's a "death tax," they said.

While the press readily accepted the Democratic word *investment* as a synonymous replacement for *spending*, they didn't go for the Republican rhetorical shift.

Throughout the 2017 tax debate, the *New York Times* and the *Washington Post* consistently referred to the tax in question as the "estate tax."

The only times that the two papers referred to the tax as the "death tax" was when the papers identified the tax as the "estate tax," and then subsequently noted that Republicans refer to the same tax by a different name. Here are the three instances when the *Post* used the term *death tax* in articles during the height of the 2017 tax debate.

"The estate tax, often described by Republicans as the 'death tax'..."[75]

"In the end, the estate tax (often called the 'death tax' by
opponents) . . ."[76]

"At one point, Phillips was shown describing the estate tax
as 'the death tax' . . ."[77]

The *Times* used *death tax* four times. Here are the first three
instances:

"An exemption for estates that owe what Republicans call the
'death tax' was lifted to $22 million from $11 million."[78]

"The House bill ultimately kills the estate tax, which Repub-
licans refer to as the death tax, because it is a tax on wealthy
estates that are left to heirs."[79]

"Almost all Republicans agree philosophically that the estate
tax—or, as they call it, the death tax—is unfair."[80]

If the *Post* and *Times* journalists were fair and consistent, they
would frame spending stories the same way they frame tax stories.
They would report that "Democrats use the term *investment*" to de-
scribe government spending or that "Democrats call spending an in-
vestment." But they don't. The media parrots the Democrats.

And then there's this—an especially loaded instance of the *Times*
printing the "death tax" nomenclature during the 2017 tax debates:

"The House bill fully repeals the so-called death tax," reported the
Times.[81] Anyone think the *Times* called Biden's trillion-dollar spend-
ing spree a "so-called investment"? It didn't.

The biased use of words is a regular tactic in the press—with terms
overwhelmingly tilted in favor of the left. Republicans refer to people
who enter the United States illegally as "illegal aliens." Democrats re-
fer to them as "undocumented immigrants," as if they just happened
to leave their paperwork lying around somewhere. Most of the media

use the Democratic phrase. The *Washington Post* in 2021 went so far as calling illegal immigration "irregular migration."[82] If someone is an "illegal alien," they're subject to deportation. If they're an "immigrant," America should welcome them. The words most often used by the press show they're neither neutral nor accurate.

Whatever action Democrats take concerning Election Day activities, the media's favorite words are "voter rights." When Republicans enact safeguards to reduce fraud or errors, including cleaning up voter rolls so they're accurate, the measures are reported as "voter suppression." The list of loaded words used by reporters to support Democratic positions is long.

Matthew Cooper describes himself as a contributing editor for *Washingtonian* magazine and *Washington Monthly*. He used to report for *Time* and *Newsweek*.[83]

In early 2021, Cooper tweeted that the Tea Party uprising of 2010—objecting to the increased spending proposals and bigger government of the Obama years—represented "the politics of resentment."

Politics of resentment? Let that sink in. A widespread, grassroots movement united around the notion that the government is too big, spends too much, is wasteful, and doesn't improve the lives of most Americans is dismissed as the "politics of resentment." Next thing you know, he'll call Republicans deplorables.

A surprising issue in the early Biden years was the treatment of transgender people. Biden entered office and quickly issued several executive orders to protect "transgender rights." As state legislatures dealt with many delicate and nuanced issues that arise from the medical procedures involved with adolescents who undergo sex change operations, much of the media decried Republicans for engaging in "culture wars."[84]

No matter what anyone's point of view is toward a young person who is figuring out how they define themselves—personally, legally, or physically—saying one side is for "rights" and the other is for a "culture war" is not good or thoughtful journalism. It's another way the press is dismissive of one side of an issue while being supportive of the other side. Once again, the framework adopted by the media matches the framework of one political party. The Democratic Party.

It's the same biased approach reporters took to President Obama's 2012 convention speech, in which he focused on social issues, a change for the Democrats. Obama, who had previously opposed gay marriage, changed his position and made it a centerpiece of his 2012 convention.[85] His campaign called for increasing immigration and mandating that health insurance plans included contraception coverage, even for Catholic nuns.[86] Much of the media lauded Obama's emphasis on social issues. To them, Obama wasn't engaging in a culture war because most of the mainstream media agreed with his positions.

When Democrats discuss social issues, the soft, supportive media coverage typically characterizes them as modern, engaging leaders. When Republicans discuss social issues, media coverage typically characterizes them as backward, intolerant people waging a culture war.

When it comes to policies, the press has preferences. Too often, the Democratic Party starts the debate in a favored position with the media while the Republican Party's positions are assumed to be bad for the country. Add that to the long list of reasons the press have lost the trust of so many people.

Chapter Ten

RACES, RIOTS,
AND COVID

In June 2020, New York State assemblyman Michael Blake ran for
Congress in a primary against New York City councilman Ritchie
Torres. Both candidates were Black Democrats. On Primary Day,
Blake found himself in second place behind Torres, a position Blake
refused to accept.

Instead of admitting defeat, Blake alleged that a series of voting
irregularities took place and charged, "Intentional black voter sup-
pression and undemocratic processes clearly don't just happen in the
South but also in the South Bronx. These incidents, among others,
are too pervasive to be a coincidence. They are a concerted effort to
suppress the Black vote."[1]

A Black candidate running against a Black candidate, in a Dem-
ocratic primary, in an overwhelmingly Democratic county (Bronx
County), in an overwhelmingly Democratic state, blamed his defeat
on race-based voter suppression.

In another Democratic congressional primary that same year in a different part of New York City, incumbent congresswoman Carolyn Maloney, a confidante of Speaker Nancy Pelosi, was challenged by Suraj Patel, a former Obama campaign aide. Maloney won on Election Day by 648 votes, but tens of thousands of absentee and mail ballots were yet to be counted. Election experts said most of the absentees were from Manhattan, which meant they would favor Maloney. Patel, realizing that his dream of defeating Maloney might slip away, alleged voter suppression.

"We're prepared to fight to the last tooth and nail to get every single vote counted," Patel told interviewer Alex Witt on MSNBC. "Voter suppression is a real thing. And it's not just real in Republican states. It's also real in the Democratic Party."[2]

Losing candidates are never happy. But when one side of a debate regularly challenges the motives of the other side, claiming racism or voter suppression, it's possible they don't have the facts on their side. Maybe they just lost, and they don't like it. So, they bring one of society's most sensitive matters—race—knowing the press will eat it up.

Maybe it's a New York thing, but in another 2020 Democratic primary—this one for the district attorney election in Queens—the race came down to a recount between Melinda Katz and Tiffany Cabán. Cabán was supported by Congresswoman Alexandria Ocasio-Cortez.[3] Katz was supported by then-governor Andrew Cuomo.[4] On Election Day, Cabán was up by about 1,100 votes, and she declared victory.[5]

Not so fast, said Katz, knowing there were thousands of absentee ballots yet to be counted. Weeks later, election officials were still counting ballots.[6] That's when the allegations of you-know-what started to fly.

"Things quickly turned exceedingly acrimonious, with the campaigns for Ms. Cabán and Ms. Katz accusing the other of suppressing votes," reported the *New York Times*.[7]

In June 2019, congressional Democrats had an internal split between their progressive caucus, championed by Ocasio-Cortez, and a more moderate block of Democrats over the amount of money to be spent on migrant children detained on the southern U.S. border. Progressives wanted more money. Moderate Democrats wanted less.

The dustup led Ocasio-Cortez's chief of staff at the time, Saikat Chakrabarti, to attack moderate Democrats, tweeting, "Instead of 'fiscally conservative but socially liberal,' let's call the New Democrats and Blue Dog Caucus the 'New Southern Democrats.' They certainly seem hell bent to do to black and brown people today what the old Southern Democrats did in the 40s."[8]

Saikat Chakrabarti
@saikatc

Instead of "fiscally conservative but socially liberal," let's call the New Democrats and Blue Dog Caucus the "New Southern Democrats." They certainly seem hell bent to do to black and brown people today what the old Southern Democrats did in the 40s.

7:08 PM · 6/27/19 · Twitter for Android

Source: Jerry Dunleavy and Julio Rosas, "AOC's Chief of Staff Deletes Tweet Calling Centrist Democrats Racist," *Washington Examiner*, June 27, 2019.

He later deleted the tweet.

Democrats do it to Democrats, and then they do it to Republicans.

Forgive me, but when Democrats accuse Republicans of being racist, as they alleged about George W. Bush in 2000, John McCain in 2008, Mitt Romney in 2012, and of course Donald Trump in 2016 and 2020, it just may be possible that Democrats who don't like to lose resort to the worst attack you can make on an opponent, calling them racists no matter what the circumstances or the truth.

These Democrats are modern-day Chicken Littles, crying the sky is falling. They use election disputes and ideological differences to stir the pot along society's most sensitive lines, counting on the press to tell the story the Democratic way. The press often obliges.

In the 2020 election, numerous ad hoc remedies were put in place at the last minute in multiple states to deal with the COVID crisis and people's fear of voting in person. Many states loosened voting procedures to allow for greater use of mail-in voting, while creating or expanding other voting options, including the use of ballot drop boxes in some places.

There is a legitimate public policy debate over how easy it should be to vote versus what safeguards should be in place to be certain the vote is honest and able to be counted reasonably quickly, avoiding the monthslong recounts that plagued New York in its 2020 primary and general election.

If there were no rules, it would be easy for anyone regardless of their residency or legal status to vote anywhere, as often as they like. If there were too many rules, voting would be too cumbersome and legitimate voters would be denied the franchise. Finding the appropriate middle ground is the essence of good government. To identify a healthy middle ground, voting laws—like any legitimate issue—need to be debated, with each side airing the pros and the cons. But for much of the press, any attempt to maintain or create a safeguard, or a middle ground, is immediately dubbed voter suppression, in accordance with the media's alignment with the left. When the press misuses the English language to depict voting policies as voter suppression, it's wrong, biased, and extreme. It's what activists do.

Falsely equating voting safeguards with Jim Crow laws is dangerous and detrimental to our democracy. Jim Crow resulted in the killing and lynching of Black Americans. It legally segregated Blacks and whites, codifying the practice of separate but equal. It created poll taxes and literacy tests, thereby denying citizens their right to vote. The intent was racist, and the results were racist.

In 2021, the state of Georgia passed into law a series of changes to its election laws. The press went nuts. CNN anchor Brianna Keilar reported, "Georgia's Republican governor has just signed a sweeping new law aiming to make it harder for people in his state to vote."[9]

Also on CNN, *CNN Tonight* anchor Don Lemon opened his report with, "We have important things to talk about right now. And, that is Jim Crow 2.0, alive and well in 2021. Georgia's governor is signing a bill that is nothing less than an assault on the right to vote."[10]

CNN senior political analyst Ron Brownstein described the law as "clearly, the broadest attempt to make it more difficult for Americans to vote since the Jim Crow era."

CBS anchor Margaret Brennan led the network's broadcast with, "The battle over voting rights. Angry protests after Georgia enacts new voting restrictions. Critics call it twenty-first-century Jim Crow."[11]

In a tweet and news story that were heavily criticized and later deleted, CBS News abandoned journalism and practiced advocacy. Not advocacy for the Republican side of an issue. Flat-out, blatant advocacy for the Democratic position. The story[12] was written by Khristopher J. Brooks, a *CBS MoneyWatch* reporter who also happens to teach at the Hunter College School of Journalism in New York City.[13]

"3 ways companies can help fight Georgia's restrictive new voting law," CBS News tweeted (and later deleted), advising readers of how they could help one side in the debate. The story listed a series of actions people could take to support the Democratic position.

At least CBS News' Twitter bio didn't include the words *Go Democrats!*

Source: CBS News. Twitter. @CBSNews. April 2, 2021.

On *NBC Nightly News with Lester Holt,* Holt led his story with "A restrictive new voting law in Georgia . . ."[14] Throughout the broadcast on the new voting laws, NBC ran this banner across the bottom of the screen: "Breaking News: Georgia Republicans Pass Law Restricting Voting Rights."[15] The banner angle mirrored that of the *NBC Nightly News* headline: "Georgia Passes Restrictive New Voting Law."[16] Across the networks, lead after lead used the phrase "new restrictive voting laws." Notice the framing. *Any* change in the law is a "restriction."

It's not. Framing laws that way would mean that any loosening of a law, as was done repeatedly in 2020, could be called a "weakening of safeguards." But most of the media did not frame it that way—because their point of view is the left's point of view. Many Democrats want to believe all Republicans are racists, and NBC, CBS, and CNN are not going to contradict them.

Take one of the most controversial provisions of the Georgia law. Anytime I hear something that sounds *so* bad that there must be more to the story, I dig to see what the press is leaving out. According to many of the news networks, the new Georgia voter law made it a crime for anyone other than poll workers to offer food and water to voters waiting in line.[17]

That sounds bad. Really bad. It conjures images of thirsty people waiting for hours, becoming dehydrated in the hot November sun. But of course, there's more to the story.

Imagine waiting in line to vote, while being approached by three or four people who are wearing MAGA (Make America Great Again) hats and carrying bottles of water. Or being approached by people with National Rifle Association shirts. Or abortion and/or anti-abortion advocates. Or Green New Deal backers. Or Jehovah's Witnesses. It doesn't matter what the cause is. Imagine waiting in line to vote when someone with an ideological ax to grind approaches a voter.

"Voter intimidation!" some people would cry. "Don't let these people near me!" These would be perfectly reasonable reactions for some citizens.

There's a legitimate reason elected officials don't want voters waiting in line to be approached by activists in any way, shape, or form. It's a perfectly reasonable, politically neutral safeguard to protect voters from real or perceived intimidation.

In Georgia, the new law said that anyone who wants to provide voters waiting in line with food or water (or anything else for that matter) had to be more than 150 feet away from a polling place and twenty-five feet away from a voter. That means a thirsty voter can walk less than ten yards—a shorter distance than a first down—to receive a bottle of water at a booth, a table, a tent—anything an organization wants to set up as a water station.[18]

The choice is up to the voter, not the activist. No one will go thirsty. Everyone is going to be protected. All you have to do is think about it, and you realize the food and water provision is no big deal and actually makes sense. But for many reporters, adding full, fair, and accurate information to inform readers and viewers of the law's impact would cut against the suppression narrative.

The American people have lost trust in the press because the press doesn't always report news that can be trusted.

THE SUMMER OF 2020 WAS violent. Following the killing of George Floyd, America's cities burst into riot. Protest was everywhere in dozens of American cities. Much of it was peaceful. Much of it was not. But the journalism profession bent over backward to minimize the violence. The same industry that will tell you that an airplane that lands safely is not news but that an airplane that crashes is big news quickly changed its standards.

Protests that were peaceful were news, but protests that were violent were not.

In April 2021, an exchange occurred between reporters and a police chief that epitomized the media's fervent journalistic desire to paper over violence. After a police officer in Brooklyn Center, Minnesota, accidentally killed Daunte Wright, a Black man, when she discharged her gun instead of her Taser, riots broke out. But, at the live news conference called by authorities to address the shooting, reporters contradicted and criticized the police chief for calling the riot a *riot*.

During the extraordinary exchange, Brooklyn Center police chief Tim Gannon stood his ground, saying, "It was [a riot]. The officers that were putting themselves in harm's way were being pelted with frozen cans of pop. They were being pelted with concrete blocks. And yes, we had our helmets on, and we had other protection here, but an officer was injured: hit in the head with a brick . . . he was transported to the hospital. We had to make decisions. We had to disperse the crowd because we can't allow our officers to be harmed."[19]

The Democratic governor of Minnesota called in the National Guard. But reporters/activists insisted that the violence in the streets, along with the looting that took place, was *not* a riot.

It was stunning to watch reporters contort themselves into verbal pretzels to explain why widespread looting, violence, and attacks on the police were "mostly peaceful," as many reporters often described events during the summer of 2020.

Democrats wanted badly to believe the protests were peaceful and righteous, and that all of the protesters were good and decent people, so that's what the media told them was happening.

No one exemplified this poor and inappropriate reporting better than CNN's Chris Cuomo.

Shortly after George Floyd's killing, as dozens of American cities enacted curfews to prevent violence, looting, and arson, the CNN anchor expressed sympathy with those committing the crimes.

"Please, show me where it says protesters are supposed to be polite and peaceful. Because I can show you that outraged citizens are what made the country what she is and led to any major milestone. To be honest, this is not a tranquil time," Cuomo said.[20]

His words bordered on encouraging protesters to engage in lawbreaking.

Cuomo was right about the summer of 2020 not being a tranquil time. But he was wrong in suggesting that protests are not supposed to be peaceful. Yes, they *are* supposed to be peaceful. Always. Regardless of the group. It doesn't matter how worthy the cause.

If Chris Cuomo's favorite cause is justified in not being peaceful, is Donald Trump's favorite cause justified? What about Sean Hannity's? Or Don Lemon's? How about Congresswoman Maxine Waters's (D-CA) favorite cause? Or Congresswoman Marjorie Taylor Greene's (R-GA) favorite cause?

The answer for all people must be that protesters *are* supposed to be peaceful. When one side is told its cause is worthy enough that violence will be tolerated, others will naturally believe their cause is also righteous enough to engage in violence over.

It's a dangerous road to travel.

In one of the more egregious examples of a reporter bending over backward to downplay the violence and arson that took place at a protest, MSNBC's Ali Velshi reported, while standing in front

MINNEAPOLIS, MN
11:07 PM

BREAKING NEWS
POLICE STATION & OTHER BUILDINGS BURNING IN MINNEAPOLIS   MSNBC   LIVE
9:07 PM PT

12:17 AM · May 29, 2020

Source: Internet Archive, *The 11th Hour with Brian Williams*, MSNBC, May 29, 2020.

of a blazing fire, "This is mostly a protest. It is not, generally speaking, unruly, but fires have been started, and this crowd is relishing that."[21]

The fire *was* a raging fire. When fires are set in the streets of American cities, when arsonists are on the loose, and when crowds relish it, that is the definition of unruly. The image of Velshi standing in front of a conflagration, using words that belied the image, made him look silly and illogical. It shows the lengths he went to play down the violence in service to what he viewed as a more important cause. His cause matched the cause of his MSNBC liberal viewers. He's telling them that the fire they see with their own eyes doesn't matter—despite the damage done and lives at risk—because the rioters are justified. This is ideological activism at its worst. It's not what reporting is supposed to be. Next time the left complains about an irrational point of view on the right from an obscure fringe group, remind them of the reporting done day in and day out to excuse violence committed by left-wing fringe groups.

It was the same story at CNN, where correspondent Omar Jimenez reported while another fire raged behind him. On the screen below Jimenez was a chyron that read, "Fiery But Mostly Peaceful

Source: Internet Archive, CNN, August 25, 2020.

Protests After Police Shooting."[22] CNN was mocked for its contorted coverage.

When reporters weren't minimizing the extent of damage from looting, burning, and rioting—which, as pointed out earlier, was among the most costly civil disorders in U.S. history[23]—they were falling over themselves, in the year of COVID-19, to dismiss the risks of COVID-19 associated with certain types of people in the streets. In contrast to the way the media routinely blamed crowds at beaches or sporting events for attending "super-spreader events," the press acted as if protesters packed together on the streets were immune from COVID-19; for the press it was as if the virus had a political consciousness and decided to skip right over street protesters, and instead infect beachgoers and sports fans. You know, people who do things that blue people do (protest) are good and people who do things that red people do (attend live sports events and go to the beach) are bad. Seldom were stories about the protests accompanied by stern lectures from news anchors reprimanding the protesters for potentially creating a super-spreader event. Seldom were there admonishments for the protesters to return home and avoid crowds. The media was too supportive of the cause for them to issue such warnings.

As the *New York Times* put it in a refreshingly candid story, "Was public health advice in a pandemic dependent on whether people approved of the mass gathering in question? To many, the answer seemed to be 'yes.'"[24]

On November 7, 2020, a college football game took place in South Bend, Indiana. Notre Dame upset top-ranked Clemson in double overtime. Students stormed the field to celebrate, as they often do after big wins in college football. The press lost its mind.

Axios headlined its story showing a picture of students on the field, "Party amid pandemic."

9. Party amid pandemic: Notre Dame sacks #1 Clemson

- **In Kansas City,** they swayed in a park to "Celebration" by Kool & the Gang. (AP)

People quickly jammed Black Lives Matter Plaza near the White House.

- **Celebrations** also filled Times Square and the Castro District in San Francisco, and broke out from L.A. to Chicago to Atlanta to Philadelphia.

Source: Mike Allen, *Axios AM*, November 8, 2020.

The very same *Axios* newsletter also had a story about Joe Biden being declared the winner of the presidency the same day as the Clemson–Notre Dame game. The headline was "America erupts" and the story cited numerous events across the country in which crowds gathered to celebrate Biden's victory. There was no mention of the pandemic for the Biden crowds, but there was for college football fans.[25]

At *Axios*, it's okay to celebrate on the street. But it's dangerous to celebrate on the field.

At the liberal outlet *Vox*, journalist Aaron Rupar threw a flag at football fans, but he celebrated with Biden fans. At 11:16 a.m. on November 7, Rupar the celebrant posted a picture of a street in front of the White House packed with people rejoicing over Biden's win and tweeted, "It's party time outside the White House."[26]

At 11:45 p.m. the same day, Rupar the scold posted a picture of Notre Dame fans on the field and tweeted, "Not ideal during a worsening pandemic."[27]

Sports radio talk-show host Clay Travis captured both tweets and summed it up well. "These tweets were less than 11 hours apart. The coronabros are complete and total hypocrites."

Source: Clay Travis. Twitter. @ClayTravis. November 8, 2020.

At the *New York Times*, journalist Jim Rutenberg also took a swipe at football fans. "Live from South Bend, it's Covid Night!" I checked his Twitter account to see if he similarly blew a whistle on Biden fans. He did not.

Time and again, a cynical, suspicious tone dominates mainstream media's coverage of Republican initiatives and motivations.

Too often, reporters approach coverage of Republican policies and behaviors with a bias that assumes they must be harmful to society or born from narrow-mindedness, misinformation, malicious intent, or lack of principle. The coverage drives Republicans crazy. More important, it has driven Republicans and most independents away from trusting the press. It's why the press is in decline and the only people left who believe the media are fair are Democrats, especially Democrats with college or graduate school degrees. The press have dug their own hole. It's likely too late for them to crawl out, assuming they even want to.

Chapter Eleven

TOO GOOD TO CHECK

A s the fourth pillar of democracy, the press is supposed to inform the American people by reporting on what is happening. They're in places that most of the public isn't, and their job is to fill us in on what they see and hear. To effectively communicate news, journalists must report it fully, fairly, and accurately. Unfortunately, today's press is falling short of its charge.

It's bad enough that reporters suppress news that helps conservatives (Hunter Biden's laptop and the role the Wuhan lab played in launching COVID), or that they deceived the American people for years about Trump colluding with Russia to win the 2016 election, or that too often reporters turn into activists, especially on behalf of Democratic policies, but still, a reader and a viewer should hope that with all the biases the media display, they could at least get their facts right. Even that, however, can sometimes be too much to expect.

The responsibility to report the news accurately is tripping up many of today's reporters. All too often, news broadcasts and stories are either wrong, hypocritical, or too friendly toward one side in a political debate. Hint: It's not the Republican side.

In March 2020, two journalists appeared on MSNBC's *The 11th Hour* to discuss the latest political news. One of them was Brian Williams, the show's host, and the other was guest Mara Gay, a member of the *New York Times* editorial board and an MSNBC contributor.

A tweet from a fellow journalist named Mekita Rivas had caught their eye, and so Williams discussed it live on the air. The Twitter handle for Rivas, with a blue check mark next to her name, says she is a "senior fashion editor @bustle" and a "contributor to @nytstyles."[1]

The since-deleted tweet read, "Bloomberg spent $500 million on ads. The U.S. population is 327 million. He could have given each American $1 million and still have money left over, I feel like a $1 million check would be life-changing for most people. Yet he wasted it all on ads and STILL LOST."

> **Mekita Rivas** ✔
> @MekitaRivas
>
> Bloomberg spent $500 million on ads. The U.S. population is 327 million. He could have given each American $1 million and still have money left over. I feel like a $1 million check would be life-changing for most people. Yet he wasted it all on ads and STILL LOST.
>
> 11:30 PM · Mar 3, 2020 · Twitter for iPhone

Source: MSNBC, *The 11th Hour with Brian Williams*, March 5, 2020.

Rivas was referring to spending by the billionaire former mayor of New York City, Michael Bloomberg, during his 2020 unsuccessful presidential bid. Williams and Gay enthusiastically agreed with Rivas. "When I read it tonight on social media it kind of all became clear. It's an incredible way of putting it," Williams said.

Gay replied, "It's true, it's disturbing, it does suggest there's too much money in politics."[2]

Keep in mind that both Williams and Gay are experienced journalists. However, neither one is good at math. If either had used a calculator, they would have figured out how glaringly inaccurate Rivas's calculations were before broadcasting the bogus figures on-air: $500 million divided by 327 million people comes out to $1.53 per person (that's *one dollar and fifty-three cents*), not $1 million per person. There's a big difference. But they didn't figure it out. Neither, amazingly, did any of those behind-the-scenes people at MSNBC, who allowed Williams and Gay to cite the inaccurate tweet, prepare and display a graphic for it on-screen, and discuss it at length on the air, while failing to read the comments pointing out that the tweet couldn't possibly be accurate in the first place!

The problem is, when you're programmed like a liberal to think money is the root of all evil, especially political evil, you don't stop to think whether the facts add up to the story you want to advocate. Since there's too much money in politics and since Bloomberg spent too much money, and people have so many needs, all that money should have gone to the people, is what Williams and Gay must have been thinking. It's called a narrative. Williams and Gay believed in it. Even if the facts didn't support it. The million dollars for the people tweet was too good to check. So MSNBC didn't check it. They reported it as the truth, live on the air.

After a deluge of criticism once the bogus story aired, the tweet was deleted, and the show apologized for its mistake.

In April 2020, CNN put out a story stating, "The US is monitoring intelligence that suggests North Korea's leader, Kim Jong Un, is in grave danger after undergoing a previous surgery, according to a US official with direct knowledge."[3]

NBC News' Katy Tur was quick with a follow-up report, claiming in a tweet, "North Korean leader Kim Jong Un is brain dead." She added, "@NBCNews confirms and adds to CNN scoop."

The only problem with these scoops, and NBC's so-called confirmation, was that they were wrong. There was nothing to confirm. Kim Jong Un was alive and kicking.

According to a story in the *Washington Post* a couple of weeks later:

> The worldwide misreporting appears to have started with a South Korean website [Daily NK] that has acknowledged that it mistranslated a single anonymous source's account of Kim's health.
>
> Daily NK's story on April 20 said that Kim was recovering from an unspecified "cardiovascular procedure," supposedly as a result of heavy smoking, obesity and fatigue, and that he reportedly was in stable condition.
>
> But Robert Lauler, the English-language editor of Daily NK, said on Tuesday that the English rendering of "cardiovascular procedure" from the site's story in Korean was inaccurately rendered as "heart surgery," a far more serious phrasing and one that found its way into other news reports.[4]

Still, Kim went from being in "stable condition" to being in "grave danger" or "brain dead." Perhaps an intelligence official—anonymous, of course—hinted there might be more to the story, but regardless, these reporters got it wrong. It's just a reminder that sometimes when reading the news, you have to count to three to be certain what you're told is correct.

If there was one person, recently, who was the subject of a torrent of wrong stories, it was Donald Trump. The former president himself could sometimes say things that were wrong. Many media organizations conducted ongoing counts of how many times the president said things they claimed weren't true. Yet, no matter what President Trump did or did not do, no matter how much he antagonized the mainstream media, none of his behavior excuses the number of errors the press made in covering him. It seemed as if, at every turn, the press leaped out of its seat to report a story that could scandalize Trump and his administration. In their overeagerness to broadcast or publish any story that could tarnish Trump's image or expose his alleged wrongdoing, journalists fast-tracked stories that should have instead been fact-checked. The result is a collection of Trump-centric stories that reveal an astonishing number of inaccuracies. Too often, these damaging stories were too good to check.

While these errors ranged from simple to substantial, they shared a common denominator: Reporters couldn't stand Donald Trump.

In May 2018, Trump convened a roundtable discussion at the White House with a group of California residents to discuss immigration and California's support for sanctuary cities.

According to a CNN report:

Complaining at the roundtable about confusion between different levels of law enforcement, Fresno County Sheriff Margaret Mims brought up the violent gang Mara Salvatrucha, better known as MS-13.

"There could be an MS-13 member I know about—if they don't have a certain threshold, I cannot tell [Immigration and Customs Enforcement] about it," Mims said.

Speaking immediately after Mims, Trump said, "We have people coming into the country, or trying to come in—and we're stopping a lot of them—but we're taking people out of the country. You wouldn't believe how bad these people are. These aren't people. These are animals. And we're taking them out of the country at a level and at a rate that's never happened before.[5]

Animals? Clearly, the president was referencing gang members in the violent, murderous MS-13. But to many in the media, that's not what Trump said. And they hit him hard.

"Trump Calls Some Unauthorized Immigrants 'Animals' in Rant," ran the headline for the *New York Times*.[6]

At *USA Today*, the headline was "Trump ramps up rhetoric on undocumented immigrants: 'These aren't people. These are animals.'"[7]

CBS News was just as misleading: "Trump calls some criminal illegal immigrants 'animals,' suggests Oakland mayor obstructed justice."[8]

Every one of these headlines could have stated that Trump was referring to MS-13. Instead, the media misled their readers and viewers to make Trump look extreme and xenophobic, calling immigrants "animals," despite the fact that if someone read deeper into the stories, the reference to MS-13 became clear.

How many people in this country still think he called immigrants animals? How many people who oppose Donald Trump would tell you it's because he called immigrants animals, colluded with Russia, stole mailboxes, and praised white supremacists as good people, even though none of those things ever happened?

Trump's MS-13 comment was defended by an unlikely source— CNN. Their senior media reporter Oliver Darcy wrote, "Several news organizations took remarks President Donald Trump made Wednesday out of context to suggest he was referring to undocumented immigrants at large as 'animals,' when in context it appears the President was likely referring to members of a violent gang."

Darcy pointed out that the Associated Press had tweeted, "Trump referred to those crossing US border illegally as 'animals' and slammed California sanctuary state laws as 'deadly.'" The tweet was subsequently deleted.

Darcy also noted, "A headline on the homepage of the *Washington Post* on Thursday morning read, 'Trump refers to some undocumented immigrants as "animals."' The story's lede said Trump had 'referred to some undocumented immigrants as "animals."' It wasn't until the newspaper's sixth paragraph that Trump's comments were put in the full context.

"And ABC News, in part, tweeted, 'Pres. Trump refers to some who cross the border illegally as "animals," not people,'" Darcy observed.[9]

Despite Darcy's fault-finding, CNN and other outlets couldn't control themselves. Eleven months later, they repeated their misleading reports after a tweet resurfaced Trump's old remarks.

The *Washington Free Beacon* reported in April 2019:

> CNN anchor Jim Sciutto [asked] a Republican guest Monday morning if Trump was helpful on border policy when "referring to immigrants as animals."
>
> Center for American Progress President Neera Tanden said on MSNBC Friday night that "this afternoon" Trump had referred to people coming across the border as "animals." Former Democratic National Committee CEO Jess O'Connell told MSNBC on Saturday, "You saw just this week, he compared immigrants to animals."
>
> Also on Saturday, liberal *Daily Beast* writer Jonathan Alter referred to Trump's comments "yesterday" as "truly shameful."
>
> "He compared people going to the border to animals," Alter said. "Now anybody who has studied any history knows that when you start calling people animals, when you dehumanize them that way, that's when the killing begins."[10]

The Twitter source for these reporters was not a journalist, but Mark Elliott, president of the New York–based Economic Mobility Corporation. Elliott deleted his tweet and wrote, "I have learned that Trump's comments were in response to a specific question about MS-13 members and not about asylum seekers more broadly. I have chosen to delete the tweet, but am copying it here. My apologies for not being more accurate."[11]

At least Elliott apologized. Most reporters who told their readers and viewers that Trump called immigrants "animals" did not.

Other times the mistakes were sweeping and relentless. Start with the COVID-19 vaccine.

In May 2020, as the world was reeling from the onslaught of the coronavirus, then-president Trump made a bold prediction. Standing in the Rose Garden, he said about the timing for a vaccine, "We're looking to get it by the end of the year if we can, maybe before."[12]

The press tore Trump apart for saying so, dismissing his prediction as an unlikely fantasy, even though Trump was right. On December 14, 2020, before the end of the year, Sandra Lindsay, an immigrant to the United States and an ICU nurse at Long Island Jewish Medical Center in New York, became the first American to receive a COVID vaccine.[13]

Lindsay's December shot in the arm followed an announcement made by Pfizer on November 9, 2020, that it had successfully tested a vaccine.[14] Pfizer's announcement came less than six months after Trump's much-maligned Rose Garden statement.

CBS News, citing "experts," had previously reported that Trump's statement that there would be a vaccine by the end of the year was "unlikely."[15]

Experts. You have to love those "experts."

In a so-called fact-check of Trump's May statement, NBC News reported, "Coronavirus vaccine could come this year, Trump says. Experts say he needs a 'miracle' to be right."[16]

The story stated, "experts say that the development, testing and production of a vaccine for the public is still at least 12 to 18 months off, and that anything less would be a medical miracle."[17] Five experts were quoted by NBC News, all of whom cast doubt on the president's statement, including Dr. Anthony Fauci. NBC News reported, "Trump's own top infectious disease expert, Dr. Anthony Fauci, told the 'Today' show that January 2021 is the earliest a vaccine could be ready but cautioned that that timeline is 'aspirational' and depends on companies producing a vaccine before researchers are sure it will work."[18]

It turns out Trump was right, and Dr. Fauci was wrong.

NBC News wasn't done with its doom-and-gloom, Trump-is-wrong coverage. Nor did they later describe him as a miracle worker.

In August, at the Republican National Convention, Trump said, "In recent months, our nation, and the entire planet, has been struck by a new and powerful invisible enemy. Like those brave Americans before us, we are meeting this challenge. We are delivering lifesaving therapies and will produce a vaccine before the end of the year, or maybe even sooner!"[19]

To which the always accurate fact-checkers at NBC wrote, "This is largely false. . . . There is also no evidence that an effective vaccine will be delivered by the end of the year. There are four vaccines currently in clinical trials in the U.S., with the one from Moderna furthest along. But it's impossible to know if these vaccines will prove effective. 'Vaccines don't always work,' one expert told NBC News earlier this year."[20]

Think about how deeply a fact-checker would have to misunderstand the word *fact* to call a prediction "largely false."

During the final presidential campaign rallies, *Washington Post* fact-checkers Glenn Kessler and Salvador Rizzo blew their whistle on Trump's repeated claim that a vaccine would be ready in weeks.

"Trump says a vaccine will be ready in weeks, while his administration's experts are much more cautious and say it won't be ready till next year," the *Post* wrote.[21]

Trump was right. Whomever Kessler and Rizzo cited was wrong.

Coverage in battleground Florida's *Miami Herald* was even worse.

"During the second and last debate before the Nov. 3 election, President Donald Trump insisted—again—that a coronavirus vaccine will be ready 'within weeks.'

"But according to scientific experts, there's no way that's happening, at least not with a vaccine that has proven safe and effective through appropriately timed clinical trials."[22]

Trump says COVID-19 vaccine is coming 'within weeks.' Experts say that's not possible

BY KATIE CAMERO
OCTOBER 23, 2020 11:07 AM, UPDATED OCTOBER 23, 2020 07:17 PM   𝕪 f ✉ ↪

Source: Katie Camero, "Trump says COVID-19 vaccine is coming 'within weeks.'
Experts say that's not possible," *Miami Herald*, October 23, 2020.

No way that's happening. Except that's precisely what happened. Trump made his "within weeks" statement on October 22, 2020. Pfizer's announcement was within weeks, on November 9, 2020.

One week before Pfizer's announcement that it had a safe and successful vaccine, Aaron Rupar, *Vox*'s associate editor of politics and policy, snidely told his nearly 670,000 Twitter followers that Trump promising people that the vaccine would be ready in "a couple of weeks" was a clear indicator that "we're not close."[23]

For most of the mainstream media, the coverage of Trump's COVID-19 initiatives fit a terrible two-part pattern. If Trump said it, it must be wrong. And if it deals with COVID-19, journalism must appeal to people's worst fears and most pessimistic takes. But the problem was deeper than that. What was really going on? That's simple: If Trump said something, the press instantly went into "how can we show he's wrong" mode. It was like a doctor striking someone on their knee to test a patient's reflexes. As soon as Trump made his statement about vaccines, the press rushed to conclude he was wrong. That's how the mainstream media reflexively reacted to much of what he did and said. Especially when it came to one of the biggest, most significant, most successful initiatives of the Trump presidency—the development of a COVID vaccine—the press was wrong and Trump was right.

That wasn't the only big error the press made in rejecting Trump's statements concerning vaccines. In September 2020, Trump announced at a White House briefing that "we expect to have enough vaccines for every American by April [2021]."[24]

CNN virtually laughed out loud at Trump, with a headline declaring "health experts say that's not likely."

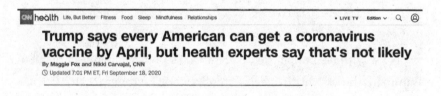

Source: Maggie Fox and Nikki Carvajal, "Trump says every American can get a coronavirus vaccine by April, but health experts say that's not likely," CNN, September 18, 2020.

CNN's story slammed Trump, stating in its first paragraph, "President Donald Trump claimed Friday there will be enough coronavirus vaccines for every American by April—a claim that doesn't match any timeline given by the federal government's health agencies, private researchers or even the companies making the vaccines."[25]

Flash forward to April 2021. CNN pretended the health agencies, private researchers, and companies making the vaccine that said Trump's timeline was wrong never existed.

"All 50 states now have expanded or will expand Covid vaccine eligibility to everyone 16 and up" was the new headline.[26] CNN should have tweeted, "Trump was right and our experts were wrong." But that's too much to expect. CNN's April 2021 story, by the way, didn't mention Trump at all. Not one single word.

Of all the COVID-19 mistakes, none were worse than stories dealing with the possibility that COVID began in a Chinese government-run lab in Wuhan and not naturally. Much of the American press corps, driven by a compulsive desire to blame Trump for his handling of the virus, turned a blind eye to the possibility that COVID-19 originated at the Wuhan Institute for Virology.

The media did worse than turn a blind eye. They derided, talked down to, and dismissed as fringe conspiracy theorists anyone who thought the Wuhan lab might be involved. They suppressed even the possibility that the virus originated there. The mainstream media failed to do its job involving COVID-19, one of the most consequential matters any journalist will ever cover. They failed to take seriously the possibility COVID-19 began in a Chinese lab because such a discussion would divert attention away from the person they preferred to blame for everything—Donald Trump.

SENATOR TOM COTTON (R-AR) WAS one of the first leaders to question the role played by the Wuhan lab. In late January 2020, before cases rapidly multiplied across the United States, Cotton told the Senate Armed Services Committee that COVID was "the biggest and most important story in the world" and "could result in a worldwide pandemic."[27]

Cotton continued, "We still don't know where coronavirus originated. Could have been a market, a farm, a food processing company. I would note that Wuhan has China's only biosafety level-four super laboratory that works with the world's most deadly pathogens to include, yes, coronavirus."[28]

Four days before Cotton's remarks, the conservative *Washington Times* reported, "The deadly animal-borne coronavirus spreading globally may have originated in a laboratory in the city of Wuhan linked to China's covert biological weapons program, said an Israeli biological warfare analyst."[29] The *Daily Mail* in England a few days earlier also noted the existence of the lab in Wuhan and floated the possibility that the virus could have originated there.[30]

Shortly after Cotton's statement, CBS News' *Face the Nation* asked Chinese ambassador to the United States Cui Tiankai about Cotton's remarks that the virus could have originated in a lab that was part of China's military biological warfare program.[31]

"Absolutely crazy," he said.[32] "It's very harmful, it's very dangerous to stir up suspicion, rumors, and spread them among the people. For one thing this will create panic. Another thing it will fan up racial discrimination, xenophobia, all these things that will really harm our general efforts to combat the virus."[33]

From that point forward, the press had its talking points.

Senator Tom Cotton Repeats Fringe Theory of Coronavirus Origins

Scientists have dismissed suggestions that the Chinese government was behind the outbreak, but it's the kind of tale that gains traction among those who see China as a threat.

Source: Alexandra Stevenson, "Senator Tom Cotton Repeats Fringe Theory of Coronavirus Origins," *New York Times*, February 17, 2020.

"Senator Tom Cotton Repeats Fringe Theory of Coronavirus Origins," reported the *New York Times* on February 17, 2020.[34]

It was the same story the same day at the *Washington Post*.

"Tom Cotton keeps repeating a coronavirus conspiracy theory that was already debunked," the *Post* told its readers.[35]

"Scientists" and "experts." Where would journalism be without them?

A little more than one year later, only after President Biden ordered America's intelligence agencies to report back to him on the possibility that COVID began in a Chinese lab, the *Post* added a prominent "correction" to its fringe theory denunciation of Cotton:

CORRECTION

Earlier versions of this story and its headline inaccurately characterized comments by Sen. Tom Cotton (R-Ark.) regarding the origins of the coronavirus. The term "debunked" and The Post's use of "conspiracy theory" have been removed because, then as now, there was no determination about the origins of the virus.

Source: Paulina Firozi, "Tom Cotton Keeps Repeating a Coronavirus Fringe Theory That Scientists Have Disputed," *Washington Post*, February 17, 2020.

Unbelievable. The original headline on the *Post* story was "Tom Cotton keeps repeating a coronavirus conspiracy theory that was already debunked."[36] The *Post* changed "conspiracy theory" to "fringe theory" and "debunked" to "disputed." When dealing with the mainstream media, that's progress, I suppose.

The real story was that so long as Donald Trump was president and so long as it was Republicans raising the possibility that COVID-19 leaked from the Wuhan lab, the press did everything in its power to delegitimize, stigmatize, and suppress the theory. But with Trump gone and Democrats now suggesting a leak might be possible, the press went along. Suddenly, what was once a conspiracy theory was now a plausible possibility. When Democrats and Joe Biden said it, it became credible. When Donald Trump and Republicans said the same thing, it was wrong.

The media wonders why Republicans don't find them credible. The media's suppression of even the possibility that the virus began in the Wuhan lab is a good example of why Republicans can't trust the press. Republicans are correct when they think the press looks down at them, dismisses their points of view, and treats them as misinformed Americans whose word is in doubt and whose motives are suspect. It's also why the Democrats typically have come to rely on and expect the mainstream media to carry their water.

Jim Geraghty, a thoughtful and thorough reporter at the conservative *National Review*, wrote extensively about the possibility of a lab leak.[37] Much of the media dismissed him for it.

In May 2021, after Biden's authorization of an investigation, Geraghty noted:

All I did was take three incontrovertible forces in human life seriously: the capacity for human error in a laboratory, the universal temptation to try to cover up a consequential mistake once it's made, and the far-reaching power of a totalitarian government when attempting to enact that cover-up. . . .

Authoritarian governments, and those who work within them, are terrified of ever admitting a mistake. Authoritarian governments need to look all-powerful and always-competent, lest the citizenry get ideas about changing who's in charge.

If I had a quarter for every time I was told I wasn't a scientist, I could play Pac-Man at the arcade for the rest of my days. I never claimed to be a scientist, nor that I played one on TV. You know what I have spent a good chunk of my adult life studying? Government bureaucracies. This is a story of viruses, yes, but it's also a story of what human beings do when they make a mistake.[38]

If only the mainstream media was as open-minded, fair, and curious as Geraghty, the media and America would be much better off.

The truth, free speech, and open debate also have a Facebook problem, especially on this issue. It's a major problem that threatens our abilities as Americans to openly debate a variety of issues.

On February 8, 2021, Facebook posted: "Today, following consultations with leading health organizations, including the World Health Organization (WHO), we are expanding the list of false claims we will remove to include additional debunked claims about the coronavirus and vaccines. This includes claims such as: COVID-19 is man-made or manufactured."[39]

But on May 26, 2021, and only after the Biden administration publicly said that COVID-19 might have originated in the Wuhan lab, Facebook reversed course. "In light of ongoing investigations into the origin of COVID-19 and in consultation with public health experts, we will no longer remove the claim that COVID-19 is man-made or manufactured from our apps," Facebook posted.[40]

In their censorship of information, there was little to no difference between how the mainstream media handled the lab leak theory and how social media companies handled it. So long as the theory came from Republicans, it was a "false claim," fit to be "removed" from Facebook and polite society. Only after Democrats acknowledged the credibility of the lab leak theory did Facebook allow it to be discussed.

This type of blatant hypocrisy, bias, and narrow-minded unfairness drives Republicans crazy and leads them to conclude that the press can't be trusted.

I wish the traditional media, along with Facebook, Twitter, and other social media platforms, would realize the damage they've done to our country. When these outlets behave as if Democratic thinking is more accurate, more high-minded, and wiser than Republican thinking, what do they think will happen? The nation becomes polarized. Unity, a traditional strength of our nation, breaks down. Democrats come to expect their points of view to be echoed by the media, while Republicans give up the belief that the media, in its many forms, will be fair. It's a terrible situation for our nation when more than half the country no longer trusts or believes in the media, including social media companies.

It doesn't matter that Facebook has the right to censor people. What Facebook did was wrong. It was antiscience, antidebate, and antidemocratic, all for an issue where the initial speculation about the lab's involvement was perfectly reasonable right from the start.

But when a Chinese ambassador says it's crazy, and Democratic politicians fear xenophobia, and so-called experts dismiss a valid hypothesis, the press falls right into line. Why are there so few independent thinkers left in the mainstream media? Aren't reporters the people who are supposed to "check everything"? How could so many, so quickly, pounce and denounce as fringe conspiracy theorists those who asked a fair and rational question about the Wuhan lab's role?

Whether it's ultimately found that the virus originated from nature, or from the Wuhan lab, or if it's never settled at all, the point remains the same: Questions about the lab's role were legitimate. The media's handling of those questions was a shameful episode of suppression journalism in service to an anti-Trump cause.

When it came to the Wuhan lab, the *New York Times* was quick to attack and dismiss theories that made China look bad. In contrast, when it came to stories that made Russia and Trump look bad, the *Times* had an itchy trigger finger.

On June 26, 2020, the *Times* broke a bombshell story about Russia.

"Russia Secretly Offered Afghan Militants Bounties to Kill US Troops, Intelligence Says" was the headline.[41]

The headline didn't say the Russians *might* have offered bounties. The story didn't say some people *allege* the Russians offered bounties. The mighty *New York Times* reported the bounties as fact. The bombshell's first paragraph began, "American intelligence officials have concluded that a Russian military intelligence unit secretly offered bounties to Taliban-linked militants for killing coalition forces in Afghanistan—including targeting American troops—amid the peace talks to end the long-running war there, according to officials briefed on the matter."[42]

The sources cited by the *Times* were, of course, anonymous. The story also stated, "The intelligence finding was briefed to President Trump, and the White House's National Security Council discussed the problem at an interagency meeting in late March, the officials said."[43]

Joe Biden, in the thick of his campaign against Trump, attacked.

"[Trump's] entire presidency has been a gift to Putin, but this is beyond the pale. It's betrayal of the most sacred duty we bear as a nation to protect and equip our troops when we send them into harm's way. It's a betrayal of every single American family with a loved one serving in Afghanistan or anywhere overseas," Biden tweeted.[44]

The rest of the mainstream media, trusting the accuracy of the *New York Times*, pounced.

The story got massive coverage. MSNBC gave the story 419 minutes. CNN dedicated 160 minutes of airtime to the bombshell. FOX covered it, too, at 146 minutes. The networks covered it extensively.[45]

On CNN, Brian Stelter called it a "stunning U.S. intel assessment."[46] ABC News called it a "bombshell report."[47] The *Washington Post* "independently confirmed" the story and upped the ante, claiming the bounties "are believed to have resulted in the deaths of several U.S. service members."[48]

In a tweet, Trump said he was never briefed about the bounties, contradicting the *New York Times,* and dismissed the allegations as a "hoax." He added that the intelligence community "did not find this info credible."[49]

Trump's press secretary, Kayleigh McEnany, explained to the press that "there is no consensus within the intelligence community on these allegations and in effect, there are dissenting opinions from some in the intelligence community with regards to the veracity of what's being reported, and the veracity of the underlying allegations continue to be evaluated."[50]

None of it mattered. The press didn't want to believe the White House denials or explanations. Their anti-Trump reflex had kicked in: If Trump said it, it must be wrong. Until the denial and explanation came from a different White House. The Biden White House.

Almost a year later, with a new administration in charge, the *Daily Beast* reported that new people were saying the same thing Trump and his team were saying. This time, the press believed them. The *Daily Beast* wrote on April 15, 2021:

> It was a blockbuster story about Russia's return to the imperial "Great Game" in Afghanistan. The Kremlin had spread money around the longtime central Asian battlefield for militants to kill remaining U.S. forces. It sparked a massive outcry from Democrats and their #resistance amplifiers about the treasonous Russian puppet in the White House whose admiration for Vladimir Putin had endangered American troops.
>
> But on Thursday, the Biden administration announced that U.S. intelligence only had "low to moderate" confidence in the story after all. Translated from the jargon of spyworld, that means the intelligence agencies have found the story is, at best, unproven—and possibly untrue.[51]

It was that simple. If team Trump said it, the press didn't believe it. If team Biden said it, it must be true.

The Biden administration's acknowledgment that yet another *New York Times* bombshell was a dud was briefly mentioned by the media. MSNBC, which gave 419 minutes to the original *Times* story, gave 3 minutes to the Biden revelation that the story didn't hold up. CNN dropped from 160 minutes' worth of coverage alleging bounties were paid to less than 3 minutes, saying they probably weren't paid. FOX pumped the Biden story hard, at 53 minutes.[52]

No one in the mainstream media apologized to Donald Trump. Nor did Joe Biden or Kamala Harris, who both used the issue against him in 2020. Stories like this were part of a pattern during the Trump presidency. Especially on any story that could make Trump look bad. Especially if reporters could claim that Trump refused to stand up to Vladimir Putin and Russia. Reporters were so invested in the collusion-must-be-true angle—despite the findings of Robert Mueller's report concluding otherwise—that they never let it go.

That is, until Joe Biden was elected and Biden aides told the press what to write. Then, with the knowledge that Trump was no longer in office, the press went along. That's not journalism. That's advocacy on behalf of a cause.

In June 2020, President Trump went for a walk.

It was a walk to St. John's Church, across from Lafayette Park, in front of the White House. For days the park had been occupied by people protesting the murder of George Floyd. In a photo op widely maligned by the media, Trump arrived at the church and held up a Bible. The press didn't like Trump being there and they especially didn't like the "fact" that Trump must have ordered the police to clear the park so he could stage his photo op.

The mainstream media was relentless in its anti-Trump coverage.

"Protesters Dispersed With Tear Gas So Trump Could Pose at Church," reported the *New York Times*.[53]

NPR went with "Peaceful Protesters Tear-Gassed To Clear Way For Trump Church Photo-Op."[54]

As the *Atlantic* magazine simply stated after a law-and-order speech Trump had given at the White House earlier in the day, "To clear the way for his planned post-speech trip to St. John's Church, police fired tear gas and rubber bullets into a crowd of peaceful demonstrators."[55]

After almost five years of leap-out-of-your-seat, "Trump is bad" and "Trump is wrong" stories, coverage of Trump's walk fit a pattern. If Trump does something, jump to the conclusion that what he did was harmful, racist, narrow-minded, or contrary to America's values. No need to stop and think. No need to ask questions. No need to check. Just blame Trump. It was a journalistic formula by then. And, once again, most reporters turned out to be flat wrong.

Trump didn't clear the park so that he could walk to the church. Trump didn't order law enforcement agencies to tear-gas protesters so that he could conduct a photo op. The accusations against Trump were groundless.

That's the conclusion of a report issued by the Department of Interior's inspector general in June 2021, one year later.

The report found, "The evidence we reviewed showed that the USPP [United States Park Police] cleared the park to allow a contractor to safely install anti-scale fencing in response to destruction of Federal property and injury to officers that occurred on May 30 and May 31. Moreover, the evidence established that relevant USPP officials had made those decisions and had begun implementing the operational plan several hours before they knew of a potential Presidential visit to the park, which occurred later that day. As such, we determined that the evidence did not support a finding that the USPP cleared the park on June 1, 2020, so that then President Trump could enter the park."[56]

When the report came out, most of the press ate its share of crow and admitted they got the story wrong.[57]

Getting the story wrong was something the mainstream media frequently did to President Donald Trump, and it hurt him badly. It hurt his image. It damaged his prospects for reelection. And it further damaged the mainstream media itself. For an institution that relies on public acceptance of its word in order to have credibility and customers, the media kept making the same mistakes time and again. That's what happens when like-minded college-educated Democratic voters who live in a self-reinforcing, anti-Trump media bubble are in charge of what many people are told.

During my interview with the former president, I asked him about mistakes like this and whether he thought the press was fair to him.

Reflecting on how the press covered him in his 2016 campaign, he told me, "The press was unbelievably ruthless, in fact to a point where you would almost say it's a miracle that you win. How do you do this? First of all, we had big tech against us. We had everybody against us."

Did you think the press would change once you were elected? I asked.

"The press was ruthless and vicious, and I said to myself when I won, the one good thing, the press will respect us greatly and the press will become a lot more fair."

That sentiment didn't last long.

"It was corrupt what they did. It was so horrible," Trump continued. "And they've only gotten worse. They had a moment—for the first month they were really starting to get good. I said, you know—I said this is going to be a great thing for the media because they're starting—but eventually that went away. It went away pretty quickly. They just couldn't do it."

"Why?" I asked.

"I have no idea," Trump answered. "I guess it's ideology. I think it's ideology. Maybe they didn't like me personally, I guess.

"I do all these things and I don't get credit for it. I noticed that very early. The economy was good. I got no credit. Jobs were good. I got no credit. I started to say, what do I have to do to get credit?"

PUBLIC AFFAIRS CONSULTANT AND FORMER congressional staffer Drew Holden is a freelance commentary writer who has penned opinion pieces for the likes of *National Review*, nytimes.com, and foxnews.com, to name a few.[58] I first came to know of Holden on Twitter.

On April 14, 2021, when President Biden announced he would bring all American troops home from Afghanistan by September 11, Holden noticed a stark difference between how the press covered Biden's announcement and how it had covered Trump's similar announcements in 2019 and 2020. Holden then tweeted this compelling thread:

← **Thread**

Drew Holden @DrewHolden360 · Apr 14
🍗THREAD🍗

Today, President Biden announced his intention to end the war in Afghanistan, to great media fanfare.

You may remember, way back in 2019 & 2020, President Trump said the same thing.

Let me know if you can spot the difference in coverage then vs. now🔽

💬 1K   🔁 14.9K   ♡ 37.5K   ⬆️

Drew Holden @DrewHolden360 · Apr 14   •••

When Trump said we were leaving, @CNN quoted the NATO Sec Gen with a "stark warning" about how "dangerous" the move would be.

But Biden's decision? Well, on that one, we just get to hear from his people.

 CNN ✔
@CNN   •••

NATO Secretary General Jens Stoltenberg issued a stark warning that any premature withdrawal from Afghanistan could be dangerous, a day after reports that President Trump is eyeing a troop drawdown against the advice of the nation's top military officials.

 CNN ✔
@CNN   •••

As President Biden prepares to lay out his plan to withdraw US troops from Afghanistan, a source familiar with his thinking tells CNN's @camanpour that he thinks no amount of US troops in the country can be a game changer anymore

---

Drew Holden @DrewHolden360 · Apr 14   •••

One of the things I've discussed before is how outlets can frame the narrative they want by focusing on people who support or oppose a certain policy. It's misleading, but also a calling card of @CNN.

"This is just reckless and it is really risky," says @BrettBruen of Trump's plan to withdraw troops from Afghanistan and Iraq.

"You're not sharing information with the incoming administration, so the likelihood that something could go wrong is very, very high."

 CNN ✔
@CNN

Former President Obama praised President Biden's "bold leadership" for his decision to withdraw US troops from Afghanistan by September 11, saying that "it is time to recognize that we have accomplished all that we can militarily" in America's longest war

Drew Holden @DrewHolden360 · Apr 14   •••

Starting to see it?

CNN politics   Live TV • ≡

Diplomats worry Trump's desire to withdraw US troops risks success of Afghan-Taliban talks

By Kylie Atwood and Jennifer Hansler, CNN

Updated 7:01 AM EDT, Fri September 11, 2020

CNN ⊘
@CNN   •••

President Biden has announced his decision to withdraw American troops from Afghanistan before September 11, the 20th anniversary of the terrorist attacks on the World Trade Center and the Pentagon that led the US into its longest war

Drew Holden @DrewHolden360 · Apr 14   •••

Replying to @DrewHolden360

This one from @TIME might be the most egregious of them all. I mean. Cmon.

TIME ⊘
@TIME   •••

Can Donald Trump accept a defeat in Afghanistan?

Can Donald Trump Accept a Defeat in Afghanistan?
time.com

TIME ⊘
@TIME   •••

"Biden's move brings to an end America's longest war, a long-simmering conflict that meant solemn sacrifice for military families and changed so much of day-to-day life for all Americans, even if they don't immediately realize it," writes @Philip_Elliott

Drew Holden @DrewHolden360 · Apr 14
@washingtonpost presented without introduction.

Trump administration to cut troop levels in Afghanistan despite Pentagon warnings

Trump administration to cut troop levels in Afghanistan and Iraq in sprint to deliver on pr...
washingtonpost.com

4:29 PM · 11/16/20 · SocialFlow

The Washington Post @
@washingtonpost

America's longest war may soon be coming to an end. President Biden is announcing that all U.S. troops will be leaving Afghanistan by the 20th anniversary of the Sept. 11, 2001, attacks. [Photo: Matt McClain/The Washington Post]

Source: Drew Holden. Twitter. @DrewHolden360. April 14, 2021.

Holden nailed it. The press takes sides by reporting the opinions of people they agree with. How can they report Trump's withdrawal from Afghanistan in such critical terms while presenting Biden's withdrawal from Afghanistan in such a thoughtful and praiseworthy manner? Because they're biased and hypocritical, that's why.

Time after time, the mainstream media covers the news differently depending on who is making it. It's almost always Republicans who get the short end of the media's stick.

After Trump's defeat in 2020, his administration did everything in its power through appointments and regulatory authority to lock into place as many conservative policies as possible.

As *Washington Examiner* journalist Byron York pointed out in a tweet,[59] the *Washington Post* blew its whistle on Trump's efforts to lock in his policies.

The *Post* headlined its story, "As Trump rants over election, his administration accelerates push to lock in policy and staffing gains."[60]

> Over the final six weeks of Trump's presidency, the adminis-
> tration has no plans to wind down its efforts to remake federal
> policies and even the government bureaucracy itself, aides said,
> despite the pending handoff to the incoming Democratic ad-
> ministration. The whirlwind of activities has *bucked tradition*
> of past presidents who have deferred on major policy actions
> during the lame-duck period, and in some cases, the moves
> could make it procedurally or politically challenging for Biden
> to fulfill campaign pledges to unwind the Trump team's actions[61]
> (emphasis added).

Bucked tradition? Here's the *New York Times'* description of Obama's postelection efforts in 2016 to lock in *his* gains: "With less than three weeks before the Obama White House is history, making way for a new administration with radically different priorities, the president is using every power at his disposal to cement his legacy and establish his priorities as the law of the land."[62]

See that? Trump bucked tradition. Obama cemented his legacy in service to the law of the land.

The hypocrisy gets worse.

As team Biden prepared to take the White House, they announced the hiring of an "all-female" senior communications team. The mainstream media fell all over itself to praise Biden for his gender-based lineup. Dozens of stories were written heralding the fact that Biden's senior communications team was all-women. The Associated Press reported it was "the first time that all of the top aides tasked with speaking on behalf of the White House and shaping the administration's message will be female."[63] Except it wasn't.

At the very moment the incoming Biden team made its announcement, an all-women senior communications team could be found in the Trump White House, a fact the press ignored. The Trump White House communications director was Alyssa Farah. The press secretary was Kayleigh McEnany. The vice president's communications director was Katie Miller. The first lady's spokeswoman was Stephanie Grisham. The second lady's spokeswoman was Kara Brooks.

You see, Democratic women get praised. Republican women get ignored.

Hypocrisy is also evident in how the media frames the narrative around illegal immigration—an issue that has been a major problem for the United States for decades. When Donald Trump was president, the Associated Press routinely called the situation on the border a "crisis."

As *Blaze News* pointed out, "The AP freely used the word 'crisis' to describe migrant surges during the Trump administration."[64]

July 2018: "Judge puts blame on Trump, Congress for immigration crisis"

June 2019: "House passes emergency funding bill for migrant care crisis"

October 2019: "Immigration official says US-Mexico border crisis not over"

June 2018: "Ivanka Trump stayed silent for days as border crisis mounted"

Yet somehow, when Joe Biden became president and there was a surge of illegal immigrants at the border—including large numbers of children who were separated from their parents—the word *crisis* was to be avoided at all costs. According to an internal Associated Press memo first obtained by Futuro Media, the AP instructed reporters to "avoid hyperbole in calling anything a crisis or an emergency."

> The current event in the news—a sharp increase in the arrival of unaccompanied minors—is a problem for border officials, a political challenge for Biden and a dire situation for many migrants who make the journey, but it does not fit the classic dictionary definition of a crisis, which is: "A turning point in the course of anything; decisive or crucial time, stage, or event," OR "a time of, or a state of affairs involving, great danger or trouble, often one which threatens to result in unpleasant consequences [an economic crisis]."
>
> Therefore, we should avoid, or at the least, be highly cautious, about referring to the present situation as a crisis on our own, although we may quote others using that language.[65]

Guess who else didn't want to call the situation a "crisis"? Joe Biden and his administration! It was a word they avoided at all costs. The Associated Press went right along with the Biden dictate, despite using that word, *crisis*, when Trump was president. Hypocrisy and activism in service of the Biden administration. That's not how journalism is supposed to work.

Sometimes the media's hypocrisy and activism show up in subtle ways—often through word choices. When Senator Elizabeth Warren ran for president in 2020, she worked to polish her national security credentials. "She is privately hosting monthly dinner seminars with policy experts to expand her command of the issues," the *New York Times* reported.[66] Seminars. I see. When George W. Bush ran for president in 2000, the same paper reported that he was receiving "tutoring" from his future national security advisor, Condoleezza Rice.[67]

Warren attends seminars. Bush needs tutoring. Got it.

In 2018, Stacey Abrams ran for governor of Georgia and lost by a sizeable margin, more than 50,000 votes, or 1.4 percentage points.[68] (For comparison's sake, Donald Trump lost Georgia in the 2020 presidential race by fewer than 12,000 votes, or 0.3 percentage points.)[69]

To this day, Abrams has refused to acknowledge that her opponent, Republican Brian Kemp, was the legitimate winner. Other Democrats allege the 2018 Georgia governor's race was "stolen"—their word. According to the *Washington Post*, "Sen. Cory Booker (D-NJ) has said the 'election is being stolen from' Democrat Stacey Abrams. Hillary Clinton has said Abrams would have won 'if she'd had a fair election.' And on Wednesday, Sen. Sherrod Brown (D-OH) went so far as to say, 'If Stacey Abrams doesn't win in Georgia, they stole it.'"[70] Failed Virginia gubernatorial candidate Terry McAuliffe said in 2021 that the Georgia race was stolen.[71]

Abrams wasn't the first candidate, backed by journalists, who refused to accept a loss.

In 2012, *New York* magazine's Jonathan Chait was *still* complaining that George W. Bush stole the 2000 election.[72]

THE NATIONAL INTEREST | JUNE 25, 2012

Yes, Bush v. Gore Did Steal the Election
By Jonathan Chait

Source: Jonathan Chait, "Yes, Bush v. Gore Did Steal the Election," *New York*, June 25, 2012.

In 2004, McAuliffe, who was then the chairman of the Democratic National Committee, also said Bush "stole" the 2000 race.[73]

Many Democrats perpetuated the claim that the 2016 election was stolen from Hillary Clinton and that Clinton was the legitimate victor. On November 8, 2017, the British newspaper the *Guardian* published a story titled, "One year on, Donald Trump is still an illegitimate president."[74]

The story's subheadline read, "It is unlikely that the presidential election will be overturned, but that is not an argument against the case that it should be."[75]

The story cited several examples of fraud, errors, or mistakes that merited the election being overturned.

Ari Berman of *Mother Jones* said that in Wisconsin, where Trump lost by fewer than 23,000 votes, as many as 45,000 voters were "prevented from casting a ballot by voter identification laws designed to disenfranchise them."

Also in Wisconsin, the *Guardian* story cited journalist Gabriel Sherman, who claimed that Hillary Clinton received 7 percent fewer votes in counties that relied on electronic voting machines compared with counties that used optical scanners and paper ballots. "Based on this statistical analysis, Clinton may have been denied as many as 30,000 votes," Sherman said.[76]

The story also said that "in many swing states, including Florida, North Carolina, Pennsylvania and Wisconsin, there were extraordinary discrepancies between the exit polls and the vote tallies."[77]

The bottom line?

"The 2016 US presidential election was so corrupted in so many ways, small and large, that there is no reason to respect its outcome or regard Donald J. Trump as the legitimate president of the United States," wrote the *Guardian*.

Clinton, who conceded to Trump the day after the 2016 election, later reversed course and sounded an awful lot like the *Guardian*.

In an interview with CBS News in September 2019, she said Trump was "an illegitimate president" and that "I believe he understands that the many varying tactics they used—from voter suppression and voter purging to hacking to the false stories—he knows that."[78]

Her words echoed former Democratic president Jimmy Carter, who said in June 2019 that Trump lost and was put into office by the Russians. "There's no doubt that the Russians did interfere in the election, and I think the interference, although not yet quantified, if fully investigated would show that Trump didn't actually win the election in 2016," Carter said. "He lost the election, and he was put into office because the Russians interfered on his behalf."[79]

The late congressman John Lewis (D-GA) said, "I don't see this president-elect as a legitimate president,"[80] one week before Trump's 2017 swearing-in, an event boycotted by more than sixty House Democrats.[81]

As soon as Trump won, a "resistance" movement was formed among many Democrats who refused to accept Trump as the legitimate winner. Many sought to overturn the November election in the Electoral College.

"At least a half-dozen Democratic electors have signed onto an attempt to block Donald Trump from winning an Electoral College majority, an effort designed not only to deny Trump the presidency but also to undermine the legitimacy of the institution," *Politico* reported in late November 2016.[82]

Hollywood joined in the act. NBC News reported:

A petition aimed at "conscientious electors" has garnered nearly 5 million signatures. The West Wing's fictitious president, Martin Sheen, and a slew of actors released a YouTube appeal pleading with electors to give the election to Clinton, or anyone other than Trump.

Filmmaker Michael Moore published an impassioned plea to

Republican members of the Electoral College "to vote your con-
science" and promising to pay the fines of electors whose states
punish them for breaking with Trump.[83]

Commentary magazine reported:

Republican electors recalled receiving "thousands of emails a
day" demanding that they abandon their duty to back Trump.
Celebrities joined with advocacy groups dedicated to over-
turning the election's results. An effort spearheaded by, among
others, House Speaker Nancy Pelosi's daughter, Christine Pelosi,
to provide electors with a classified briefing on Russian inter-
ference in the 2016 election prior to the certification of the vote
received the support of Hillary Clinton's campaign chief. "Elec-
tors have a solemn responsibility under the Constitution and we
support their efforts to have their questions addressed," Clinton
campaign chairman John Podesta wrote in December 2016. . . .

In the *Washington Post*, Harvard University law professor
Lawrence Lessig insisted that it would violate "the fundamental
principle of one person, one vote" if electors didn't back Clinton.
It would take just 37 Republicans "with the courage to perform
their moral duty and protect the nation" to stave off the disaster
of a Trump administration, observed *Post* columnist Kathleen
Parker. "Please, be brave," Parker wrote.

In the *New York Times*, Columbia Law School professor Da-
vid Pozen noted that there were few state-level legal obstacles
and no constitutional impediments before would-be renegade
electors. Moreover, given the candidate Americans backed at
the polls, "the practice of sticking with the state's top vote-getter
loses moral force." And even if Trump does emerge with the
requisite votes to be inaugurated, the trauma of 2016 should

become a torch forever borne by his opponents. Anger over the "tainted election" "shouldn't be allowed to cool," *Times* columnist Paul Krugman wrote.[84]

Instead of criticizing such extraordinary efforts to overturn a legitimate election, much of the media treated the anti-Trump effort as a sign of how polarizing Donald Trump was. NBC News said the overturn efforts would turn out to be "a great big civics lesson."[85]

When it came time for Congress to certify the results of the 2016 election, numerous Democratic members of the House objected, including:

Jim McGovern (D-MA) objected to Alabama's votes.

Jamie Raskin (D-MD) objected to Florida's votes.

Pramila Jayapal (D-WA) objected to Georgia's votes.

Raul Grijalva (D-AZ) objected to North Carolina's votes.

Sheila Jackson Lee (D-TX) objected to the votes from North Carolina in addition to votes from South Carolina and Wisconsin. She also stood up and objected to "massive voter suppression" after Mississippi's votes were announced.

Barbara Lee (D-CA) brought up allegations of Russian interference in the election and malfunctioning voting machines when she objected following the announcement of Michigan's votes.

Maxine Waters (D-CA) rose and said, "I do not wish to debate. I wish to ask 'Is there one United States senator who will join me in this letter of objection?'" after the announcement of Wyoming's votes.[86]

Once again, the media treated most of these objections as a sign of the times, with Trump being the one who caused the trouble. There was hardly any condemnation of those who sought to undermine the integrity of the 2016 election. The mainstream media did not rise up in a feeding frenzy against Democrats who said the election was stolen, just as they didn't rise up against Stacey Abrams. Some stories chided the Democrats for using the word *steal*, but mostly the media lionized Abrams and other resistance Democrats. MSNBC's Chris Hayes in 2018 called Abrams "a star."[87]

In contrast, as the *Washington Post* framed the story in May 2021, after Trump and his allies objected to the 2020 results, "The escalating rhetoric by the former president and his backers shows that he is intent on keeping alive the falsehood that the 2020 race was rigged, a claim that critics say has perilous implications for the country and the public's faith in how they select their leaders."[88]

So it's okay for Jimmy Carter, Hillary Clinton, John Lewis, Cory Booker, Sherrod Brown, and numerous liberal reporters to delegitimize election results that they don't like, but it's perilous when Trump does the same thing.

What about the implications for the country and the public's faith in how leaders are selected due to the sustained effort by Democrats to resist, overturn, and boycott Trump's 2016 victory by calling him illegitimate?

The mainstream media failed America by tacitly, and in some cases overtly, accepting the Democrats' narrative that Trump was the illegitimate winner of the 2016 race. Most of the media instantly and overwhelmingly condemned Trump's claims that he won the 2020 campaign, but they failed in their duty to condemn Democratic challenges to Trump's legitimacy. Instead, much of the media thought Trump's 2016 election was suspect because of Russian interference, which, of course, turned out to be wrong.

When one side in America's political debates sees the other side get away with extremist language challenging the results of an election, that side will respond in kind. In our divided country, if the media give a pass to one side, it only encourages the other side to escalate.

Pretty soon every candidate will think they can act like Stacey Abrams and Hillary Clinton, questioning the legitimacy of the candidate who defeated them. Candidates who lose close races in both parties will believe they should get away with such claims. When that happens, it will weaken confidence in election results and erode our democracy. The mainstream media may never acknowledge their role in the weakening of our nation's belief in the fairness and accuracy of elections. But their hypocritical reactions to parallel events undermine the faith much of the country has in the media to be fair, objective, and nonpartisan. In so many ways, the media has dug its own grave. (And this has nothing to do with the January 6, 2021, riot. The press objected to Trump's statements about his election defeat prior to January 6, and they did it in ways totally unlike how they covered objections to Hillary's 2016 defeat.)

If the mainstream press criticized Abrams, Clinton, *and* Trump, they would have more credibility. If they were fair, our nation would be stronger. If they weren't hypocritical, they would have more readers and viewers who trust them.

For the record, on November 7, 2020, when the media called the election for Joe Biden, I said live on FOX News that "I'm an American before I'm a Republican. I'm an American before I'm a pro-Trump voter. And so, congratulations to President-elect Joe Biden."[89]

I try to be consistent, which is more than I can say about America's mainstream media.

ONE HUNDRED DAYS INTO THE Biden administration, the Pew Research Center released a study of how the press covered Biden over the first sixty days of his tenure, compared to the first sixty days of Biden's four predecessors.[90]

The study showed that Biden got the softest coverage of the

presidents they studied. According to Pew, only 19 percent of the stories about Biden "had an overall negative assessment."

That contrasted with coverage of Trump's early days in office. At that time, 62 percent of news stories had an overall negative assessment. The study also showed that media coverage was easier on Biden than Obama, which tells you all you need to know about today's press corps.[91] They covered Biden with kid gloves. It's hard to get softer coverage than Barack Obama, but Joe Biden got it.

Comparing the five presidents, the three Democrats (Biden, Obama, and Clinton) got the least negative coverage, while the two Republicans (Bush and Trump) got the most negative coverage over their first sixty days. (Bush and Clinton tied each other with a 28 percent negative assessment.)[92]

The softness for Joe Biden came early and often. In October 2020, with Election Day in sight, NBC News held a town hall with the Democratic candidate in Miami. NBC's Lester Holt was the moderator. The audience was billed by NBC as a group of "undecided Florida voters."[93]

As the debate opened, Holt told those watching, "Welcome to tonight's town hall, where we are surrounded by dozens of undecided voters and where Democratic candidate Joe Biden will answer our questions and make his case tonight."[94]

"Undecided" voters. That sounds good.

One such voter, Peter Gonzalez, asked Biden, "Cuban American and Venezuelan voters here in South Florida are being targeted with messages by the Trump campaign claiming that a vote for Joe Biden is a vote for the radical left and socialism, and even communism. What can you tell people in my family, my friends—who are understandably concerned with that issue—that would make them feel comfortable voting for Joe Biden and Kamala Harris?"

Another voter, Ismael Llano, said, "Hi, Mr. Vice President. You talk a lot about your unity and division, but it seems now more than ever there's a divisiveness in the country that goes way beyond disagreeing with policy or whether you've made the right decision or not. It's either, 'You're with me or you're against me.' The role of president, in my opinion, should be to unify as much as possible, so what three actions will you take as president to get us back to being one country versus several little fiefdoms that are trying to yell at each other about who's wrong and right?"[95]

Nothing wrong with the questions but there was something wrong with NBC. Neither voter was undecided. They were both for Biden, a fact known to MSNBC.

According to the *Washington Free Beacon*, "Both Gonzalez and Llano . . . were featured in an MSNBC segment in August to explain why they support Biden. 'If we get four more years of Trump, good luck, and good luck with the future attracting younger voters,' Gonzalez said as an MSNBC chyron noted he was 'voting for Biden.' Llano was also identified as 'voting for Biden' and offered praise for the former vice president."[96]

I don't watch MSNBC, but maybe NBC should.

How could NBC bill its town hall as one with undecided voters when MSNBC previously reported it included Biden voters? This is poor journalism.

NBC's gathering wasn't the media's only tilted town hall.

On September 17, 2020, amid coronavirus restrictions, CNN hosted an unconventional drive-in town hall between Biden and Pennsylvania voters in a minor-league baseball stadium parking lot in Moosic, Pennsylvania.[97] According to Curtis Houck at the Media Research Center, during the town hall "Biden faced 16 total audience questions with 13 coming from Democrats to just three Republicans."[98] The primary was over. This was during the general election in 50-50 Pennsylvania. I know that media pollsters often undersample

Republicans. It looks like the producers who put on these town halls also undercount the GOP.

On December 2, 2020, President-elect Biden made a bold prediction about COVID-19 deaths. "I don't want to scare anybody here but understand the facts. We're likely to lose another 250,000 people dead between now and January. You hear me?"[99]

Biden was wrong. He grossly exaggerated the number of deaths. According to Johns Hopkins University, 72,267 people died between the date of Biden's warning and January 1, 2021.[100]

It's easy to see what was happening here. Biden's strategy was to exaggerate how bad things were prior to his taking office so he could receive credit for how much better conditions would eventually become. It's a common political tactic, the kind of thing most reporters are aware of and cautious about.

When January 1 came and went, did the mainstream media go back to Biden's frightening prediction and hold him to account? Of course not. When Biden manipulated numbers to serve his cause, the press gave him a pass. When Trump did it, they hammered him. Time and again, the press refuses to cover Biden in the same, skeptical, tough way it covers other public figures.

Campaigning in Iowa during the Democratic primaries in May 2019, Biden dismissed China's rising status as a threat to the United States, telling a crowd, "China is going to eat our lunch? Come on, man."[101]

Sitting in the Oval Office less than two years later, Biden told reporters, "Last night, I was on the phone for two straight hours with [Chinese president] Xi Jinping. . . . [I]f we don't get moving, they're going to eat our lunch."[102]

When a president flip-flops on a major issue, especially how he assesses the threat from China, you would think the 180-degree turn would be a major issue for the media, leading to substantial negative coverage for the new president. That's how the White House press corps covered Trump and Bush. That's not how they covered Biden. None of the mainstream networks erupted in a feeding frenzy over Biden's flip-flop. CNN and the *Washington Post* ignored it. The *New York Times* buried it at the very end of a larger piece.[103] FOX News dedicated more than fifteen minutes to the story.[104]

Joe Biden flip-flopped on China, but his base will never know, because the press that his base watches didn't tell them.

At Biden's first White House press conference, in March 2021, PBS correspondent Yamiche Alcindor stated that the surge in illegal immigrants at the southern border was because "the perception of you that got you elected—as a moral, decent man—is the reason a lot of immigrants are coming to this country and entrusting you with unaccompanied minors."[105]

A "moral, decent man." "Entrusted" by illegal immigrants.

Joe Biden is the man who, when campaigning for reelection as vice president in 2012, told a predominantly Black audience that Republicans under Mitt Romney would "put y'all back in chains."[106] It was one of the most divisive, wrong, and immoral attack lines ever delivered by a politician. I guess it never occurred to Alcindor that there may be many Americans who don't see Biden as moral and decent. But she does. Good for her. She's biased. And she's proud to show it.

Reporters, especially White House reporters, are supposed to be tough. They're supposed to ask hard questions, regardless of whom they cover. It should not matter to them if they like a president's policies or personality. It should not matter to them if the president is mean to them or nice to them. It shouldn't matter if the president is a fan of chocolate chocolate-chip ice cream and *Mario Kart,* two trivial items the Biden press corps swooned over when they heard Biden talk about them.[107]

Too often, in the Trump years and beyond, the mainstream media abandoned journalistic impartiality. They were wrong, hypocritical, didn't check their facts, and were way too friendly. They had an agenda—an anti-Trump, anti-Republican, don't-let-facts-get-in-the-way, suppress-it-if-necessary, deceive-when-helpful agenda—to support.

They still don't understand why they've lost the trust of people who aren't Democrats.

Chapter Twelve

WHAT COMES NEXT?

E very bit of suppression, deception, activism, and snobbery— replete with misleading headlines, retracted stories, erroneous anonymous sources, and editorialized stories—robs the American people of any belief that they can rely on the media to learn the truth about important national events. When the importance of sensationalism and subscriptions, aligned with taking sides in favor of Democrats and liberal causes, eclipses neutrality and fairness, our democracy breaks a little bit more.

Is the mainstream media capable of change? Will it keep getting worse? Do they even *want* to change or are they satisfied with the way they are perceived?

They are not satisfied, but that doesn't mean they'll change.

Within our mainstream media, there are good reporters whose work reflects the values of solid, down-the-middle journalism. But today, these reporters are a fading breed. If there is any group in Washington that is convinced it is right and stuck in its ways, it's the majority of reporters within the mainstream media. They're painfully aware of the polls that show most Americans don't trust them. They know they're perceived as biased. And they're scared to death about the looming loss of viewership or readership, and what that means for their livelihoods.

Most of today's newsrooms have been at it too long, doing it the same way, made up largely of the same type of people. When a newsroom is ideologically homogeneous, it's easy for like-minded reporters to think that their reporting is mostly full, fair, and accurate. If readers or viewers question the fullness, fairness, or accuracy of a story (remember that Gallup poll showing most Americans don't have confidence the press tells the news fully, fairly, or accurately), then, in the eyes of many reporters and editors, the fault lies with those viewers or readers, not with themselves. Especially if those viewers and readers are Republicans.

The capacity for today's media to be worthy of trust hinges on the media's commitment to supporting newsrooms that are ideologically diverse. It requires that they report stories that can be believed by most Americans, not just a slice of them.

For me, the real indictment of the press was the Pew Research Center poll showing that most Americans don't think the press understands them. Understanding people and keeping an open mind should not be hard, especially for curious people who want to be reporters. Open-mindedness and curiosity should be hallmarks of who journalists are and what they do.

When the only group of Americans who think the press understands them are college-educated Democrats, it should come across like a siren that the journalism profession has veered far off course and become out of touch.

But for too many reporters, in too many newsrooms, this warning siren is muffled by the resounding chorus of fellow college-educated Democratic voters. The words they use, the framing of their stories, their definition of what is news, and the bias they bring with them favor Democrats. This bias leads them to disregard—or speak derisively of—a significant percentage of the population who don't view the world through the same liberal, college-educated lens. Those most maligned by the media are Trump-supporting, conservative Republicans—especially Trump supporters who carry guns, think abortion is murder, or wear MAGA hats. If you don't think wearing a MAGA hat makes you guilty in the eyes of many reporters, just ask Nicholas Sandmann, the teenager in a MAGA hat from Covington Catholic High School whom many reporters excoriated for his "altercation" with a Native American on the steps of the Lincoln Memorial.

It would be shortsighted to think that the problems plaguing the press will vanish if Donald Trump vanishes. While Trump magnified preexisting problems and often stirred the pot, he didn't create the problems. The decay in the media's credibility has been decades in the making.

Now, after more than five years of finding their activist voices on behalf of a cause, the mainstream media is not about to mute themselves, especially when the business model of the media is polarized, with mainstream reporters and editors knowing their audiences consist mostly of Democrats. They can't *afford* to let it go, and many of them just don't want to anyway.

If Tom Cotton, Ted Cruz, Mike Pompeo, Ron DeSantis, Mike Pence, Kristi Noem, or pretty much any other conservative or populist Republican becomes the GOP presidential nominee in 2024, the press will do to them what they've done to Trump and his supporters. The press will quickly deride these candidates as dishonest, sexist, xenophobic, narrow-minded people who probably are racist and homophobic, too, not to mention that their policies hurt most Americans. The business model and advocacy habits of today's press corps demand it. Plus, it's become fun. An opportunity to tip the scale has become an enjoyable driving force for many of today's reporters and their news organizations. The classic restraint of neutral, down-the-middle journalism is an increasingly quaint practice of the pre-internet era.

As anyone watching CNN can see, reporters there have been licensed by their bosses to blend opinion and reporting, almost always in ways that favor Democrats over Republicans, and certainly anti-Trumpers over Trumpers. In a 2024 Biden or Kamala Harris race against any of the Republicans named above, is there anyone who thinks CNN will be neutral? Or if it's Donald Trump against either Biden or Harris, or any Democrat, Katy bar the door.

When confronted with what they've done wrong, reporters sometimes admit it, but then, all too often, they blame it on Trump. Take the reaction to the news when the Biden administration in the spring of 2021 said the Wuhan lab might actually have caused the release of coronavirus, contrary to a year's worth of absolute denial in the media.

"[Y]es, I think a lot of people have egg on their face," ABC News chief Washington correspondent Jonathan Karl said. "This was an idea that was first put forward by Mike Pompeo, secretary of state, Donald Trump. And look, some things may be true even if Donald Trump said them. And there was—because Trump was saying so much else, it was just out of control. And because he was, you know, making a frankly racist appeal talking about Kung Flu, and the China virus . . . he said flatly that this came from that lab was widely dismissed," Karl noted.[1]

In other words, reporters said it was *impossible* because Trump and Pompeo said it was *possible*.

Karl is admitting that the press didn't dig into possible facts. Possible facts were dismissed because they were put forth by Trump and his people. If that's not suppression and deception, what is?

Also referring to the possibility that Trump and Pompeo were right about the origin of the COVID-19 virus, *New York Times* reporter David Leonhardt belatedly reached a conclusion about bias and suppression. He told CNN, "I think people made this mistake, I think a lot of people on the political left, and a lot of people in the media, made this mistake, they said, 'wow if Tom Cotton is saying something, it can't be true.' Or they assumed that. And that's not right," Leonhardt said.[2] "Tom Cotton does deal in disinformation," Leonhardt alleged, but added, "that doesn't mean that everything he says is wrong."[3]

See, it's not just wrong if Donald Trump says it. It's wrong if Tom Cotton says it, too. You can see where this will be going in 2024 and beyond. If you think the press is one-and-done, you're wrong. Our nation may be closely divided, but journalists are not.

In the words of acclaimed journalist Lance Morrow, formerly of *Time* magazine, "in the *annus insanus* of 2020, we are afflicted by a pandemic of media phoniness. Plastering the facts with attitude—tilting the story to the party line, moralizing it, sentimentalizing it, propagandizing it—is the way of noisy, distracted cable news and, increasingly, of all media. Not a sparrow falls without the New York Times, in its news columns, telling the reader that the bird was shot by a 'white supremacist.' News is laid before the citizen's mind so packaged and tarted up with a narrative line that the simple facts are often impossible to discern."[4]

"This is not honest reporting but garish, partisan fabulation," Morrow wrote.

The elements sowing and sustaining this phony narrative draw strength from journalism's original sin: its homogeneity of thought. With newsrooms composed of too many similarly minded people, groupthink trounces individuality. Narratives defeat diversity of thought. Questioning authority depends on who the authorities are. Question Trump? Yes. Question Biden or Obama? Sometimes yes.

Often no. Going beyond prevailing narratives is too risky, especially for stories about social justice, especially in newsrooms full of younger reporters who want to move the needle. It's the same mindset that results in tough questions for anyone who wants to reduce government spending, cut business taxes, eliminate regulations, enact pro-life measures, or pass voting reforms. *Those* are problematic ideas. But those who seek to increase spending, raise taxes, advocate for abortion, promote so-called equity, or get rid of voting safeguards—*those* are forward-thinking, helpful measures.

Journalism needs a booster shot of independent thought. The few reporters left willing to challenge overwhelmingly liberal, cut-from-the-same-cloth narratives are not rewarded. They're driven out of the profession or relegated to Substack or some other independent forum where several, but not many, have flourished.

For journalism to reclaim its important role as a pillar of American society, executives at media companies will need to be courageous enough to do something anathema. They will need to hire journalists who think differently. They will need newsrooms with plenty of people, not a token one or two, who sound like America. They will need writers and editors who will raise uncomfortable issues and push back on prevailing liberal notions. They will need editors who run their publication for the entire country, not the loudest people on the internet, or the most noisy protesters in the streets, and definitely not for the most liberal faction of young social warriors in their newsrooms. The same-mindedness of newsrooms has turned mainstream outlets into redundant readouts for liberal and anticonservative narratives to be told over and over again, only with more edge and attitude than the last time the same tale was told.

If only newsrooms had more ideological diversity, the number of stories that were wrong, hypocritical, or too friendly toward the Democrats would decline. An entire new pool of readers and viewers might be convinced they could learn something, or get their news, from one of these outlets.

Is that too much to ask?

If I ran the admissions department at a journalism school, and I realized that all my students came from Manhattan, I would think that's a problem. If all my students came from east of the Mississippi, I would think that's a problem. If all my students were one race, religion, or gender, I would think that's a problem.

This brings me back to Columbia Journalism School and every other journalism school in the United States. Don't these top journalism schools want to graduate reporters who represent diversity of thought instead of a crop of reporters who all think the same way (poll after poll, and candid journalist after journalist, acknowledges the lopsided ideology in which they operate)? Don't these schools want to graduate reporters who understand our country? Not half the country but the entire country? That means turning out reporters who understand how to engage issues and people through the eyes of Trump voters, gun owners, those who hold only high school degrees, people who go to church every week, and people who are proudly pro-life.

I'm not talking about teaching largely liberal students how to travel, explore, and ask questions to people who have nothing in common with them. I'm talking about teaching people who grew up with guns, in rural towns, with a different approach to life, being recruited and welcomed into newsrooms.

Fixing journalism will require journalism schools and newsrooms everywhere to think deeply about the critical role they play in diversifying the field of journalism through the diversity of thought. Conservative thought cannot be anathema to journalists if the industry is to have a future.

I asked an unlikely source about the future of journalism.

Former president Trump isn't prone to introspection or dispassionate analyses of the media. (During our interview, he did call CBS White House correspondent Weijia Jiang "crazy"; CNN's Jim Acosta was "a maniac" and "a loser"; and CBS's Paula Reid was a "wackjob.")

If he had won the 2020 election, I asked him, "Do you think you as president would do something different in your second term about how you handle the press?"

"I don't think it would matter. I think they would treat me the same," he replied.

"What's the future for Republicans? How should Republicans handle the press?" I asked.

"I think the public is to a certain extent tuned out. You can't get worse publicity than I get. I think the public gets it. I think the public is very smart actually. It's something that is highly underrated."

The public is tuned out, he observed. The public gets it.

Trump's take is not all that different from the numerous poll results we've examined here, including the Gallup poll indicating that most Americans agree the press doesn't understand them (except for college-educated Democrats).

Don't the media *want* the public to tune them in? To watch, read, and listen, because the public knows they're getting the news fully, fairly, and accurately?

That would require reporters to be neutral and balanced. That would require newsrooms to crack down on advocacy, in print, on the air, and online.

That would require reporters to simply report the facts and the truth and leave the interpretations of what that means to their readers and viewers.

That would require the media to be composed of people who are different from those who make up the mainstream media today.

It would require news executives to do something their current crop of reporters won't like, welcome, or accept.

The rehabilitation of journalism is a heavy lift, one requiring the dedication and commitment of journalism school admission officers, reporters, and media executives. With work, newsrooms could start to see differing opinions not simply as *opposition* but as *opportunity*. An opportunity to understand half the country whose different ways of thinking have endured, and whose thought represents a valuable American contribution to our common cause, something to respect, not deride or look down upon.

Virtually all Americans—regardless of whether their ideals and beliefs align with those of liberal newsrooms—deserve respect. They also deserve a media that speaks *to* them instead of *at* them. A mainstream media that understands them and appeals to them rather than one that marginalizes, stereotypes, and often talks down to them.

Americans deserve a mainstream media that doesn't suppress news it doesn't like, a media that doesn't deceive people like they did with collusion in a way that immeasurably helped the Democrats, and a media that doesn't consist of activists for a cause.

It's not too late to have a media that sees its cracks not as unfixable fissures, but as a chance to reshape itself to fulfill its commitment to the American people.

Is that too much to ask?

Acknowledgments

Writing a book like this is a labor of love. I take seriously the media's important role in America and want the press to be a respected, trusted institution. It would be better for our country if the press could return to an era of trust, which is what inspired me to write this book.

I'm grateful to Eric Nelson, executive editor at HarperCollins, for contacting me out of the blue several years ago to suggest I write such a book. Thinking about how much work a book would be, I politely told him no. Eric accepted my reaction, but then said if the day ever comes when you can't stop thinking about something and you believe you could add to the conversation, you might want to write about it.

That's about when I started to watch the mainstream media increasingly abandon neutrality in reporting and become activists for a cause. I kept watching them tilt the news, being unfair in service to saving the Republic from the legitimately elected president of the United States, Donald Trump. As anyone who watches me on FOX knows, I support President Trump when he deserves it and I speak out against him when I think it's warranted. But the press was brutal and biased against Trump, and that's what inspired me to write this book.

Eric planted a seed and I'm glad he did. He not only launched me on this journey; his edits, suggestions, ideas, and reordering of thoughts have been spot on. Every writer needs a good editor, and I'm fortunate to have one of the very best.

This is the second book I've published with HarperCollins. Thank you to Doug Jones for making this possible. Also to James Neidhardt for his hard work in ushering the book along, crossing *T*s, dotting *I*s, and keeping things on schedule. Thanks also to Theresa Dooley and Tom Hopke for their efforts to promote and launch the book. I am grateful to have the support of everyone at HarperCollins.

A book like this relies on good fact-checkers and researchers. I'm fortunate to have two smart, hardworking, dedicated researchers, without whom I couldn't have written this. Bobby and Jane worked valiantly, checking, double-checking, and triple checking important details. Thanks to both of you for answering my hundreds of emails and being the professionals you are. Thanks also to Steve Guest from the Republican National Committee and Rich Noyes from Newsbusters for their tips and guidance that helped get the research done.

There is nothing I can do without the help of my executive assistant, Mary Beth Reilly. Mary Beth keeps me moving and makes me stay on time. Without her superb organizing skills and ability to juggle numerous balls at once, I would not have been able to write this. Thank you, MB.

Despite my many criticisms, I'm grateful to our nation's press corps. I've described here what they get wrong and how too many have lost their way. But I will never give up hope. The one question I hear more than any other is "Where can I go to get the news straight, without bias?" The country yearns for solid reporting. It's a good feeling to read a story or watch the news and tell myself I learned something

I didn't know, thanks to the reporters who told me about it. That remains the job of journalists everywhere, and despite the changes the industry is going through, there remain many reporters who want to get it right. I hope this book inspires journalism schools, journalists, and media executives to ask hard questions about their profession. Our nation needs it.

Finally, thank you to my wonderful family. To my mother, my brothers, their wives and significant others, my children, and of course Kitushtorte, thank you for your love and support. You mean everything to me.

Notes

Chapter One: Original Sin

1. *CNN Tonight*, January 25, 2020, CNN transcripts, http://transcripts.cnn.com/TRANSCRIPTS/2001/25/cnnt.01.html.
2. https://www.cnn.com/election/2016/results/exit-polls.
3. https://ballotpedia.org/Presidential_election,_2020.
4. Pew Research Center, "Two-thirds of U.S. adults say they've seen their own news sources report facts meant to favor one side," November 2, 2020, https://www.pewresearch.org/fact-tank/2020/11/02/two-thirds-of-u-s-adults-say-theyve-seen-their-own-news-sources-report-facts-meant-to-favor-one-side/.
5. Pew Research Center, "Americans See Skepticism of News Media as Healthy, Say Public Trust in the Institution Can Improve," August 31, 2020, https://www.journalism.org/2020/08/31/americans-see-skepticism-of-news-media-as-healthy-say-public-trust-in-the-institution-can-improve/.
6. Pew Research Center, "Nearly three quarters of Republicans say the news media don't understand people like them," January 18, 2019, https://www.pewresearch.org/fact-tank/2019/01/18/nearly-three-quarters-of-republicans-say-the-news-media-dont-understand-people-like-them/.
7. Pew Research Center, "U.S. Media Polarization and the 2020 Election: A Nation Divided," January 24, 2020, https://www.journalism.org/news-item/u-s-media-polarization-and-the-2020-election-a-nation-divided/.
8. https://twitter.com/JimVandeHei.
9. https://www.axios.com/2020-lessons-media-america-b6b6c184-ea46-4fc5-a6dd-0f5ad3dda082.html?utm_source=newsletter&utm_medium=email&utm_campaign=newsletter_axiosam&stream=top.
10. https://journals.sagepub.com/doi/10.1177/1077699018778242.
11. https://www.cjr.org/covering_the_election/campaign_donations

_journalists.php?utm_content=buffere88be&utm_medium=social& utm_source=twitter.com&utm_campaign=buffer.

12. https://hughhewitt.com/the-new-york-times-jane-coaston-on-whether -legacy-media-is-left-left-left-an-extension-of-the-democratic-party.

13. https://www.politico.com/f/?id=0000015d-e70d-d36c-a17f- e7ddb75c0000 Question POL 5_1.

14. https://nypost.com/2017/10/21/the-other-half-of-america-that-the-liberal -media-doesnt-cover.

15. https://knightfoundation.org/wp-content/uploads/2020/08/American -Views-2020-Trust-Media-and-Democracy.pdf, p. 17.

16. Ibid., p. 19.

17. Ibid.

18. Ibid.

19. Ibid.

20. https://www.politico.com/newsletters/playbook/2021/01/17/chuck-todd -to-republicans-quit-ducking-the-sunday-shows-491438.

21. Felix Salmon, "Media Trust Hits New Low," *Axios*, January 21, 2021, https://www.axios.com/media-trust-crisis-2bf0ec1c-00c0-4901-9069 -e26b21c283a9.html.

22. https://www.axios.com/media-trust-crisis-2bf0ec1c-00c0-4901-9069 -e26b21c283a9.html?utm_source=newsletter&utm_medium=email &utm_campaign=newsletter_axiosam&stream=top.

23. Interview with Michael Steel, November 6, 2020.

24. Ibid.

Chapter Two: Deceptions and Double Standards

1. Tweet by Donald J. Trump (@realDonaldTrump) on October 16, 2019.

2. "Trump tried to insult 'unhinged' Pelosi with an image. She made it her Twitter cover photo," *Washington Post*, October 17, 2019, https://www .washingtonpost.com/nation/2019/10/17/trump-insults-pelosi-over -meeting-photo-she-made-it-her-twitter-cover/.

3. *Morning Joe*, MSNBC, October 17, 2019, https://archive.org/details /MSNBCW_20191017_100000_Morning_Joe/start/720/end/780; https:// archive.org/details/MSNBCW_20191017_100000_Mornin g_Joe/start/660/end/720.

4. *New Day with Alisyn Camerota and John Berman*, CNN, October 17, 2019, https://archive.org/details/CNNW_20191017_110000_New_Day _With_Alisyn_Camerota_and_John_Berman/start/660/end/720.

5. https://www.nytimes.com/2019/10/18/us/politics/trump-pelosi-photo. html.

6. https://arizonadailyindependent.com/2019/10/17/brewer-calls-out-media -hypocrites-for-hailing-pelosi-pointing-finger-at-trump.

7. Chris Matthews, *MSNBC Hardball with Chris Matthews*, January 26,

2012, https://archive.org/details/MSNBC_20120127_000000_Hardball_With_Chris_Matthews/start/2160/end/2220.

8. John King, CNN, January 26, 2012, https://archive.org/details/CNN_20120126_230000_John_King_USA/Start/2160/end/2220.

9. Ashleigh Banfield, *Early Start*, CNN, January 26, 2012, https://archive.org/details/CNN_20120126_100000_Early_Start/start/0/end/60.

10. *CBS Evening News with Scott Pelley*, January 26, 2012, https://archive.org/details/WUSA_20120126_233000_CBS_Evening_News_With_Scott_Pelley/start/120/end/180.

11. Brian Williams, *NBC Nightly News*, January 26, 2012, https://archive.org/details/KNTV_20120127_013000_NBC_Nightly_News/start/0/end/60.

12. "In Airport Run-in, Democrats See Help for Obama Among Hispanics," *New York Times*, January 26, 2012, https://www.nytimes.com/2012/01/27/us/politics/in-airport-run-in-democrats-see-help-for-obama-among-hispanics.html.

13. https://nyti.ms/2FW99Zm.

14. https://news.gallup.com/poll/355526/americans-trust-media-dips-second-lowest-record.aspx.

15. https://news.gallup.com/poll/1663/media-use-evaluation.aspx.

16. Federal Bureau of Investigation, Boston Bureau, press release, April 17, 2013, https://archives.fbi.gov/archives/boston/press-releases/2013/no-arrest-made-in-bombing-investigation.

17. "The F.B.I. Criticizes the News Media After Several Mistaken Reports of an Arrest," *New York Times*, April 17, 2013, https://www.nytimes.com/2013/04/18/business/media/fbi-criticizes-false-reports-of-a-bombing-arrest.html.

18. "Coverage Rapid, And Often Wrong, In Tragedy's Early Hours," *Morning Edition*, National Public Radio, December 18, 2012, https://www.npr.org/2012/12/18/167466320/coverage-rapid-and-often-wrong-in-tragedys-early-hours.

19. https://archive.org/details/CNNW_20171208_130000_New_Day/start/540/end/600.

20. MSNBC, https://www.msnbc.com/msnbc/watch/sources-email-shows-effort-to-give-trump-camp-hacked-wikileaks-documents-1112367171825.

21. "CNN Corrects Story on Email to Trumps About Wikileaks," CNN Business, December 8, 2017, https://money.cnn.com/2017/12/08/media/cnn-correction-email-story/index.html.

22. https://www.washingtonpost.com/news/the-fix/wp/2017/12/09/cnn-botched-a-story-about-trump-jr-who-claims-without-evidence-that-reporters-got-played.

23. https://edition.cnn.com/2017/12/08/politics/email-effort-give-trump-campaign-wikileaks-documents/index.html.

24. https://money.cnn.com/2017/12/08/media/cnn-correction-email-story /index.html.

25. https://theintercept.com/2017/12/09/the-u-s-media-yesterday-suffered -its-most-humiliating-debacle-in-ages-now-refuses-all-transparency-over -what-happened.

26. Glenn Greenwald, *The Intercept*, December 9, 2017, https://the intercept.com/2017/12/09/the-u-s-media-yesterday-suffered-its-most -humiliating-debacle-in-ages-now-refuses-all-transparency-over-what -happened.

27. https://thefederalist.com/2021/03/16/washington-post-accuses-trump-of -a-crime-based-on-fabricated-quotes.

28. https://www.washingtonpost.com/politics/trump-call-georgia -investigator/2021/01/09/7a55c7fa-51cf-11eb-83e3-322644d82356 _story.html.

29. https://thefederalist.com/2021/03/16/washington-post-accuses-trump -of-a-crime-based-on-fabricated-quotes.

30. https://twitter.com/ron_fournier/status/948718790409445376.

31. ABC News, December 2, 2017, https://abcnews.go.com/US/abc-news -statement-michael-flynn-report/story?id=51536475.

32. https://www.washingtonpost.com/news/arts-and-entertainment/wp/2017 /12/03/abc-news-apologizes-for-serious-error-in-trump-report-suspends -brian-ross-for-four-weeks.

33. "Opinion: ABC News upgrades cowardly 'clarification' to 'correction' over bogus Flynn-Trump story," *Washington Post*, December 2, 2017, https:// www.washingtonpost.com/blogs/erik-wemple/wp/2017/12/02/abc-news -upgrades-cowardly-clarification-to-correction-over-bogus-flynn-trump -story.

34. https://www.salon.com/2007/04/11/abc_response/.

35. https://www.washingtonexaminer.com/opinion/surprise-report-claiming -us-has-the-worlds-highest-rate-of-children-in-detention-is-bogus.

36. https://www.npr.org/2019/11/20/781279252/u-n-expert-clarifies-statistic -on-u-s-detention-of-migrant-children#:~:text=Expert%20Clarifies%20 Statistic%20On%20U.S.%20Detention%20Of%20Migrant%20Children, -Facebook&text=The%20author%20of%20a%20sweeping,children%20 in%20migration%2Drelated%20detention.

37. https://www.washingtonexaminer.com/opinion/surprise-report-claiming -us-has-the-worlds-highest-rate-of-children-in-detention-is-bogus.

38. https://news.gallup.com/poll/116500/presidential-approval-ratings-george -bush.aspx.

39. https://www.mrc.org/media-reality-check/tv-buries-bad-news-public %E2%80%99s-rejection-obama%E2%80%99s-presidency.

40. https://news.gallup.com/poll/116479/barack-obama-presidential-job -approval.aspx.

41. Gallup, September 2, 2014, approval ratings, https://news.gallup.com /poll/113980/Gallup-Daily-Obama-Job-Approval.aspx.

42. https://www.mrc.org/media-reality-check/tv-buries-bad-news-public %E2%80%99s-rejection-obama%E2%80%99s-presidency.

43. https://cnn.it/3galfvD.

44. CNN, June 25, 2020, https://www.cnn.com/2020/06/25/politics/donald -trump-swing-state-polls-new-york-times-siena/index.html.

45. https://wapo.st/3lFztG3.

46. https://ballotpedia.org/Election_results,_2014.

47. https://www.nytimes.com/2014/10/31/us/why-republicans-keep-telling -everyone-theyre-not-scientists.html.

48. https://www.washingtonpost.com/news/the-fix/wp/2014/10/22/people -dont-like-mitch-mcconnell-thats-why-alison-lundergan-grimes-has-a -chance.

49. Ibid.

50. https://archive.org/details/CNNW_20141021_100000_New_Day/start /5400/end/5460.

51. https://archive.org/details/MSNBCW_20140426_120000_Up_WSteve _Kornacki/start/120/end/180.

52. https://justthenews.com/politics-policy/elections/pollster-john-mclaugh lin-says-election-polls-were-meant-depress-trump.

53. https://www.latimes.com/politics/story/2019-09-25/trump-california -unpopular-poll-2020-election.

54. https://nymag.com/intelligencer/2020/12/republicans-claw-back-four -california-congressional-seats.html.

55. https://www.langerresearch.com/wp-content/uploads/1216a52020StateB attlegrounds-MIWI.pdf.

56. https://int.nyt.com/data/documenttools/az-fl-pa-wi/bc6b622f38350414 /full.pdf.

57. Federal Election Commission, Official 2020 Presidential General Election Results, https://www.fec.gov/resources/cms-content/documents/2020 presgeresults.pdf.

58. http://cdn.cnn.com/cnn/2020/images/10/31/rel2_nc.pdf.

59. https://www.nbcnews.com/politics/meet-the-press/poll-biden-leads -trump-six-north-carolina-n1245468.

60. https://www.fec.gov/resources/cms-content/documents/2020presgere sults.pdf.

61. https://poll.qu.edu/florida/release-detail?ReleaseID=3683.

62. https://www.fec.gov/resources/cms-content/documents/2020presgere sults.pdf.

63. https://poll.qu.edu/kentucky/release-detail?ReleaseID=3673.

64. https://ballotpedia.org/United_States_Senate_election_in_Maine, _2020.

65. https://www.nbcnews.com/politics/meet-the-press/poll-biden-leads
-trump-six-north-carolina-n1245468.

66. https://ballotpedia.org/United_States_Senate_election_in_North
_Carolina,_2020.

67. https://nyti.ms/3mU4SpJ.

68. https://www.nytimes.com/2020/10/17/us/politics/joni-ernst-iowa
-republican-senate.html.

69. https://ballotpedia.org/United_States_Senate_election_in_Iowa,_2020.

70. https://nyti.ms/36WyjSs.

71. https://www.nytimes.com/2020/10/27/us/politics/democrats-house
-elections.html.

72. https://www.nytimes.com/interactive/2020/11/03/us/elections/results
-indiana-house-district-5.html.

73. https://wapo.st/3gsEkJz.

74. https://www.washingtonpost.com/politics/house-trump-democrats
-republicans/2020/10/25/685717ae-1550-11eb-82af-864652063d61_story
.html.

75. https://www.politico.com/news/2021/02/08/2020-house-anthony-brindisi
-concedes-467560.

76. https://www.realclearpolitics.com/epolls/2020/president/us/general
_election_trump_vs_biden-6247.html.

77. https://www.cnbc.com/2020/11/02/2020-election-polls-biden-leads
-trump-in-six-swing-states.html.

78. https://www.documentcloud.org/documents/7280263-200986-NBCWSJ
-Late-October-Poll.html.

79. https://poll.qu.edu/national/release-detail?ReleaseID=3681.

80. https://www.pewresearch.org/fact-tank/2021/01/28/turnout-soared-in
-2020-as-nearly-two-thirds-of-eligible-u-s-voters-cast-ballots-for
-president.

81. https://www.cfr.org/blog/2020-election-numbers; https://www.fec.gov
/resources/cms-content/documents/2020presgeresults.pdf.

82. https://www.niemanlab.org/2016/11/has-election-2016-been-a-turning
-point-for-the-influence-of-the-news-media.

83. https://www.presidency.ucsb.edu/statistics/data/2020-general-election
-editorial-endorsements-major-newspapers.

Chapter Three: Reporters Have Lost Their Minds

1. CNBC, full transcript, published October 29, 2015, https://www.cnbc
.com/2015/10/29/cnbc-full-transcript-cnbcs-your-money-your-vote-the
-republican-presidential-debate-part-2.html.

2. https://www.washingtonpost.com/news/book-party/wp/2018/04/20/amy
-chozick-covered-hillary-clinton-for-a-decade-heres-what-she-learned
-and-what-she-endured/?noredirect=on.

3. https://www.wsj.com/articles/the-liberal-leaning-media-has-passed-its-tipping-point-11590430876.
4. "FBI's Spreadsheet Puts a Stake Through the Heart of Steele's Dossier," *The Hill*, July 16, 2019, https://thehill.com/opinion/white-house/453384-fbis-spreadsheet-puts-a-stake-through-the-heart-of-steeles-dossier.
5. "Bomb Threats to Jewish Community Centers and Organizations," ProPublica, March 23, 2017, https://projects.propublica.org/graphics/jcc-bomb-threats.
6. https://www.nytimes.com/2017/02/28/us/jewish-community-center-donald-trump.html?auth=login-email&login=email.
7. https://www.thedailybeast.com/trump-appears-to-suggest-bomb-threats-against-jews-are-false-flags?source=twitter&via=desktop.
8. Ibid.
9. *New Day*, CNN, February 21, 2017, http://www.cnn.com/TRANSCRIPTS/1702/21/nday.03.html.
10. https://observer.com/2017/03/juan-thompson-anti-semitic-jcc-bomb-threats.
11. "The Dangers of Blaming Trump for Anti-Semitism," *Atlantic*, March 24, 2017, https://www.theatlantic.com/politics/archive/2017/03/the-dangers-of-blaming-trump-for-anti-semitism/520692.
12. *Guardian*, https://www.youtube.com/watch?v=yAaFzbOsG3s.
13. https://bit.ly/3ERj5vA.
14. https://www.cnn.com/2017/11/06/politics/donald-trump-koi-pond-japan/index.html.
15. https://www.washingtonexaminer.com/cnn-others-spread-honest-to-goodness-fake-news-about-trumps-japan-visit.
16. ABC News, Twitter, @ABC, November 5, 2017, https://twitter.com/BC/status/927400010890833926?ref_src=twsrc%5Etfw%7Ctwcamp%5Etweetembed%7Ctwterm%5E927400010890833926%7Ctwgr%5E%7Ctwcon%5Es1_&ref_url=https%3A%2F%2Fmashable.com%2F2017%2F11%2F06%2Fdonald-trump-feeds-koi-fake-news%2F.
17. Jezebel, Twitter, @Jezebel, November 6, 2017, https://twitter.com/jezebel/status/927442529104035840.
18. Alana Abramson, "Donald Trump Was Criticized for Overfeeding Fish in Japan. But the Prime Minister Did It First," *Time*, November 6, 2017, https://time.com/5011386/donald-trump-fish-koi-japan.
19. https://thehill.com/opinion/white-house/358983-media-shows-why-its-so-mistrusted-after-falsified-trump-fish-feeding.
20. Interview with President Trump, April 28, 2021, Mar-a-Lago, Palm Beach, Florida.
21. https://www.cnn.com/2020/08/22/politics/melania-trump-rose-garden-restoration/index.html.
22. https://www.usatoday.com/story/opinion/2020/08/25/melania-trump

-and-rose-garden-renovations-leave-dull-and-pale-column/3426365
001.

23. https://www.foreignaffairs.com/articles/2018-08-13/how-we-got-iran
-deal.

24. https://www.architecturaldigest.com/story/the-full-story-behind-the
-controversial-rose-garden-redesign.

25. https://muckrack.com/howardfineman.

26. Alan Taylor, "Not My President: Thousands March in Protest," *Atlantic*,
November 10, 2016, https://www.theatlantic.com/photo/2016/11/not-my
-president-thousands-march-in-protest/507248.

27. https://washingtonpost.com/news/the-fix/wp/2016/03/07/the-hitler
-ification-of-donald-trump/.

28. https://nymag.com/intelligencer/2016/07/donald-trump-and-hitlers-rise
-to-power.html.

29. https://www.nytimes.com/politics/first-draft/2015/06/16/choice-words
-from-donald-trump-presidential-candidate.

30. https://www.bostonglobe.com/metro/2016/03/23/congressman-seth
-moulton-compares-rise-donald-trump-election-hitler/5nbZpv2d4B25N2
A3hgOldP/story.html.

31. https://encyclopedia.ushmm.org/content/en/article/kristallnacht.

32. Christiane Amanpour, CNN transcripts, November 12, 2020, http://trans
cripts.cnn.com/TRANSCRIPTS/2011/12/ampr.01.html.

33. https://www.washingtonpost.com/washington-post-live/2020/11/23/
transcript-cape-up-live-rep-ilhan-omar-with-jonathan-capehart/.

34. *Morning Joe*, MSNBC, June 22, 2018, https://archive.org/details/MSN
BCW_20180622_100000_Morning_Joe/start/1075/end/1135?q=donny
+deutsch.

35. https://www.nationalreview.com/2018/06/comparing-trump-administra
tion-to-nazis-trivializes-holocaust/.

36. MSNBC, *Morning Joe*, September 23, 2020, https://archive.org/details
/MSNBCW_20200923_100000_Morning_Joe/start/4260/end/4320.

37. https://thefederalist.com/2020/08/17/6-myths-about-u-s-postal-service
-and-the-election-debunked.

38. https://twitter.com/taylorswift13/status/1294685437362155522.

39. https://about.usps.com/who-we-are/postal-history/mail-collection-boxes
.pdf.

40. Rebecca Heilweil, "How a Viral Photo of USPS Collection Boxes Became a
Lesson in Misinformation," *Vox*, August 19, 2020, https://www.vox.com
/recode/2020/8/19/21375303/mailboxes-removed-usps-postal-service
-collection-boxes-mail-in-voting.

41. https://www.uspsoig.gov/blog/where-have-all-collection-boxes-gone.

42. https://www.nbcnewyork.com/news/local/usps-mailboxes-removed-in
-some-new-york-neighborhoods/2569908.

43. https://www.sfchronicle.com/bayarea/article/U-S-Postal-Service-removes
-collection-boxes-in-15523485.php.

44. https://www.independent.co.uk/news/world/americas/us-politics/2020
-election-mail-box-removal-trump-ballots-voting-postal-service
-a9671951.html.

45. https://www.npr.org/2020/08/16/903056927/pelosi-calls-back-lawmakers
-to-vote-on-postal-service.

46. Michael Shear, "Trump Envisions a Parade Showing Off American
Military Might," *New York Times*, September 18, 2017, https://www
.nytimes.com/2017/09/18/us/politics/trump-4th-of-july-military-parade
.html.

47. https://twitter.com/repmcgovern/status/961032422249975808?lang=da.

48. *Anderson Cooper 360*, CNN, February 7, 2018, https://www.cnn.com
/videos/politics/2018/02/07/jackie-speier-military-parade-napoleon-sot
-ac360.cnn.

49. https://www.vox.com/the-big-idea/2018/2/12/17003600/trump-military-
parade-bastille-day-washington.

50. NBC News, https://www.nbcnews.com/politics/donald-trump/trump
-plans-elaborate-july-4th-party-d-c-critics-say-n1021276.

51. Peter Baker, "Trump Sets Off Fireworks of a Different Sort with Fourth
of July Speech Plan," *New York Times*, June 5, 2019, https://www.nytimes
.com/2019/06/05/us/politics/trump-4th-of-july.html.

52. C-SPAN, July 4, 2019, full transcript, https://www.c-span.org/video
/?462091-1/president-trump-speaks-4th-july-celebration.

53. Ibid.

54. Ibid.

55. https://www.cnn.com/videos/politics/2019/07/04/trump-july-4th-speech
-military-phil-mudd-reaction-sot-tsr-vpx.cnn.

56. Stephen Collinson, CNN, https://www.cnn.com/2019/07/05/politics
/trump-july-4th-speech/index.html.

57. Ibid.

58. CNN transcripts, November 7, 2020, http://transcripts.cnn.com/TRANS
CRIPTS/2011/07/se.20.html.

59. Karla Adam, "No, Paris didn't ring church bells for Biden. And London
fireworks had more to do with Guy Fawkes," *Washington Post*, November
9, 2020, https://www.washingtonpost.com/world/europe/paris-bells
-london-fireworks-biden/2020/11/09/aba7b5c8-22a6-11eb-9c4a-0dc62
42c4814_story.html.

60. "Piers Morgan Mocks ABC News After They Claim Bonfire Night Fire-
works Were For Joe Biden," Simple News, November 9, 2020, https://
simplenews.co.uk/general/piers-morgan-mocks-abc-news-after-they
-claim-bonfire-night-fireworks-were-for-joe-biden.

61. Tim Graham, Media Research Center, *NewsBusters*, November 9, 2020,

https://www.newsbusters.org/blogs/nb/tim-graham/2020/11/09/morons
-brits-laugh-abc-cnn-msnbc-thinking-uk-fireworks-were-biden.

62. *The Week with Joshua Johnson*, MSNBC, November 8, 2020, https://
archive.org/details/MSNBCW_20201109_040000_The_Week_With
_Joshua_Johnson/start/2640/end/2700.

63. https://apnews.com/article/fact-checking-9692562784.

64. "2017 Super Bowl Champions White House Visit," C-SPAN, April 19, 2017,
https://www.c-span.org/video/?427236-1/president-trump-welcomes
-england-patriots-white-house.

65. Victor Mather, "Tom Brady Skips Patriots' White House Visit Along With
Numerous Teammates," *New York Times*, April 19, 2017, https://www
.nytimes.com/2017/04/19/sports/-new-england-patriots-visit-white
-house-donald-trump.html.

66. https://www.yahoo.com/now/melania-trump-gets-mocked-wearing
-timberland-boots-visiting-troops-221926377.html.

67. https://www.teenvogue.com/story/melania-trump-puerto-rico-heels
-timberland-boots-backlash.

68. https://thefederalist.com/2020/09/17/media-timberland-boots-only-look
-fabulous-on-democrats.

69. Ibid.

Chapter Four: The Way It Was

1. https://news.gallup.com/poll/1663/media-use-evaluation.aspx.

2. "Cronkite Podcast: The Most Trusted Man in America," Journalism His-
tory, July 19, 2020, https://journalism-history.org/2020/07/19/cronkite
-podcast-the-most-trusted-man-in-america/.

3. https://news.gallup.com/poll/1663/media-use-evaluation.aspx.

4. https://www.cjr.org/special_report/how-does-journalism-happen-poll
.php.

5. https://reutersinstitute.politics.ox.ac.uk/digital-news-report/2021/dnr
-executive-summary.

6. https://www.journalism.org/chart/network-tv-evening-news-overall
-viewership-since-1980.

7. https://www.axios.com/newsletters/axios-am-3390b186-c31b-4336-973f
-7032d63ad79a.html?chunk=8&utm_term=emshare#story8.

8. https://www.journalism.org/fact-sheet/newspapers.

9. https://www.vox.com/2015/5/3/11562248/the-new-york-times-will-soon
-hit-1-million-digital-subscribers-but.

10. https://www.statista.com/statistics/273503/average-paid-weekday
-circulation-of-the-new-york-times/#:~:text=In%202019%2C%20the%
20average%20weekday,for%20the%20last%20few%20years.

11. https://www.cnbc.com/2016/11/29/new-york-times-subscriptions-soar
-tenfold-after-donald-trump-wins-presidency.html.

12. https://www.vox.com/recode/2020/11/5/21551379/new-york-times
    -subscribers-q3-2020-trump-election-pandemic.
13. https://www.cjr.org/special_report/when-all-the-news-that-fits-is-trump
    .php.
14. https://www.latimes.com/entertainment-arts/business/story/2020-11-23
    /cable-tv-news-donald-trump-fox-news-cnn-msnbc.
15. https://shorensteincenter.org/news-coverage-donald-trumps-first-100
    -days/#_ftnref18.
16. Ibid.
17. https://www.cjr.org/politics/cable-news-trump-obsession.php.
18. Ibid.
19. https://shorensteincenter.org/news-coverage-donald-trumps-first-100
    -days/#_ftnref18.
20. https://www.nytimes.com/2020/05/04/opinion/letters/joe-biden-tara
    -reade.html.
21. Ibid.
22. https://millercenter.org/the-presidency/presidential-speeches/march-12
    -1933-fireside-chat-1-banking-crisis.
23. https://www.politico.com/story/2018/03/27/redesign-editors-note-484867.
24. https://www.c-span.org/video/?508155-1/swearing-ceremony-biden
    -administration-appointees.
25. https://www.politico.com/newsletters/playbook/2021/01/21/democrats
    -caught-flat-footed-by-total-control-of-washington-491476.
26. https://www.politico.com/newsletters/playbook-pm/2021/01/27/dems
    -are-over-impeachment-too-491546?nname=playbook-pm&nid=0000015
    a-dd3e-d536-a37b-dd7fd8af0000&nrid=0000014f-88f9-d780-a9ef-9dfb
    d4c60000&nlid=964328.
27. https://www.politico.com/playbook/0607/7.html.
28. https://www.politico.com/newsletters/playbook/2021/01/19/the-washing
    ton-trump-leaves-behind-491443.
29. https://www.axios.com/china-spy-california-politicians-9d2dfb99-f839
    -4e00-8bd8-59dec0daf589.html.
30. https://www.nytimes.com/2021/06/20/us/politics/liz-cheney-republican
    -party-trump.html.
31. https://www.newsbusters.org/blogs/nb/rich-noyes/2021/05/19/liberal-tv
    -touts-gop-civil-war-over-bidens-policy-debacles.
32. https://www.pewresearch.org/fact-tank/2020/02/14/fast-facts-about
    -the-newspaper-industrys-financial-struggles/#:~:text=U.S.%20newspaper
    %20circulation%20fell%20in,first%20year%20with%20available%20
    data.&text=Newspaper%20revenues%20declined%20dramatically%20
    between,2018%2C%20a%2062%25%20decline.
33. https://www.brandknewmag.com/why-digital-media-is-killing-tv
    -advertising.

34. Journalist and author Matt Taibbi presented a lecture on his book *Hate Inc.: Why Today's Media Makes Us Despise One Another*. This event was cosponsored by Penn State's McCourtney Institute for Democracy and Donald P. Bellisario College of Communications. https://www.youtube.com/watch?v=mG1qJeDI9Ok.

35. https://www.thedailybeast.com/more-than-100-politico-staffers-send-letter-to-ceo-railing-against-publishing-ben-shapiro.

36. https://www.pewresearch.org/fact-tank/2020/04/01/americans-main-sources-for-political-news-vary-by-party-and-age/.

37. Ibid.

38. Ibid.

39. Ibid.

40. https://www.washingtonpost.com/news/the-fix/wp/2017/08/02/stephen-miller-vs-jim-acosta-sent-the-white-house-press-briefing-completely-off-the-rails/?utm_term=.24eb22b5364d.

41. https://www.rand.org/pubs/research_reports/RR2960.html.

42. https://www.vanityfair.com/news/2016/11/bill-plante-signs-off.

43. https://www.realclearpolitics.com/video/2017/03/05/bill_plante_to_journalists_dont_share_how_you_feel_about_trump_if_youre_offended_keep_it_to_yourself.html; https://edition.cnn.com/videos/tv/2017/03/05/dc-veterans-say-this-drama-is-unprecedented.cnn.

44. https://www.theatlantic.com/politics/archive/2020/12/media-after-trump/617503/.

45. Ibid.

46. Ibid.

47. Ibid.

48. Ibid.

Chapter Five: Suppression

1. https://www.britannica.com/event/Logan-Act.

2. https://www.washingtonpost.com/politics/2020/06/26/michael-flynn-barack-obama-trumps-claims-treason.

3. Ibid.

4. https://www.c-span.org/video/?475947-1/fbi-director-james-comey-testimony-russia-investigation.

5. https://www.goodmorningamerica.com/news/story/biden-pushes-back-trumps-testing-claims-labels-coronavirus-70624491.

6. https://www.msnbc.com/transcripts/the-last-word/2020-05-14-msna1357196.

7. https://www.washingtonpost.com/national-security/new-justice-dept-disclosures-cast-fresh-doubt-on-trump-russia-investigation/2020/09/25/f08ccfb0-ff61-11ea-9ceb-061d646d9c67_story.html.

8. Ibid.

9. Original research.
10. https://bit.ly/3u6Zm6T.
11. https://bluevirginia.us/2021/05/video-virginia-democratic-lt-governor -candidates-debate.
12. https://www.washingtonpost.com/local/virginia-politics/sam-rasoul -muslim-faith-debate/2021/05/26/90d37938-be25-11eb-b26e-53663e6be 6ff_story.html.
13. Original research.
14. https://www.nytimes.com/2017/09/28/us/amy-coney-barrett-nominee -religion.html.
15. https://www.hsgac.senate.gov/imo/media/doc/Statement%20for%20 Record-OSC%20Report%20Redacted-2017-07-14.pdf.
16. https://www.washingtonpost.com/politics/postal-service-broke-law-in -pushing-time-off-for-workers-to-campaign-for-clinton-investigation -finds/2017/07/19/3292741c-6ca0-11e7-b9e2-2056e768a7e5_story .html.
17. https://www.nytimes.com/search?dropmab=true&end-Date=20210527 &query=USPS%20hatch%20act%20or%20clinton&sort=best&startDate =20170701.
18. https://www.cnn.com/2017/07/19/politics/osc-usps-hillary-clinton-hatch -act/index.html.
19. Original research.
20. https://www.nytimes.com/2020/06/11/us/politics/steve-huffman-african -americans-coronavirus.html?referringSource=articleShare.
21. https://www.foxnews.com/politics/texas-dem-official-faces-demands-to -step-down-after-calling-tim-scott-an-oreo.amp?__twitter_impression =true.
22. https://www.nytimes.com/search?dropmab=true&end- Date=20210528&query=oreo&sort=best&startDate=20210425.
23. Original research.
24. Original research.
25. https://www.miamiherald.com/news/local/community/miami-dade /article145327079.html.
26. https://www.nytimes.com/2017/04/21/us/florida-senator-frank-artiles -resigns-racist-rant.html.
27. https://www.dailymail.co.uk/news/article-9661781/Hunter-Biden-used -n-word-multiple-times-casual-conversation-text-messages-show.html.
28. https://www.dailymail.co.uk/news/article-9689809/No-yellow-Hunter -Biden-referred-Asians-slur-2019-texts.html.
29. https://www.snopes.com/news/2017/11/02/dnc-white-males.
30. Original research.
31. https://www.washingtonpost.com/world/national-security/gop-aides -online-dig-at-obama-daughters-creates-backlash/2014/11/29/688305

0a-7806-11e4-a755-e32227229e7b_story.html?wpisrc=nl-most&
wpmm=1&itid=lk_inline_manual_5.

32. https://www.nytimes.com/politics/first-draft/2014/12/01/g-o-p-aide
-quits-over-remarks-critical-of-obama-daughters/?searchResult
Position=1.

33. https://archive.org/details/tv?q=Elizabeth%20Lauten.

34. GOP Communications Aide Criticizes Obama's Daughters on Facebook
Post Coverage.docx.

35. https://thehill.com/homenews/media/504103-melania-trumps-spokes
woman-slams-inappropriate-and-insensitive-comments-about.

36. https://www.nytimes.com/2017/09/05/us/politics/barron-tiffany-trump
-school.html?searchResultPosition=1; https://www.google.com/search
?q=washington+post+barron+daily+caller&oq=washington+post+barron
+daily+caller&aqs=chrome.69i57.9939j1j4&sourceid=chrome&ie=UTF-8;
https://archive.org/details/CNNW_20170822_190000_CNN_News
room_With_Brooke_Baldwin/start/3502/end/3562?q=%28barron
+trump+and+daily+caller%29+AND+date%3A%5B2017-08-20+TO+20
17-9-1%5D; https://archive.org/details/tv?q=%28barron%20trump%20
and%20daily%20caller%29%20AND%20date%3A%5B2017-08-20%20
TO%202017-9-1%5D.

37. https://onlinelibrary.wiley.com/doi/full/10.1111/1468-0009.12368.

38. https://www.politico.com/story/2019/01/29/coke-obesity-sugar-research
-1125003.

39. https://www.washingtonpost.com/news/powerpost/paloma/the
-health-202/2019/01/29/the-health-202-coca-cola-emails-reveal-how
-soda-industry-tries-to-influence-health-officials/5c4f65dd1b326b29
c3778cf1.

40. https://www.cnn.com/2019/01/29/health/coca-cola-cdc-emails-study
/index.html.

41. https://nypost.com/2021/05/01/teachers-union-collaborated-with-cdc-on
-school-reopening-emails.

42. Original research.

43. https://wapo.st/3imMohK.

44. https://www.newsbusters.org/blogs/nb/brent-bozell/2018/08/28/bozell
-graham-column-corrupt-democrats-are-not-news.

45. https://www.nytimes.com/2021/05/06/us/corrine-brown-conviction
-overturned-florida.html.

46. https://www.rev.com/transcript-editor/shared/Qd6ISebt6xIXQ
lpttsT15YuX8oZmekdjwKK5xj9M3FkPhhNDXaOK7m1AXHS0A9
7OqQe8AuT8ZWVbaeJWUu6eWe8v9oc?loadFrom=PastedDeeplink&ts
=700.98.

47. https://1drv.ms/b/s!AoiWGeTm2ZIFhTHeniqplcEDhbsc?e=wymWsY.

48. http://transcripts.cnn.com/TRANSCRIPTS/2009/12/smer.01.html.

49. Original research.
50. https://archive.org/details/FOXNEWSW_20200910_220000_Special _Report_With_Bret_Baier/start/960/end/1020.
51. https://www.nytimes.com/2020/02/21/us/politics/biden-south-africa -arrest-mandela.html.
52. https://archive.org/details/CNNW_20200228_130000_New_Day_With _Alisyn_Camerota_and_John_Berman/start/2580/end/2640.
53. https://www.cbsnews.com/news/south-carolina-democratic-debate-full -transcript-text.
54. https://www.cbsnews.com/news/biden-cognitive-test-why-the-hell-would -i-take-a-test.
55. https://www.nytimes.com/2020/08/05/us/elections/trump-vs-biden.htm l?searchResultPosition=1.
56. Original research.
57. https://nypost.com/2020/10/14/email-reveals-how-hunter-biden-intro duced-ukrainian-biz-man-to-dad.
58. https://www.nytimes.com/2020/10/14/us/politics/hunter-biden-ukraine -facebook-twitter.html.

Chapter Six: Viewership Views

1. The data is the result of two U.S. surveys conducted April 23–26, 2021, and June 24–25, 2021, each with a 1,000-respondent national sample. Interviews were conducted online. The demographics (age, gender, party ID, income, education, race, etc.) were weighted to reflect turnout in the 2020 presidential election. Margin of error was +/- 2.2 percent.
2. https://www.pbs.org/wnet/firing-line/video/stacey-abrams-4x42pr.
3. Original research.
4. https://www.nydailynews.com/news/politics/new-york-elections-govern ment/ny-noncitizen-voting-new-york-municipal-elections-20210224-biok lbqwwbgbpafjncqomnyvpe-story.html.
5. Ibid.
6. https://www.nytimes.com/2021/12/09/nyregion/noncitizens-voting -rights-nyc.html.
7. https://ballotpedia.org/Laws_permitting_noncitizens_to_vote_in_the _United_States.
8. https://www.foxnews.com/politics/vermont-senate-dems-override-gop -governors-vetoes-on-noncitizen-voting.
9. https://www.washingtonpost.com/politics/in-flag-burning-com ments-trump-again-plays-to-the-base-voters-that-elected-him/2016 /11/29/31ee203c-b64e-11e6-a677-b608fbb3aaf6_story.html.
10. https://www.washingtonpost.com/news/post-politics/wp/2016/11/29 /trump-suggests-loss-of-citizenship-or-jail-for-those-who-burn-u-s-flags.
11. https://www.washingtonpost.com/politics/in-flag-burning-comments

-trump-again-plays-to-the-base-voters-that-elected-him/2016/11/29/31ee
203c-b64e-11e6-a677-b608fbb3aaf6_story.html.

Chapter Seven: CNN

1. https://www.nytimes.com/2006/06/26/business/media/26carr.html.
2. https://www.journalism.org/2020/01/24/americans-are-divided-by-party
   -in-the-sources-they-turn-to-for-political-news/.
3. https://freebeacon.com/media/nearly-half-of-cnns-republican-comment
   ators-are-voting-for-biden.
4. Ibid.
5. Ibid.
6. https://theintercept.com/2019/01/20/beyond-buzzfeed-the-10-worst-most
   -embarrassing-u-s-media-failures-on-the-trumprussia-story/.
7. https://www.washingtonpost.com/lifestyle/style/the-story-behind-a
   -retracted-cnn-report-on-the-trump-campaign-and-russia/2017/08/17
   /af03cd60-82d6-11e7-ab27-1a21a8e006ab_story.html.
8. https://thehill.com/blogs/blog-briefing-room/336871-cnn-issues
   -correction-after-comey-statement-contradicts-reporting; https://www
   .cnn.com/2017/06/06/politics/comey-testimony-refute-trump-russian
   -investigation.
9. https://www.cnn.com/2017/09/18/politics/paul-manafort-government
   -wiretapped-fisa-russians/index.html.
10. https://www.cnn.com/2018/07/26/politics/michael-cohen-donald-trump
    -june-2016-meeting-knowledge/index.html.
11. Chris Cillizza, "Michael Cohen just dropped a collusion bombshell in the
    Russia investigation," CNN Politics, July 27, 2018, https://www.cnn
    .com/2018/07/26/politics/michael-cohen-donald-trump-russia-meeting
    /index.html.
12. https://www.washingtonpost.com/politics/attorney-for-michael-cohen
    -backs-away-from-confidence-that-cohen-has-information-about-trumps
    -knowledge-on-russian-efforts/2018/08/26/09d7f26e-a876-11e8-97ce-cc9
    042272f07_story.html.
13. https://archive.org/details/CNNW_20180802_120000_New_Day_With
    _Alisyn_Camerota_and_John_Berman/start/2520/end/2580.
14. https://www.nytimes.com/2017/10/27/us/politics/trump-dossier-paul
    -singer.html.
15. https://www.nytimes.com/2017/10/24/us/politics/clinton-dnc-russia
    -dossier.html.
16. https://www.lamag.com/citythinkblog/michael-avenatti-lawsuits-2021.
17. https://www.cnn.com/2021/07/08/politics/michael-avenatti-prison-nike
    -extortion/index.html.
18. https://www.newsbusters.org/blogs/nb/bill-dagostino/2019/04/11/update
    -tv-news-hosted-michael-avenatti-254-times-one-year.

19. https://www.newsbusters.org/blogs/nb/bill-dagostino/2018/05/02/one
-day-cnn-hosts-porn-stars-lawyer-michael-avenatti-59-times.

20. Ibid.

21. Original research.

22. https://archive.org/details/CNNW_20210121_120000_New_Day_With
_Alisyn_Camerota_and_John_Berman/start/180/end/240.

23. White House press briefing, January 21, 2021, https://www.whitehouse
.gov/briefing-room/press-briefings/2021/01/21/press-briefing-by-press
-secretary-jen-psaki-january-21-2021/.

24. https://twitter.com/AriFleischer/status/1352256196313559043.

25. https://www.newsbusters.org/blogs/nb/mike-ciandella/2017/09/27/cnn
-ignores-menendez-trial-barely-skipped-day-ted-stevens-08.

26. https://www.govinfo.gov/content/pkg/DCPD-201700815/html/DCPD
-201700815.htm.

27. https://www.nbc26.com/news/national/trump-asks-japan-to-build-cars
-in-the-us.

28. https://www.cnn.com/videos/politics/2020/05/21/chris-andrew-cuomo
-swabs-test-joke-cpt-vpx.cnn.

29. https://www.cnn.com/videos/politics/2020/06/30/chris-cuomo-ron-desan
tis-florida-coronavirus-cpt-vpx.cnn.

30. https://ag.ny.gov/press-release/2021/attorney-general-james-releases
-report-nursing-homes-response-covid-19.

31. Cuomo Sexual Assault First Allegation Coverage_.docx.

32. https://www.washingtonpost.com/politics/chris-cuomo-andrew-cuomo
/2021/05/20/99579382-b7f9-11eb-bb84-6b92dedcd8ed_story.html.

33. https://ag.ny.gov/sites/default/files/2021.08.03_nyag_-_investigative
_report.pdf.

34. https://www.cnn.com/2021/05/20/media/chris-cuomo-andrew-cuomo
-strategy-sessions/index.html.

35. https://www.cnn.com/2021/12/04/media/cnn-fires-chris-cuomo/index
.html.

36. https://www.bea.gov/news/2020/gross-domestic-product-2nd-quarter
-2020-advance-estimate-and-annual-update.

37. https://www.congress.gov/bill/116th-congress/house-bill/748.

38. https://www.cbpp.org/research/federal-budget/cares-act-measures
-strengthening-unemployment-insurance-should-continue#:~:text
=Federal%20Pandemic%20Unemployment%20Compensation%20
(FPUC,Act%20measures%2C%20through%20July%2031.

39. https://www.washingtonpost.com/business/2020/08/06/600-dollar
-unemployment-benefit/.

40. http://transcripts.cnn.com/TRANSCRIPTS/2007/30/nday.06.html.

41. http://archives.cnn.com/TRANSCRIPTS/2008/04/cnr.01.html.

42. https://mms.tveyes.com/MediaCenterPlayer.aspx?u=aHR0cDovL21lZGl

hY2VudGVyLnR2ZXllcy5jb20vZG93bmxvYWRnYXRld2F5LmFzcHg
/VXNlcklEPTc3MTkyNSZNRElEPTEzNTcwMTk0Jk1EU2VlZD02Njkz
JlR5cGU9TWVkaWE%3D.

43. https://www.cnbc.com/2020/12/21/covid-relief-bill-extends-and-enhances
-unemployment-benefits.html.

44. https://www.bls.gov/opub/ted/2020/unemployment-rate-16-point-1
-percent-in-massachusetts-4-point-5-percent-in-utah-in-july-2020.ht-
m#:~:text=U.S.%20unemployment%20rate%3A%2010.2%25%20in
%20July%202020.

45. https://www.bls.gov/news.release/pdf/laus.pdf.

46. https://www.dol.gov/ui/data.pdf.

47. https://mms.tveyes.com/MediaCenterPlayer.aspx?u=aHR0cDovL21lZGl
hY2VudGVyLnR2ZXllcy5jb20vZG93bmxvYWRnYXRld2F5LmFzcHg
/VXNlcklEPTc3MTkyNSZNRElEPTE0NDMwODQ1Jk1EU2VlZD0
xNTY0JlR5cGU9TWVVkaWE%3D.

48. Ibid.

49. https://www.cnn.com/profiles/jeff-zeleny-profile#about.

50. https://www.c-span.org/video/?285574-3/presidential-news-conference&
event=285574&playEvent.

51. https://twitter.com/chuckwoolery/status/1282499347117215745.

52. https://archive.org/details/CNNW_20200713_120000_New_Day_With
_Alisyn_Camerota_and_John_Berman/start/1020/end/1080.

53. https://archive.org/details/CNNW_20200713_120000_New_Day_With
_Alisyn_Camerota_and_John_Berman/start/1080/end/1140.

54. https://bit.ly/384xTIV.

55. https://bit.ly/2NKswZf.

56. https://bit.ly/30Rg8ur.

57. Ibid.

58. https://www.cnn.com/2020/04/13/politics/trump-coronavirus-defense
-fauci/index.html.

59. https://www.cnn.com/2020/07/04/opinions/trump-mount-rushmore
-speech-monuments-rhetoric-dantonio/index.html.

60. https://www.cnn.com/2010/POLITICS/01/25/voter.anger/index.html.

61. https://www.cnn.com/2014/10/27/politics/cnn-poll-angry-voters/index
.html.

62. https://mms.tveyes.com/MediaCenterPlayer.aspx?u=aHR0cDovL21lZGl
hY2VudGVyLnR2ZXllcy5jb20vZG93bmxvYWRnYXRld2F5LmFzcHg
/VXNlcklEPTc3MTkyNSZNRElEPTE1MTI0NzI3Jk1EU2VlZD0xMDk
mVHlwZT1NZWRpYQ%3D%3D.

63. https://twitter.com/acosta/status/1083411819354558467?lang=en.

64. https://www.nytimes.com/2020/03/11/us/politics/trump-coronavirus
-speech.html and https://www.c-span.org/video/?470284-1/president
-trump-travel-europe-us-suspended-30-days-uk.

65. https://archive.org/details/CNNW_20200312_050000_Cuomo_Prime _Time/start/780/end/840.

66. Ibid.

67. https://twitter.com/mrctv/status/1238186498433966081.

68. https://www.cnn.com/2020/03/17/politics/trump-china-coronavirus /index.html.

69. https://www.cnn.com/2021/01/11/politics/justice-democrats-endorse -nina-turner-ohio-congress/index.html.

70. http://archives.cnn.com/TRANSCRIPTS/2008/21/cnr.12.html.

71. https://archive.org/details/CNNW_20201002_140000_CNN_News room_With_Poppy_Harlow_and_Jim_Sciutto/start/3494/end/3554?q= surrogate+putin.

72. https://www.thedailybeast.com/cnn-staffers-demoralized-by-hiring-of -gop-operative-sarah-isgur-to-oversee-2020-coverage.

73. https://www.cnn.com/2019/02/20/media/reliable-sources-02-19-19/index .html.

74. https://abcnews.go.com/GMA/george-stephanopoulos-good-morning -america-anchor-biography/story?id=133369.

75. https://www.nbcnews.com/id/wbna25148636.

76. https://www.foxnews.com/person/p/dana-perino.

77. https://www.cnn.com/profiles/laura-jarrett#about.

78. Ibid.

79. https://www.cnn.com/profiles/laura-jarrett.

80. https://www.timesunion.com/local/article/A-Cuomo-top-aide-resigning -4283655.php.

81. https://www.nbcnews.com/media/zucker-lieutenant-top-candidate -replace-cnns-helm-rcna287.

82. https://www.nytimes.com/2022/02/18/business/media/allison-gollust -cnn-cuomo.html.

83. https://chiefexecutive.net/author/jgagliano1/; https://ctc.usma.edu/a-view -from-the-ct-foxhole-james-a-gagliano-former-fbi-hostage-rescue-team -counterterrorist-operator.

84. http://transcripts.cnn.com/TRANSCRIPTS/1609/21/ebo.01.html.

85. https://www.nytimes.com/2017/10/01/nyregion/chelsea-bombing-trial .html.

86. http://transcripts.cnn.com/TRANSCRIPTS/1901/12/ndaysat.02.html.

87. Interview with James Gagliano, February 26, 2021.

88. https://www.nytimes.com/2018/06/14/us/politics/fbi-texts-trump.html.

89. https://www.cnn.com/videos/tv/2019/08/22/lead-james-gagliano-live.cnn.

90. https://www.cnn.com/2019/09/15/politics/crossfire-hurricane-josh -campbell-james-comey-trump-tower/index.html.

91. https://www.washingtonpost.com/politics/cnn-hires-former-acting -fbi-chief-andrew-mccabe-drawing-fire-from-trumps-son-campaign

-and-others/2019/08/23/77ece630-c5b0-11e9-9986-1fb3e4397be4_story
.html.

92. https://twitter.com/jamesagagliano/status/1299817031299194882?lang
=en.

Chapter Eight: *The New York Times*

1. Jill Abramson, *Merchants of Truth* (New York: Simon & Schuster, 2019),
   ch. 12.
2. https://www.c-span.org/video/?180472-1/journalism-ethics.
3. https://www.nytimes.com/2020/06/03/opinion/tom-cotton-protests
   -military.html.
4. https://www.cnn.com/2020/06/03/media/new-york-times-tom-cotton
   -op-ed/index.html.
5. https://slate.com/news-and-politics/2020/06/new-york-times-tom-cotton
   -staff-reaction.html.
6. Ibid.
7. https://www.nyguild.org/post/our-statement-on-the-new-york-times-op
   -ed-send-in-the-troops.
8. https://www.nytimes.com/2020/06/03/opinion/tom-cotton-protests
   -military.html.
9. https://www.washingtonpost.com/graphics/2019/national/amp-stories
   /a-tragic-american-weekend.
10. https://trumpwhitehouse.archives.gov/briefings-statements/remarks
    -president-trump-mass-shootings-texas-ohio.
11. https://www.thenation.com/authors/joan-walsh/.
12. https://www.foxnews.com/opinion/new-york-times-headline-change
    -mob-lost-its-mind-dan-gainor.
13. https://www.politico.com/magazine/story/2019/08/06/liberals-new-york
    -times-trump-headline-227507.
14. Ibid.
15. https://slate.com/news-and-politics/2019/08/new-york-times-meeting
    -transcript.html.
16. https://www.nytimes.com/2021/02/14/business/media/new-york-times
    -donald-mcneil.html?referringSource=articleShare.
17. https://dailynorthwestern.com/2019/11/06/campus/students-protest-jeff
    -sessions-speech-police-presence.
18. "Students protest Jeff Sessions' speech, police presence," *Daily Northwest
    ern*, November 6, 2019, https://dailynorthwestern.com/2019/11/06/cam
    pus/students-protest-jeff-sessions-speech-police-presence/.
19. https://dailynorthwestern.com/2019/11/10/lateststories/addressing-the
    -dailys-coverage-of-sessions-protests.
20. https://www.nytimes.com/2019/11/12/business/media/northwestern
    -university-newspaper.html.

21. Interview with Senator Tom Cotton, March 23, 2021.
22. https://cronkite.asu.edu/content/paola-boivin-digital-director-cronkite -news-phoenix-sports-bureau.
23. Interview with Paola Boivin, December 18, 2020.
24. https://twitter.com/ron_fournier/status/948718790409445376.
25. https://money.cnn.com/2018/03/27/media/journalism-activism-reliable -sources/index.html.
26. https://www.nationaljournal.com/staff.
27. https://longreads.com/2018/03/29/is-journalism-a-form-of-activism /#:~:text=Evans%20on%20journalism%2Das%2Dactivism,with%20 the%20information%20they%20have.
28. https://www.journalofexpertise.org/articles/volume1_issue1/JoE_2018 _1_1_Wai_Perina.pdf.
29. Ibid.
30. https://www.pewresearch.org/fact-tank/2020/04/01/americans-main -sources-for-political-news-vary-by-party-and-age/.
31. https://slate.com/news-and-politics/2019/08/new-york-times-meeting -transcript.html.
32. https://www.pewresearch.org/fact-tank/2020/04/01/americans-main -sources-for-political-news-vary-by-party-and-age.
33. https://www.theatlantic.com/politics/archive/2020/12/media-after -trump/617503.
34. https://www.huffpost.com/entry/new-york-times-clinton-email-scoop _n_6911502.
35. https://www.nytimes.com/2017/02/09/us/politics/donald-trump-admin istration.html.
36. https://www.nytimes.com/2021/02/27/nyregion/cuomo-charlotte-bennet t-sexual-harassment.html.
37. https://nyti.ms/2OT9qk1.
38. https://nyti.ms/38NXEi6.
39. https://newsbusters.org/blogs/nb/curtis-houck/2021/03/19/rewind-cnn -msnbc-spent-50-mins-analyzing-trumps-ramp-walk-water.
40. https://archive.org/details/CNNW_20210319_200000_The_Lead _With_Jake_Tapper/start/1020/end/1080 (segment is 15.06 seconds).
41. https://archive.org/details/MSNBCW_20210319_170000_MTP_Daily /start/600/end/660 (segment was just under a minute).
42. https://www.washingtonpost.com/blogs/erik-wemple/wp/2018/04/24 /new-york-times-corrects-its-curious-example-of-a-far-right-conspiracy.
43. https://www.nytimes.com/2018/04/21/technology/facebook-campbell -brown-news.html.
44. https://law.yale.edu/emily-bazelon.
45. https://www.nytimes.com/2018/10/01/us/politics/kavanaugh-bar-fight .html.

46. https://www.cnn.com/2018/10/02/media/new-york-times-kavanaugh -tweet.

47. https://www.foxnews.com/media/new-york-times-katie-benner-deletes -tweets.

48. https://www.mprnews.org/story/2020/09/27/npr-woman-charged-with -attempted-murder-after-driving-into-pro-trump-protesters.

49. https://www.latimes.com/california/story/2021-01-20/orange-county -rally-organizer-new-charges-assault.

50. https://www.nydailynews.com/news/national/ny-california-driver -protest-murder-20200927-2eymmpwihbhy3iyhi6khvawa4m-story.html.

51. https://www.nytimes.com/2020/09/27/us/tatiana-turner-yorba-linda -protest.html.

52. Ibid.

53. https://nyti.ms/3lB0LyU.

54. https://nyti.ms/3r7cw1a.

55. https://nyti.ms/3r1Khkw.

56. https://www.claimsjournal.com/news/national/2020/06/02/297361 .htm.

57. https://www.nbcnewyork.com/news/local/nearly-400-nypd-officers-hurt -during-nycs-two-weeks-of-protest-over-george-floyds-death/2455285.

58. https://news.wttw.com/2020/06/06/george-floyd-protests-1258-arrested -130-police-officers-injured-chicago.

59. https://nypost.com/2020/06/08/more-than-700-officers-injured-in -george-floyd-protests-across-us.

60. https://www.claimsjournal.com/news/national/2020/06/02/297361.htm.

61. https://www.cnn.com/us/live-news/george-floyd-protests-05-30-20/h _dc6ce9f14c78f97c4b6c40430a781b45.

62. https://www.cnn.com/2020/06/01/us/national-guard-protests-states -map-trnd/index.html.

63. https://www.npr.org/2020/08/12/901859883/riots-that-followed-anti -racism-protests-come-at-great-cost-to-black-owned-busin.

64. Ibid.

65. Ibid.

66. https://blacklivesmatter.com/wp-content/uploads/2017/10/Toolkit -WhitePpl-Trayvon.pdf?__cf_chl_jschl_tk__=7b9f315151bc6ebf
894811ce2593da8ea15993db-1620864660-0-AfkEX7cITcJRlBG
NYqyYsCRoUbvB13Oi81oiYr7ZLGBEOztYHBYzczp1NILfc4GOawam2U
LKGFkFkhe8bmY6RYWqQantLXDNSSFePr0eplh0GH-qBzO5nQmMkG
l6nbNzdC4QSKG88mWN1c8NqwVIdBwzn7UajfEzoOJxb8R8RRC5FS73
PDbLpXfm05DdS75dW6eVn8MUy6rQGMXyqyPr0-8aF2YEHTqaXfY
WkMOG7CXUcc3SoegpI3UYveHwVYNRBkATVxTA-he1g016qN4Gb87k
xhUj5p5XINnPkUb8AZ6_gdTZ7U27ZY2Rw9Qg3dOBN3Eifvtuhn199n
JMwpnTnCslr6nfWfP2AZ9sjL24MoZyNV1EFovD3zzZ6LjyfO9Uiv

XuhqAemsPJFE9ZV5Ub67Gn4UdAxVT01RqCEUtzRxnzerFSRSd
_XmRPOUrAVvQrB5OXDBC1u5e-EMXKwdUebR8GGIduCeIY8eY
Vn-sDTDlImhAeTgMCud2kpBzuz3c9r0LDSsxWXFMwZ9EJseLR7gU.

67. https://www.wral.com/nikki-haley-s-view-of-new-york-is-priceless-her
-curtains-52-701-/17841777/.

68. https://www.washingtonpost.com/blogs/erik-wemple/wp/2018/09/14
/new-york-times-wrongs-nikki-haley-with-curtain-headline.

69. Ibid.

70. http://newsdiffs.org/diff/1867667/1868026/https%3A/www.nytimes
.com/2018/09/13/us/politics/nikki-haley-curtains.html.

71. https://www.nytimes.com/2018/09/13/us/politics/state-department
-curtains.html.

72. https://www.nytimes.com/search?dropmab=true&end-Date=2017
0111&query=dossier&sort=best&startDate=20170110.

73. https://www.nytimes.com/2017/01/11/us/politics/donald-trump-russia
-intelligence.html.

74. https://www.nytimes.com/2017/02/14/us/politics/russia-intelligence-com
munications-trump.html.

75. https://www.pulitzer.org/winners/staffs-new-york-times-and-washington
-post.

76. https://www.judiciary.senate.gov/imo/media/doc/Annotated%20New%20
York%20Times%20Article.pdf.

77. Ibid.

78. https://taibbi.substack.com/p/aaugh-a-brief-list-of-official-russia
?r=36mlt&utm_campaign=post&utm_medium=email&utm_source=
copy.

79. https://www.washingtonpost.com/lifestyle/media/anonymous-miles
-taylor-new-york-times-senior-official/2020/10/28/73634c0a-1959-11eb
-82db-60b15c874105_story.html.

80. https://www.nytimes.com/2018/09/05/opinion/trump-white-house-anony
mous-resistance.html.

81. https://www.nytimes.com/2018/09/06/us/politics/trump-pence-pompeo
-anonymous-op-ed.html.

82. https://www.bariweiss.com/resignation-letter.

Chapter Nine: Activists for a Cause

1. http://www.washingtonpost.com/wp-dyn/content/article/2008/12/24
/AR2008122402590.html.

2. http://transcripts.cnn.com/TRANSCRIPTS/2101/19/se.10.html.

3. https://georgewbush-whitehouse.archives.gov/news/releases/20010123-5
.html.

4. https://www.kff.org/global-health-policy/fact-sheet/mexico-city-policy
-explainer.

5. https://www.govinfo.gov/content/pkg/WCPD-1993-01-25/pdf/WCPD -1993-01-25-Pg88-2.pdf.
6. https://www.c-span.org/video/?162079-1/white-house-daily-briefing.
7. https://www.c-span.org/video/?37746-1/white-house-daily-briefing.
8. News coverage examples from Ari Fleischer, *Taking Heat: The President, the Press, and My Years in the White House* (New York: William Morrow, 2005).
9. https://www.theatlantic.com/national/archive/2013/04/why-dr-kermit -gosnells-trial-should-be-a-front-page-story/274944/; https://cdn.cnsnews .com/documents/Gosnell,%20Grand%20Jury%20Report.pdf.
10. http://gosnellmovie.com.
11. https://www.washingtonpost.com/opinions/the-ignored-story-of -americas-biggest-serial-killer/2018/12/07/6379964a-f986-11e8-8c9a-860 ce2a8148f_story.html.
12. https://www.washingtonpost.com/news/wonk/wp/2013/04/15/the-gosnell -case-heres-what-you-need-to-know.
13. https://www.buckscountycouriertimes.com/opinion/20181014/mullane -with-gosnell-another-media-blackout.
14. https://www.tvinsider.com/69819/timeline-of-real-trials-shown-on-tv.
15. https://archive.org/details/CNNW_20130321_200000_The_Lead_With _Jake_Tapper/start/936/end/996?q=%28kermit%29+AND+date%3 A2013-03-21.
16. https://archive.org/details/CNNW_20130412_200000_The_Lead_With _Jake_Tapper/start/3221/end/3281?q=%28kermit%29+AND+date%3 A2013-04-12.
17. https://www.nytimes.com/2013/04/16/us/online-furor-draws-press-to -abortion-doctors-trial.html.
18. https://www.msnbc.com/morning-joe/watch/philadelphia-doctor-who -performed-abortions-charged-with-murder-26125891848.
19. Original research.
20. https://www.washingtontimes.com/news/2013/mar/27/harper-a-shameful -silence-on-abortion-clinic-scand.
21. https://www.forbes.com/sites/mikeozanian/2013/04/05/it-is-disturbing -that-mike-rice-gets-more-coverage-than-kermit-gosnell-and-kathy-boud in/?sh=222d4dae19e9.
22. Ibid.
23. https://www.usatoday.com/story/opinion/2013/04/10/philadelphia -abortion-clinic-horror-column/2072577.
24. Ibid.
25. https://slate.com/news-and-politics/2013/04/kermit-gosnell-the-alleged -mass-murderer-and-the-bored-media.html.
26. https://www.washingtonpost.com/news/the-fix/wp/2013/06/26/key -moments-from-wendy-daviss-11-hour-filibuster.

27. https://www.cnn.com/2013/06/26/politics/wendy-davis-profile.
28. https://www.vogue.com/article/stand-and-deliver-texas-senator-wendy
    -davis.
29. Ibid.
30. https://www.nytimes.com/2013/07/24/us/24iht-letter24.html?search
    ResultPosition=35.
31. https://twitter.com/hashtag/StandWithWendy?src=hashtag_click.
32. https://twitter.com/BarackObama/status/349703625616011264.
33. https://www.usmagazine.com/celebrity-news/news/wendy-davis
    -abortion-filibuster-elizabeth-banks-mark-ruffalo-ricky-gervais-other
    -celebrities-react-2013266.
34. https://abcnews.go.com/ThisWeek/video/sunday-spotlight-wendy-davis
    -19537028.
35. https://abbyj.com/about.
36. https://www.youtube.com/watch?v=xycB0a7_ik4.
37. https://thefederalist.com/2020/08/26/nbc-labels-pro-life-rnc-speaker
    -abby-johnson-opponent-of-abortion-rights.
38. https://abcnews.go.com/Politics/transcript-joe-biden-kamala-harris-joint
    -interview-abcs/story?id=72541513.
39. https://taxfoundation.org/federal-income-tax-data-2021.
40. https://www.nytimes.com/2017/09/27/us/politics/trump-tax-plan-wealthy
    -middle-class-poor.html.
41. https://www.washingtonpost.com/news/wonk/wp/2017/09/25/trumps
    -tax-reform-looks-like-tax-cuts-for-the-rich.
42. https://archive.org/details/CNNW_20170927_140000_CNN_Newsroom
    _With_John_Berman_and_Poppy_Harlow/start/1980/end/2040.
43. https://www.bloomberg.com/news/articles/2020-09-15/u-s-median
    -household-income-jumped-6-8-in-2019-poverty-fell?cmpid=socialflow
    -twitter-business&utm_medium=social&utm_campaign=socialflow
    -organic&utm_content=business&utm_source=twitter&sref=ohmt
    MHdW.
44. https://www.washingtonpost.com/opinions/the-10-best-things-trump
    -has-done-in-2018/2018/12/31/a2de64b6-0d1b-11e9-84fc-d58c33d6c8c7
    _story.html.
45. https://www.wsj.com/articles/the-wealth-gap-shrinks-11601420393.
46. https://www.washingtonpost.com/news/the-fix/wp/2017/12/20/
    republicans-are-about-to-pass-a-tax-bill-democrats-think-theyre-signing
    -their-death-certificate.
47. Ibid.
48. https://www.nytimes.com/2021/01/14/business/economy/biden-economy
    .html.
49. Ibid.
50. https://www.jct.gov/publications/2017/jcx-67-17.

51. https://www.nytimes.com/2021/01/15/business/dealbook/biden-economy-deficit.html.
52. https://static01.nyt.com/images/2021/03/07/nytfrontpage/scan.pdf.
53. https://www.nytimes.com/2021/03/07/us/politics/child-tax-credit-stimulus.html
54. https://www.washingtonpost.com/business/2021/03/08/reparations-black-farmers-stimulus/.
55. https://www.taxpolicycenter.org/briefing-book/how-did-tcja-change-standard-deduction-and-itemized-deductions.
56. https://www.taxpolicycenter.org/briefing-book/how-did-tcja-change-taxes-families-children#:~:text=The%202017%20Tax%20Cuts%20and,ineligible%20for%20the%20%242%2C000%20credit.
57. https://wapo.st/32WT4uj.
58. https://www.washingtonpost.com/us-policy/2021/02/19/schumer-pledges-final-passage-19-trillion-relief-bill-ahead-march-14-unemployment-insurance-deadline.
59. Ibid.
60. https://email.punchbowl.news/t/ViewEmail/t/68C226F97991F81C2540EF23F30FEDED/B827D62DB555E31C148F9D201EEB5695.
61. Ibid.
62. https://www.census.gov/newsroom/press-releases/2020/income-poverty.html.
63. https://democrats.org/where-we-stand/party-platform/building-a-stronger-fairer-economy/. The term *invest* is used at least forty-one times in describing the economic platform.
64. https://www.whitehouse.gov/briefing-room/speeches-remarks/2021/03/31/remarks-by-president-biden-on-the-american-jobs-plan.
65. https://www.whitehouse.gov/briefing-room/speeches-remarks/2021/04/07/remarks-by-president-biden-on-the-american-jobs-plan-2.
66. https://www.nytimes.com/live/2021/03/31/us/biden-news-today.
67. https://www.washingtonpost.com/us-policy/2021/03/31/biden-infrastructure-climate-plan/.
68. https://www.nytimes.com/2021/04/09/business/biden-details-1-52-trillion-spending-proposal-to-fund-discretionary-priorities.html?referringSource=articleShare.
69. https://www.washingtonpost.com/us-policy/2021/04/09/biden-2022-budget.
70. Ibid.
71. http://edition.cnn.com/TRANSCRIPTS/2104/02/es.03.html.
72. http://transcripts.cnn.com/TRANSCRIPTS/2103/31/cnnt.02.html.
73. http://edition.cnn.com/TRANSCRIPTS/2105/03/es.03.html.
74. https://email.punchbowl.news/t/ViewEmail/t/1B3F93BE3588B

A7D2540EF23F30FEDED/B827D62DB555E31C148F9D201EEB
5695.

75. https://wapo.st/3gGzJ99.
76. https://wapo.st/32bnE38.
77. https://wapo.st/3wR4ayQ.
78. https://nyti.ms/32A0Qdz.
79. https://nyti.ms/2QpHJjP.
80. https://nyti.ms/3nbMx8G.
81. https://nyti.ms/3ng4PWk.
82. https://www.washingtonpost.com/politics/harris-assigned-to-tackle
    -volatile-issues-quietly-builds-a-network/2021/09/25/5440d8ac-163c-11ec
    -9589-31ac3173c2e5_story.html.
83. https://twitter.com/mattizcoop?lang=en.
84. https://www.google.com/search?q=media+republicans+culture
    +war+transgender&oq=media+republicans+culture+war+transgender
    &aqs=chrome.69i57.6317j0j4&sourceid=chrome&ie=UTF-8.
85. https://time.com/3816952/obama-gay-lesbian-transgender-lgbt-rights.
86. https://slate.com/news-and-politics/2012/06/obamas-gay-marriage-and
    -immigration-moves-how-the-president-is-outfoxing-romney.html.

Chapter Ten: Races, Riots, and COVID

1. https://www.nydailynews.com/news/politics/ny-blake-black-voter
   -suppression-bronx-congressional-20200626-3jx2oerp2ndhbaguzfpnzcje
   re-story.html.
2. https://archive.org/details/MSNBCW_20200627_160000_Weekends
   _With_Alex_Witt/start/6420/end/6480.
3. https://www.nytimes.com/2019/05/22/nyregion/tiffany-caban-aoc
   -endorsement-queens-da.html.
4. https://www.nydailynews.com/new-york/queens/guv-loves-katz-article
   -1.1499291.
5. https://www.nytimes.com/2019/07/03/nyregion/katz-caban-recount
   -queens.html.
6. https://www.nytimes.com/2019/07/04/nyregion/katz-caban-recount
   -queens-da.html.
7. https://www.nytimes.com/2019/07/15/nyregion/queens-da-recount
   -caban-katz.html.
8. https://www.washingtonexaminer.com/news/aocs-chief-of-staff-deletes
   -tweet-calling-centrist-democrats-racist.
9. http://www.cnn.com/TRANSCRIPTS/2103/26/cnr.09.html.
10. https://archive.org/details/CNNW_20210327_020000_CNN_Tonight
    _With_Don_Lemon/start/0/end/60.
11. https://archive.org/details/KPIX_20210327_013000_CBS_Evening
    _News_With_Norah_ODonnell/start/0/end/60.

12. https://www.cbsnews.com/news/georgia-voting-law-coca-cola-ups
    -home-depot-voter-rights-ups-delta-for-the-people-act/?ftag=CNM-00
    -10aab7e&linkId=115231493.
13. https://fm.hunter.cuny.edu/journalism/index.php/faculty/.
14. https://archive.org/details/KNTV_20210327_090600_NBC_Nightly
    _News_With_Lester_Holt/start/600/end/660.
15. https://archive.org/details/KNTV_20210327_090600_NBC_Nightly
    _News_With_Lester_Holt/start/660/end/720.
16. https://www.nbcnews.com/nightly-news/video/georgia-passes-restrictive
    -new-voting-law-109157957531.
17. https://archive.org/details/tv?q=makes%20it%20a%20crime%20and%20
    offer%20food%20and%20water%20to%20anyone%20waiting%20in%20
    line%20AND%20date%3A%5B2021-03-24%20TO%202021-03-30%5D.
18. https://www.legis.ga.gov/api/legislation/document/20212022/201121.
19. http://edition.cnn.com/TRANSCRIPTS/2104/12/cnr.08.html.
20. https://bit.ly/3ea9gxG.
21. https://bit.ly/3n4XuZA.
22. https://bit.ly/3xcAWdP.
23. https://www.claimsjournal.com/news/national/2020/06/02/297361
    .htm.
24. https://www.nytimes.com/2020/07/06/us/Epidemiologists-coronavirus
    -protests-quarantine.html?referringSource=articleShare.
25. https://www.axios.com/newsletters/axios-am-704df021-3478-4c4f-bade
    -51dccbe1da69.html?utm_source=newsletter&utm_medium=email
    &utm_campaign=newsletter_axiosam&stream=top.
26. https://twitter.com/claytravis/status/1325441315769896960?lang=en.
27. Ibid.

Chapter Eleven: Too Good to Check

1. https://twitter.com/MekitaRivas?ref_src=twsrc%5Egoogle%7Ctwcamp
   %5Eserp%7Ctwgr%5Eauthor.
2. https://bit.ly/33RzLDu.
3. https://www.cnn.com/2020/04/20/politics/kim-jong-un-north-korea
   /index.html.
4. https://www.washingtonpost.com/lifestyle/media/kim-jong-un-appears
   -to-be-alive-after-all-so-how-did-his-death-make-the-news/2020/05/05
   /e9cf7f0e-8d6c-11ea-a0bc-4e9ad4866d21_story.html.
5. https://money.cnn.com/2018/05/17/media/media-trump-animals
   -immigrants/index.html.
6. https://www.nytimes.com/2018/05/16/us/politics/trump-undocumented
   -immigrants-animals.html.
7. https://www.usatoday.com/story/news/politics/2018/05/16/trump-
   immigrants-animals-mexico-democrats-sanctuary-cities/617252002/.

8. https://www.cbsnews.com/news/trump-hosts-california-sanctuary-state -roundtable-live-updates/.

9. https://money.cnn.com/2018/05/17/media/media-trump-animals -immigrants/index.html.

10. https://freebeacon.com/politics/msnbc-cnn-spreads-false-impression -that-trump-called-immigrants-animals/.

11. https://twitter.com/markmobility/status/1115290958113976321.

12. https://trumpwhitehouse.archives.gov/briefings-statements/remarks -president-trump-vaccine-development/.

13. https://www.washingtonpost.com/health/2020/12/14/sandra-lindsay -first-covid-vaccine/.

14. https://www.pfizer.com/news/press-release/press-release-detail/pfizer -and-biontech-announce-vaccine-candidate-against.

15. https://twitter.com/NorahODonnell/status/1261426582448558080.

16. https://www.nbcnews.com/politics/donald-trump/fact-check-coronavirus -vaccine-could-come-year-trump-says-experts-n1207411.

17. Ibid.

18. Ibid.

19. https://abcnews.go.com/Politics/full-text-donald-trumps-2020-republican -national-convention/story?id=72659782.

20. https://www.nbcnews.com/politics/2020-election/live-blog/2020-08-27 -rnc-updates-n1238267/ncrd1238620#blogHeader.

21. https://www.washingtonpost.com/politics/2020/11/02/fact-checking-final -arguments-biden-trump/.

22. https://www.miamiherald.com/news/coronavirus/article246661043 .html.

23. https://twitter.com/atrupar/status/1323409524728995842?s=20.

24. https://trumpwhitehouse.archives.gov/briefings-statements/remarks -president-trump-press-briefing-september-18-2020/.

25. https://www.cnn.com/2020/09/18/health/trump-coronavirus-vaccine -april-promise-bn/index.html.

26. https://www.cnn.com/2021/03/30/health/states-covid-19-vaccine -eligibility-bn/index.html.

27. https://twitter.com/SenTomCotton/status/1222923797503803392; https://www.cotton.senate.gov/news/videos/watch/january-30-2020 -senator-cotton-urges-china-travel-ban-in-wake-of-coronavirus.

28. https://twitter.com/SenTomCotton/status/1222971592403226628; https://www.cdc.gov/media/releases/2020/p0121-novel-coronavirus -travel-case.html.

29. https://www.washingtontimes.com/news/2020/jan/26/coronavirus-link -to-china-biowarfare-program-possi.

30. https://www.dailymail.co.uk/health/article-7922379/Chinas-lab-studying -SARS-Ebola-Wuhan-outbreaks-center.html.

31. https://www.cbsnews.com/video/chinese-ambassador-to-u-s-dismisses
-coronavirus-theories-as-absolutely-crazy.
32. Ibid.
33. Ibid.
34. https://www.nytimes.com/2020/02/17/business/media/coronavirus-tom
-cotton-china.html.
35. https://www.businessinsider.com/wapo-corrects-article-describing
-wuhan-lab-leak-claim-as-conspiracy-theory-2021-6.
36. https://www.wsj.com/articles/the-virus-lab-theorys-new-credibility
-11622066808?st=ls13168g95m1qrl&reflink=article_email_share.
37. https://www.nationalreview.com/author/jim-geraghty?q=china.
38. https://www.nationalreview.com/the-morning-jolt/even-xavier-becerra
-jumps-on-the-lab-leak-bandwagon.
39. https://about.fb.com/news/2020/04/covid-19-misinfo-update/#removing
-more-false-claims.
40. Ibid.
41. https://www.nytimes.com/2020/06/26/us/politics/russia-afghanistan
-bounties.html.
42. Ibid.
43. Ibid.
44. https://twitter.com/joebiden/status/1277318851160506369?lang=en.
45. Russia Bounty Coverage TV_updated.docx.
46. http://transcripts.cnn.com/TRANSCRIPTS/2006/28/rs.01.html.
47. https://abc.com/shows/world-news-tonight/episode-guide/2020-06/29
-monday-june-29-2020.
48. https://www.washingtonpost.com/national-security/russian-bounties
-to-taliban-linked-militants-resulted-in-deaths-of-us-troops-according
-to-intelligence-assessments/2020/06/28/74ffaec2-b96a-11ea-80b9-40ece
9a701dc_story.html.
49. https://bit.ly/2SKHoJA.
50. https://www.rev.com/blog/transcripts/press-secretary-kayleigh-mcenany
-press-conference-transcript-june-29.
51. https://www.thedailybeast.com/us-intel-walks-back-claim-russians-put
-bounties-on-american-troops.
52. Russia Bounty Retraction Coverage_.docx Updated.docx.
53. https://www.nytimes.com/2020/06/01/us/politics/trump-st-johns-church
-bible.html.
54. https://www.npr.org/2020/06/01/867532070/trumps-unannounced
-church-visit-angers-church-officials.
55. https://www.theatlantic.com/politics/archive/2020/06/trumps-biblical
-spectacle-outside-st-johns-church/612529/.
56. https://doioig.opengov.ibmcloud.com/sites/doioig.gov/files/Final%20
Statement_0.pdf.

57. https://www.google.com/search?q=corrections+june+2021+inspector
    +general+report+trump+park&oq=corrections+june+2021+inspector
    +general+report+trump+park&aqs=chrome.69i57.9960j1j7&sourceid
    =chrome&ie=UTF-8.
58. https://muckrack.com/drew-holden/articles.
59. https://twitter.com/ByronYork/status/1335780338719727619.
60. https://www.washingtonpost.com/politics/trump-lame-duck-policies
    /2020/12/06/8165088c-3661-11eb-a997-1f4c53d2a747_story.html.
61. Ibid.
62. https://www.nytimes.com/2016/12/31/us/politics/obama-last-days-trump
    -transition.html.
63. https://www.post-gazette.com/news/nation/2020/11/29/Joe-Biden-all
    -female-senior-communications-team-director-press-secretary-Kate
    -Bedingfield-Jen-Psaki-Neera-Tanden/stories/202011290196.
64. https://www.theblaze.com/news/associated-press-tells-reporters-not-to
    -say-crisis.
65. https://twitter.com/julito77/status/1375195739530354695.
66. https://www.nytimes.com/2017/09/19/us/politics/bernie-sanders
    -elizabeth-warren-democrats-presidential-election.html.
67. https://www.nytimes.com/2000/06/16/world/2000-campaign-advisor
    -bush-s-foreign-policy-tutor-academic-public-eye.html.
68. https://www.cnn.com/election/2018/results/georgia/governor.
69. https://www.cnn.com/election/2020/results/state/georgia.
70. https://www.washingtonpost.com/politics/2018/11/15/democrats-are
    -now-going-there-stolen-elections.
71. https://www.nationalreview.com/news/terry-mcauliffe-embraces-stacey
    -abrams-stolen-election-conspiracy-theory.
72. https://nymag.com/intelligencer/2012/06/yes-bush-v-gore-did-steal-the
    -election.html.
73. https://www.nationalreview.com/news/terry-mcauliffe-embraces-stacey
    -abrams-stolen-election-conspiracy-theory.
74. https://www.theguardian.com/commentisfree/2017/nov/08/donald-trump
    -illegitimate-president-rebecca-solnit.
75. Ibid.
76. Ibid.
77. Ibid
78. https://www.cbsnews.com/news/hillary-rodham-clinton-trump-is-a
    -corrupt-human-tornado/.
79. https://www.washingtonpost.com/politics/jimmy-carter-says-trump
    -wouldnt-be-president-without-help-from-russia/2019/06/28/deef1ef0
    -99b6-11e9-8d0a-5edd7e2025b1_story.html.
80. https://www.politico.com/story/2017/01/john-lewis-donald-trump-not
    -legitimate-president-233607.

81. https://www.npr.org/2017/01/19/510534005/number-of-democrats -boycotting-trump-inauguration-grows.

82. https://www.politico.com/story/2016/11/democrats-electoral-college -faithless-trump-231731.

83. https://www.nbcnews.com/politics/politics-news/drama-filled-electoral -college-vote-fitting-ending-2016-election-n697521.

84. https://www.commentarymagazine.com/noah-rothman/the-last-time -they-tried-to-steal-an-election/?utm_source=ActiveCampaign&utm _medium=email&utm_content=The+Last+Time+They+Tried+to ++Steal+an+Election&utm_campaign=Daily+newsletter+12%2F14%2F20.

85. https://www.nbcnews.com/politics/politics-news/drama-filled-electoral -college-vote-fitting-ending-2016-election-n697521.

86. https://www.congress.gov/congressional-record/2017/01/06/house-section /article/H185-8?loclr=askfaq.

87. https://archive.org/details/MSNBCW_20181120_010000_All_In_With _Chris_Hayes/start/2040/end/2100.

88. https://www.washingtonpost.com/politics/trump-2020-election-audits /2021/06/02/95fd3004-c2ec-11eb-8c34-f8095f2dc445_story.html.

89. https://archive.org/details/FOXNEWSW_20201107_170000_Fox_News _Democracy_2020_Election_Coverage/start/5700/end/5760.

90. https://www.journalism.org/2021/04/28/at-100-day-mark-coverage-of -biden-has-been-slightly-more-negative-than-positive-varied-greatly-by -outlet-type.

91. https://www.journalism.org/2021/04/28/at-100-day-mark-coverage-of -biden-has-been-slightly-more-negative-than-positive-varied-greatly-by -outlet-type/pj_2021-04-28_biden-100-days_0-04.

92. Ibid.

93. https://www.nbcnews.com/politics/2020-election/nbc-news-hold-town -hall-joe-biden-miami-n1241406.

94. https://www.rev.com/blog/transcripts/joe-biden-nbc-town-hall-transcript -october-5.

95. Ibid.

96. https://freebeacon.com/media/undecided-voters-at-nbc-town-hall -previously-told-network-they-were-voting-biden.

97. https://www.cnn.com/2020/09/17/politics/cnn-drive-in-town-hall-joe -biden/index.html.

98. https://www.newsbusters.org/blogs/nb/curtis-houck/2020/09/18/total -joke-cnns-biden-town-hall-filled-softballs-versus-abcs.

99. https://www.theguardian.com/world/video/2020/dec/03/joe-biden -warns-of-250000-further-us-covid-deaths-between-now-and-january -video.

100. https://www.stardem.com/emergency_notice/where-joe-biden-s

-prediction-of-250-000-new-covid-deaths-stands/article_6c9c29e9
-359b-5165-9834-e10a81b4ae90.html.

101. https://www.washingtonpost.com/politics/biden-says-china-is
-not-competition-for-us-prompting-pushback-from-republicans/2019/05
/01/4ae4e738-6c68-11e9-a66d-a82d3f3d96d5_story.html.

102. https://www.whitehouse.gov/briefing-room/speeches-remarks
/2021/02/11/remarks-by-president-biden-before-meeting-with-senators
-on-the-critical-need-to-invest-in-modern-and-sustainable-american
-infrastrucutre.

103. https://www.nytimes.com/2021/03/10/business/china-us-tech-rivalry
.html?searchResultPosition=4.

104. Original research.

105. https://www.whitehouse.gov/briefing-room/speeches-
remarks/2021/03/25/remarks-by-president-biden-in-press-conference.

106. https://www.reuters.com/article/us-usa-campaign-biden/biden-draws
-romneys-ire-with-chains-comment-idUSBRE87E00W20120815.

107. https://nypost.com/2021/05/27/press-slammed-for-asking-biden
-questions-about-his-ice-cream; https://www.msn.com/en-us/news
/politics/yes-the-media-is-going-easy-on-the-biden-administration
/ar-BB1dLYn7.

Chapter Twelve: What Comes Next?

1. https://abcnews.go.com/Politics/week-transcript-30-21-secretary-pete
-buttigieg-cia/story?id=77982655.

2. https://www.cnn.com/videos/business/2021/05/30/why-is-the-lab-leak
-theory-back-in-the-news-now.cnn/video/playlists/business-media.

3. Ibid.

4. https://www.wsj.com/articles/before-reporting-became-journalism
-11600879803.

Index

Eisele, Kitty, 55
election of 1996, journalism
    students and, 5
election of 2000, 275
election of 2014, 39–40
election of 2016
    Harwood's question to Trump,
        49
    journalists and support for
        Clinton, 6, 10, 46
    left's sureness that Trump
        would lose, 90
    polls and reporting on, 41–42,
        44–45
    reporters' surprise at results
        of, 4
    reports and mocking of voters
        for Trump, 1–2
    USPS support for Clinton,
        109–110
election of 2020
    European fireworks
        interpreted as reaction to
        Biden's election, 68–72
    journalism students and, 6
    media coverage of Biden's
        election victory celebrations
        versus football game
        celebrations, 242–244
    media endorsements of Biden
        versus Trump, 46
    media's lack of understanding
        of voters for Trump, 6
    polls and reporting on, 38–45
    reporting on Biden's' victory
        in, 4
    reporting on voting in Georgia,
        31–33
    story of Trump removing
        mailboxes, 62–65, 101
    Trump and policies through
        end of term, 271–272
    voter turnout, 65

Elliott, Mark, 253
Equal Time (MSNBC program),
    92
Ernst, Joni, 42–43
estate taxes, 228

Facebook, 45, 111, 116–117, 123,
    125, 189–190, 261–262
facts, abandoned for narratives
    unfavorable to Republicans,
    246–247, 285–286
    anonymously sourced story
        about Russian bounties on
        US troops, 262–265
    Biden, Trump and all-female
        senior communications staff,
        272–273
    Bloomberg's unconfirmed
        2020 political contributions,
        247–248
    coverage of Biden's first
        few days contrasted with
        previous presidents',
        281–285
    coverage of refusals to accept
        election results, 275–281
    COVID-19 and Trump's
        comments about vaccines,
        253–257
    COVID-19 and Wuhan lab leak
        theory, 257–262
    damage done to Trump before
        2020 election, 267
    differing coverage of Trump
        and Biden and withdrawal
        from Afghanistan, 268–
        271
    rumors about health of Kim
        Jong Un, 248–249
    Trump and policies after 2020
        election, 271–272
    Trump's supposed comments
        about immigrants, 249–253

About the Author

ARI FLEISCHER was the White House press secretary from 2001 to 2003. He served as spokesman during September 11, two wars, and the anthrax attacks. His previous book, *Taking Heat*, detailed his years in the White House and reached number seven on the *New York Times* bestseller list. Since leaving the White House, Ari has run a communications company that helps corporations and sports organizations with their media needs. He is a FOX News contributor and a graduate of Middlebury College in Vermont, and he now resides in Westchester County, New York.